Ironwork
Fer forgé
Schmiedeeisen
Hierro forjado
Изделия из металла

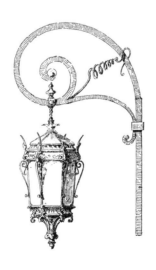

L'Aventurine

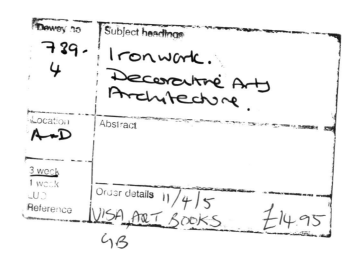
Textes : William Wheeler

Français: C. S.
English: William Wheeler
Deutsch: Annett Richter
Español: Stéphanie Lemière
Русский: Тина Золотова

© L'Aventurine, Paris, 2004
ISBN 2-914199-38-4

Русский текст - ООО "МАГМА", Москва ЛР 065019

• Contents • Sommaire • Inhalt •
Índice • Содержание

Foreword

Thanks to its strength, resistance but also its malleability, iron can be transformed in innumerable ways answering completely different needs. This was traditionally the work of the blacksmith who forged the numerous architectural elements decorating the interior and exterior of buildings: balconies, balustrades, stair railings, fan lights, canopies, porch roofs, signs, as well as coping, cresting, and finials on roof tops. They also executed grilles of all types used for defensive or ornamental purposes. Locksmiths contributed decorative, utilitarian bolts, locks, and various types of hinges including ornate strap hinges. Still other craftsmen made caldrons, pots, andirons, firedogs, shoes and spurs for horses anchors and chains for ships and cannons and munitions for warfare.

Iron craftsmen sought inspiration for their models in the pattern books published throughout Europe beginning in the 16th century. Arabesques, tracery and foliated scrolls are the bases of this vocabulary where classic styles can be found alongside more novel trends. The technological advances in metallurgy in the late 18th and the early 19th century opened the way for metallic architecture. Henceforth, iron would replace stone and wood in the structural framework of buildings and bridges. With significantly lower manufacturing costs, cast iron, which, as its name specifies, was poured into molds, progressively replaced wrought iron which became a luxury item. Affordable by the masses, cast iron allowed a wide array of constructions and objects to be designed such as furniture, garden structures, fireplaces and heating apparatus, urban furniture, decorative objects, etc.

All the illustrations in this book are stored on a CD-ROM you can use on Mac or PC. The images are in high resolution (TIFF format), and ready to use for any non-commercial purpose. For any professional/commercial purposes, please contact the publishers at :
laventurine@wanadoo.fr
The enclosed CD is free and cannot be sold separately.

Avant-propos

Grâce à sa robustesse, sa résistance, mais aussi sa maniabilité, le fer peut être transformé d'innombrables façons répondant à des besoins très divers. Traditionnellement, ce travail est le domaine du forgeron qui réalise les nombreux éléments architecturaux qui ornent l'intérieur et l'extérieur des bâtiments : balcons, balustrades, rampes d'escalier, imposts, marquises, auvents, enseignes, crêtes, faîtières et épis sur les toitures. Ces artisans exécutent également des grilles de toutes sortes, qui servent de protection ou d'ornement, décorant principalement portes et fenêtres. Les serruriers participent eux aussi à l'élaboration d'éléments utilitaires ou décoratifs tels que les verrous, les clefs, les serrures, les pentures et les gonds. D'autres artisans fabriquent des objets de la vie quotidienne : chaudrons, casseroles, landiers, chenêts, fers et éperons pour les chevaux, ancres et chaînes pour les bateaux, canons et boulets pour la guerre…

Les artisans du fer puisent leurs modèles d'ornementation dans des recueils de dessins publiés à travers l'Europe à partir du XVIᵉ siècle. Arabesques, entrelacs et rinceaux sont les bases du vocabulaire où le classicisme côtoie les plus grandes fantaisies. Les avancées technologiques dans le domaine de la métallurgie à la fin du XVIIIᵉ siècle et au début du XIXᵉ siècle ouvrent la voie à l'architecture métallique. Désormais, le fer remplace la pierre et le bois dans les charpentes des bâtiments, des ponts et des passerelles. Fabriqué à moindres frais, le fer de fonte, coulé dans un moule, remplace peu à peu le fer forgé ou battu, qui devient un produit de luxe. Accessible au plus grand nombre, la fonte permet alors d'imaginer une foule d'objets et de structures d'une diversité étonnante : mobilier, constructions du jardin, cheminées et appareils de chauffage, mobilier urbain, objets de décoration, etc.

Vorwort

Die Bearbeitung des Eisens gehört zu den schönsten Eroberungen des Menschen. Eisen kann, dank seiner Zähigkeit und Wiederstandsfähigkeit, unzählige Male umgeformt und wiederverwendet werden und somit auf die verschiedensten Bedürfnisse antworten. Traditionsgemäß wurde diese Arbeit von den Händen eines Schmiedes ausgeführt, eine Handwerkskunst, welche die Architekturkunst mit zahlreichen Dekorationselementen für den Schmuck von Gebäuden, Balkone, Geländern, Treppengeländern, Beleuchtungen, Vordächern, Dachk olben, Schildern oder auch Kämme bereicherte. Schmiedearbeiten, wie z.B. Gitter welche hauptsächlich Türen und Fenstern dekorierten und Schutz lieferten, wurden von den Kunsthandwerkern in immer gleicher Art und Weise gefertigt. Aber auch Schlosser beteiligten sich an der Fertigung von Riegeln, Schlüsseln, Schlössern und Angeln, die nicht nur als Gebrauchselement zu sehen waren sondern auch ausgesprochen dekorativ sind. Andere Schmiede fertigten aus Eisen wiederum Gebrauchsgegenstände des täglichen Lebens wie Töpfe, Küchenpfannen, Tiegel, Fesseln und Sporen für Pferde, Anker und Ketten für Boote, Geschütze, Kugeln und andere Kriegsutensilien.

Kunstschmiede entnahmen ihre Ideen oder Modelle für Verzierungen aus Sammlungen und Zeichnungen, welche seit dem 16. Jh. in Europa veröffentlich wurden. Eingangshallen, Dachrinnen und Arabesken sind aus dem Vokabular des Klassizismus, einer Epoche grosser Ideen und Phantasien, nicht wegzudenken. Der technische Fortschritt in der Metallindustrie Ende des 18. Jh. sowie Beginn des 19. Jh. eröffneten der Eisenhandwerkskunst völlig neue Möglichkeiten und somit den Weg in die metallische Architektur. Von nun an wurden Stein und Holz bei Konstruktionen von Häusern, Brücken und Fussgängerbrücken von Eisen ersetzt. Mit geringen Vertigungskosten, da nun in Formen gissbar, ersetzt Gusseisen nach und nach das geschmiedete oder auch geschlagene Eisen und wird zu einem ausgesprochenen Luxusobjekt. Gusseisen, nun mit grosser Stückzahl produzierbar, ermöglicht alle Art von Strukturen oder Objekten herzustellen. So lassen sich Mobiliar, Gartenkonstruktionen, Kamine und andere Heizungs-konstruktionen mit einer erstaunlichen Vielfalt wiederfinden.

Alle Illustrationen dieses Buches sind auch auf der beigepackten CD-ROM (PC und Mac) hoch auflösend (tiff Format) gespeichert. Ihr Einsatz im privaten und nicht kommerziellen Bereich ist gebührenfrei. Bei kommerzieller Anwendung bittet der Verlag um Kontaktaufnahme unter: laventurine@wanadoo.fr
Die beigelegte CD ist gratis und darf nicht separat verkauft werden.

Prólogo

Gracias a su robustez, su resistencia, y también su maleabilidad, el hierro se puede transformar de innumerables maneras para responder a necesidades muy diversas. Tradicionalmente, esta tarea depende de la competencia del herrero quien realiza los numerosos elementos arquitectónicos que adornan el interior y el exterior de los edificios: balcones, balaustradas, barandillas, montantes, marquesinas, tejadillos, letreros, coronaciones, caballetes y espigones para tejados. Estos artesanos ejecutan también verjas de todo tipo, para proteger o adornar, que guarnecen principalmente las puertas y las ventanas. Los cerrajeros participan también en la elaboración de elementos utilitarios o decorativos tales como los cerrojos, las llaves, las cerraduras, los pernios y los goznes. Otros artesanos fabrican objetos de la vida cotidiana: calderos, cacerolas, morillos, herraduras y espuelas para caballos, anclas y cadenas para barcos, cañones y balas para la guerra.

Los artesanos del hierro sacan sus modelos de ornamentación de las colecciones de dibujos publicados por toda Europa a partir del siglo XV. Arabescos, mocárabes y follajes son las bases del vocabulario en el que el clasicismo juega con las mayores fantasías.

Los adelantos tecnológicos en el campo de la metalurgia a fines del siglo XVIII y a principios del siglo XIX dan a luz la arquitectura metálica. A partir de este momento, el hierro reemplaza la piedra y la madera en los armazones de los edificios, de los puentes y de las pasarelas. Más económico, el hierro colado, moldado, sustituye poco a poco el hierro forjado o batido, que se vuelve un producto de lujo. Accesible para muchos, el hierro colado permite entonces imaginar una multitud de objetos y estructuras de una sorprendente diversidad: muebles, construcciones para el jardín, chimeneas y aparatos de calefacción, mobiliario urbano, objetos decorativos, etc.

Todas las ilustraciones del presente libro están contenidas en un CD-ROM (Mac/PC). Las imágenes están en alta resolución (formato TIFF), y pueden ser utilizadas a fines no comerciales. Por toda utilización comercial, contacte el editor a la siguiente dirección :
laventurine@wanadoo.fr
El CD es gratuito y no puede venderse separadamente.

Предисловие

Из железа, благодаря его прочности, упругости и ковкости, можно изготовить бесконечное множество изделий, отвечающих самым разным потребностям. Традиционно этим занимаются кузнецы; они создают архитектурные элементы, которые украшают интерьеры домов и их внешний облик: балконы, балюстрады, перила лестниц, стойки, навесы, крыши, табло, венцы, окон и коньки крыш. Эти умельцы делают также разнообразные решетки на двери и окна, служащие для надежности или красоты. Важную роль играют слесари, которые обрабатывают полезную или декоративную утварь вроде засовов, ключей, замков, петель и крючков. Из железа выполняют и другие вещи, необходимые для повседневной жизни: котлы, кастрюли, подставки для дров, уздечки, подковы, якоря и корабельные цепи, а также пушки и ядра.

В качестве моделей для декора мастера используют коллекции рисунков, издающихся по всей Европе начиная с XVI века. Арабески, банты и листья составляют основу орнаментального словаря, где классицизм причудливо сочетается с фантазией автора. Технические достижения в области металлургии конца XVII - начала XIX века сделали возможным применять металл в архитектуре. С этого времени железо заменяет камень и дерево в каркасах зданий, мостов и опор. Менее дорогая формованная прокатная сталь постепенно вытесняет кованое железо, которое превращается в предмет роскоши. Сталь, доступная более широкому кругу потребителей, позволяет создавать удивительные по красоте изделия и конструкции: мебель, садовый инвентарь, камины, нагревательные приборы, предметы городского быта, декоративные детали и многие другие полезные вещи.

Названия печатных первоисточников приведены в книге на языке оригинала.

Все иллюстрации в этой книге представлены на компакт-диске, которые могут использоваться как на PC, так и на Mac компьютерах.

Изображения сохранены в файлах формата TIFF высокого разрешения и могут свободно применяться в некоммерческих целях. Для использования в коммерческих или профессиональных целях просьба обращаться к издателям: laventurine@wanadoo.fr.

Прилагаемый диск CD является бесплатным и не может продаваться отдельно от данной книги.

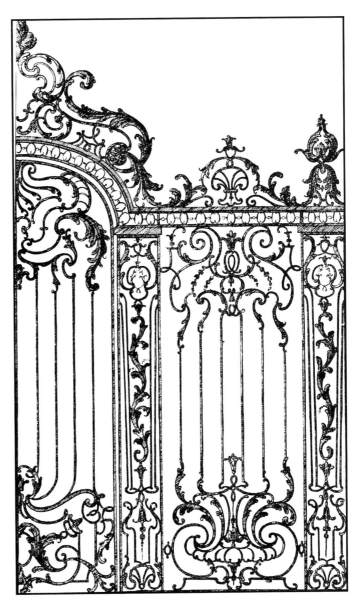

13

• Gates • Portails • Portale
• Pórticos • Ограды •

13: Gateway.
Grille d'entrée.
Eingangstore.
Cancela.
Ограда.

J. Jores, *A New Book of Iron Work containing a great variety of Designs*, London, 1759.

14-1: Jean Lamour. Detail of the gates,
Place Royale in Nancy.
Jean Lamour. Détail de la grille d'entrée,
Place Royale à Nancy.
Jean Lamour. Detail des Eingangstores,
Place Royale in Nancy.
Jean Lamour. Detalle de la cancela,
Place Royale en Nancy.
Жан Лямур. Деталь решетки.
Пляс Рояль, Нанси.

Héré de Corny, *Recueil des Fondations et Établissements faits par le roi de Pologne… dans la ville de Nancy.* Lunéville, 1762.

14-2: Gate.
Grille.
Gitterzaun.
Cancela.
Ограда.

Colin Campbell, *Vitruvius Britannicus*, London, 1717.

15: Gate of a public park, France, 19th century.
Grille d'entrée d'un parc public, France, XIXᵉ siècle.
Eingangstor eines öffentlichen Parks.
Frankreich, 19. Jh.
Cancela de uno parco público. Francia, siglo XIX.
Вход в общественный парк. Франция, XIX век.

Établissement métallurgique A. Durenne.

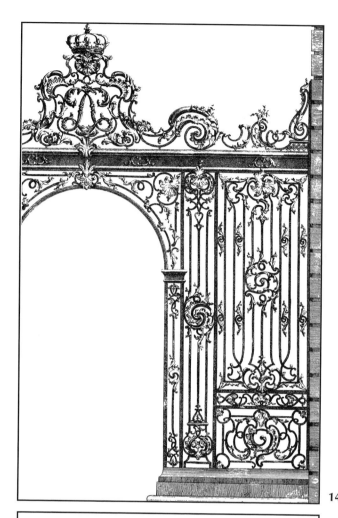

14-1

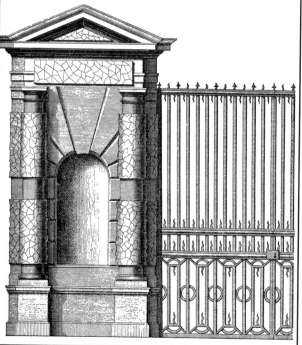

14-2

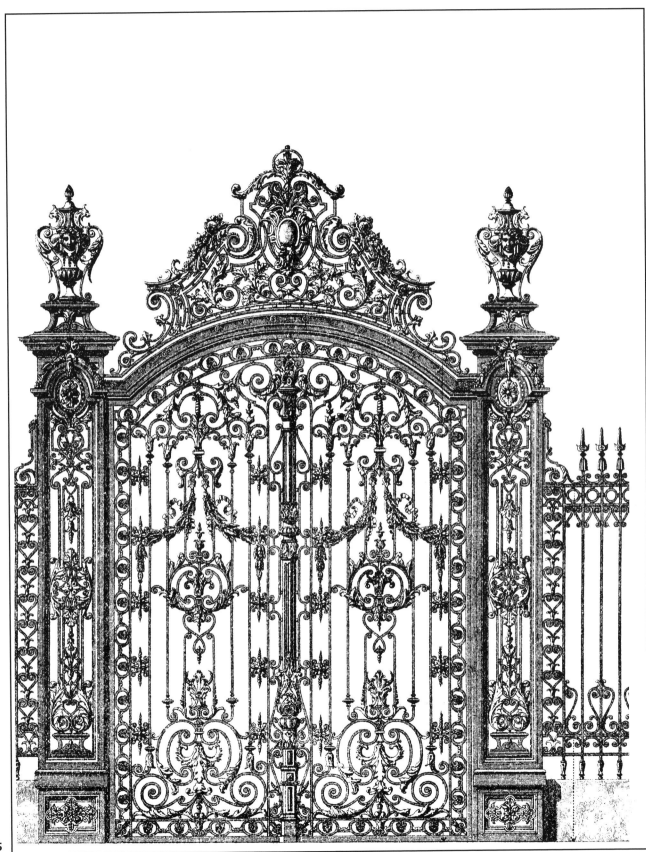

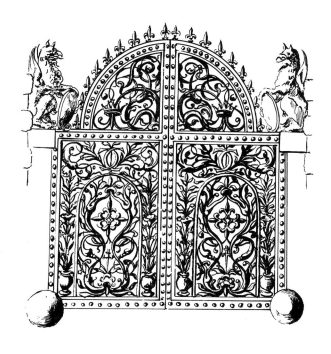

16-1

16-1: Balthasar Gerbier. Gateway, England, *c.* 1662.
Balthasar Gerbier. Grille d'entrée, Angleterre, vers 1662.
Balthasar Gerbier. Eingangstor, England, um 1662.
Balthasar Gerbier. Cancela, Inglaterra, hacia 1662.
Балтазар Джерби. Ограда, Англия, ок. 1662.

16-2: Hants Weovil. Gateway, England, 1704.
Hants Weovil. Grille d'entrée, Angleterre, 1704.
Hants Weovil. Eingangstor, England 1704.
Hants Weovil. Cancela, Inglaterra. 1704.
Хантс Уовил. Ограда, Англия 1704.

17: Gate.
Grille.
Gittertor.
Cancela.
Ограда.

Diderot & D'Alembert, *L'Encyclopédie*, Paris, 1751–1772.

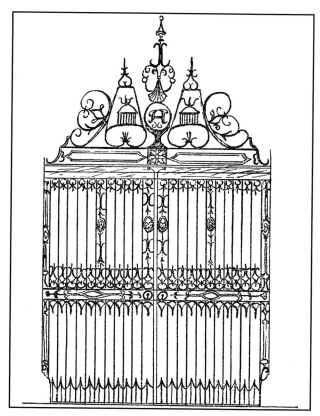

16-2

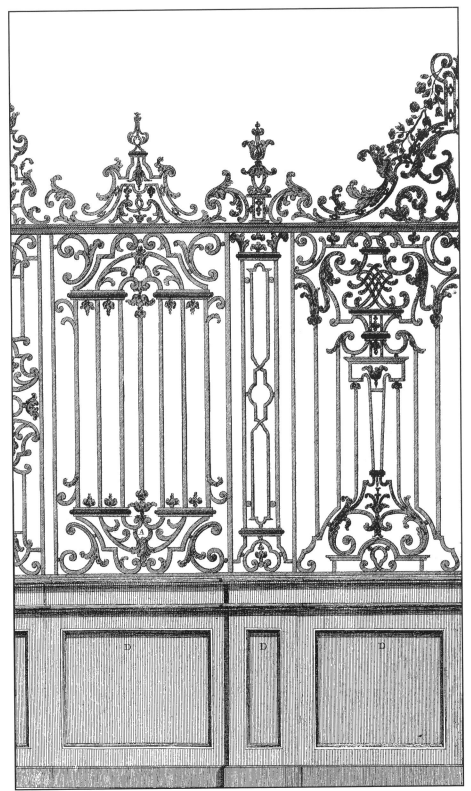

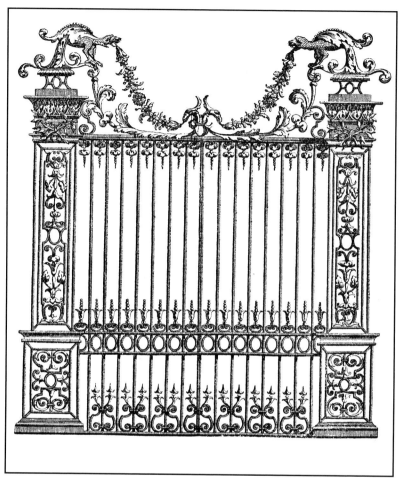

18/20: Gates.
Grilles.
Gitter.
Cancelas.
Ограды.

Jean Tijou, *A New Book of Drawings Invented and Designed by Jean Tijou*, London, 1690.

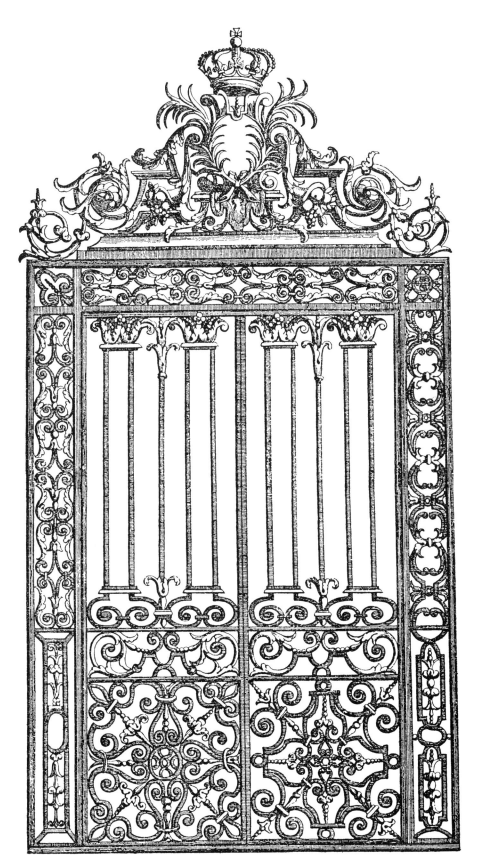

19

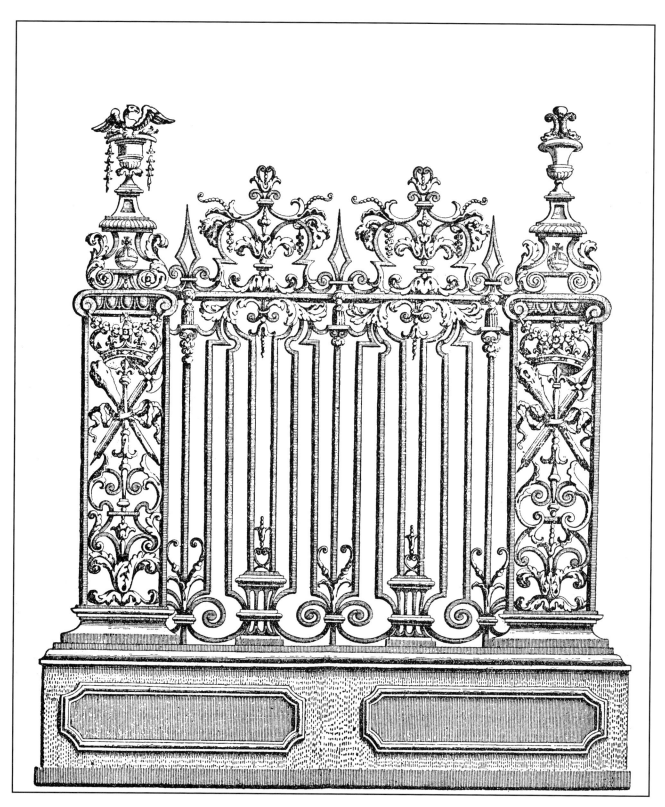

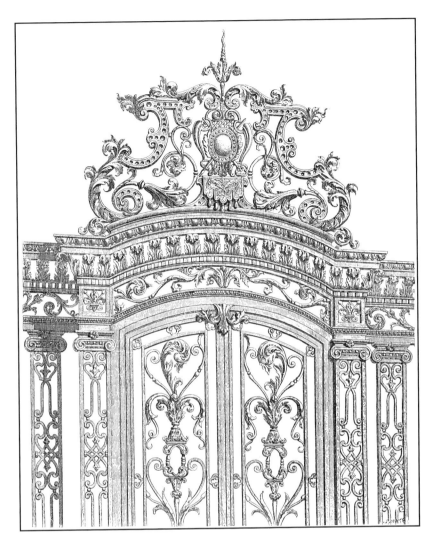

21

21: Detail of the choir grille in the church of Saint-Ouen de Rouen, France, 17th century.
Fragment de la grille du chœur de l'église Saint-Ouen de Rouen, France, XVIIe siècle.
Fragment des Torgitters der Kirche Saint-Ouen in Rouen, Frankreich 17. Jh.
Fragmento de la alambrera del coro de la iglesia Saint-Ouen de Rouen, Francia, siglo XVII.
Деталь решетки для хоров в церкви Сэнт-Уэн де Руан, Франция, XVII век.

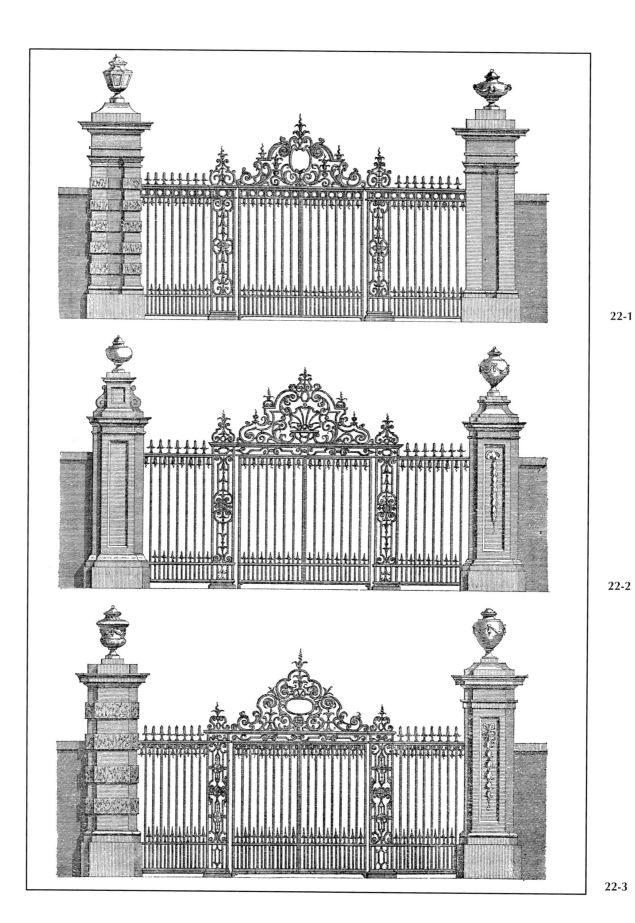

22-1

22-2

22-3

22

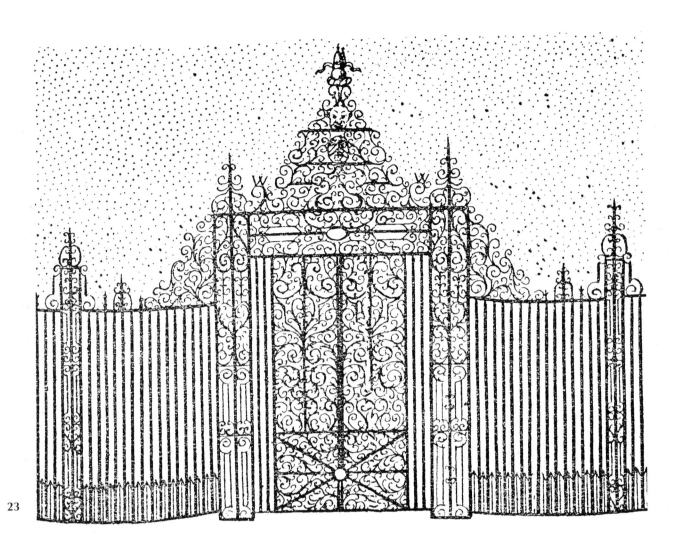

23

22: Gateways.
Grilles d'entrée.
Eingangstor.
Cancelas.
Ограды ворот.

James Gibbs, *A Book of Architecture*, London, 1728.

23: Thomas Robinson. Gateway of New College, Oxford.
Thomas Robinson. Grille d'entrée du New College, Oxford.
Thomas Robinson. Eingangstor des New College, Oxford.
Thomas Robinson. Cancela del New College, Oxford.
Томас Робинсон. Ограда Нью-Колледжа, Оксфорд.

William Williams, *Oxonia Depicta*, Oxford 1723-1733.

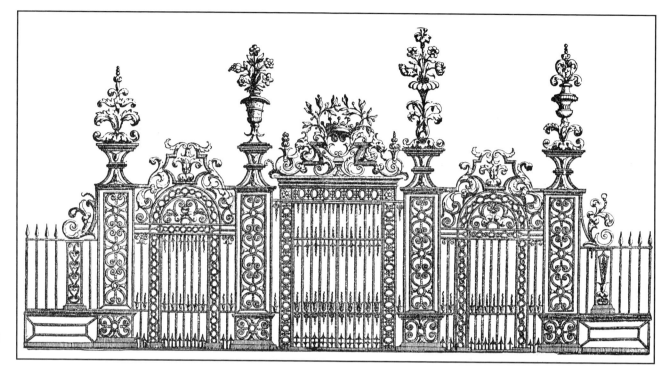

24-1

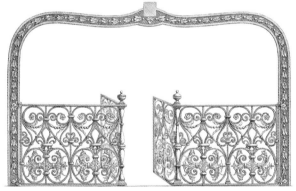

24-2

24-1: Gate.
Grille.
Tor.
Cancela
Решетка.

Jean Tijou, *A New Book of Drawings Invented and Designed by Jean Tijou*, London, 1690.

24-2: Wrought iron and gilt grille from the Royal gallery of Louis XIV, France, 18th century.
Grille en fer forgé et doré de la galerie royale de Louis XIV, France, XVIIᶜ siècle.
Geschmiedetes vergoldetes Gitter der galerie réale de Louis XIV, Frankreich, 17. Jh.
Cancela en hierro forjado y dorado de la galería Reale de Louis XIV, Francia, siglo XVII.
Решетка из кованого позолоченного железа королевской галереи Людовика XIV, Франция, XVIII век.

25: Gateway at Trinity College, Oxford.
Grille d'entrée du Trinity College, Oxford.
Eingangstor des Trinity College, Oxford.
Cancela del Trinity College, Oxford.
Решетка ворот Тринити Колледжа, Оксфорд.

William Williams, *Oxonia Depicta*, Oxford 1723-1733.

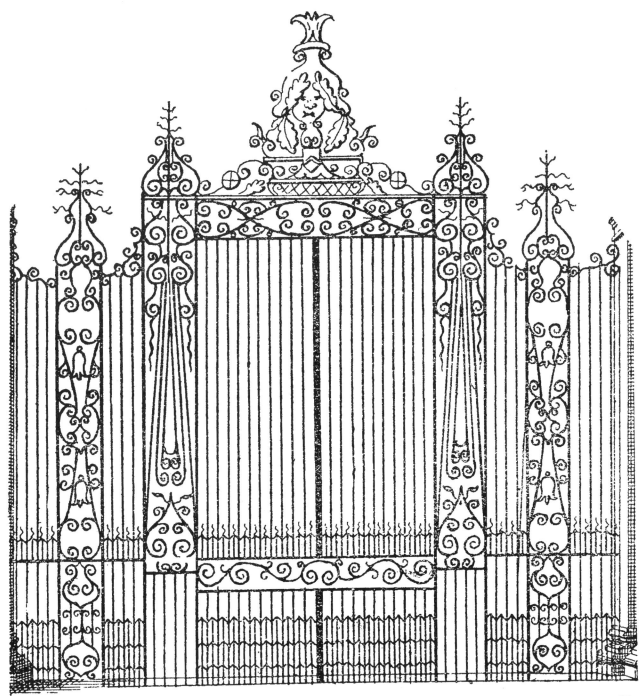

25

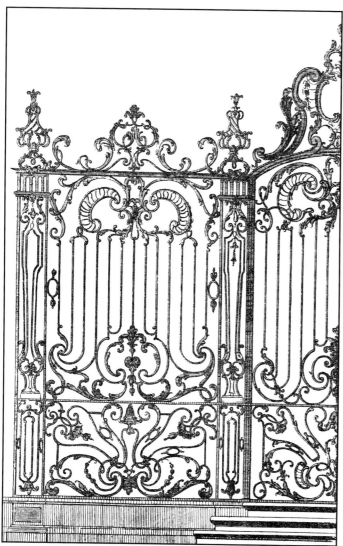

26-1

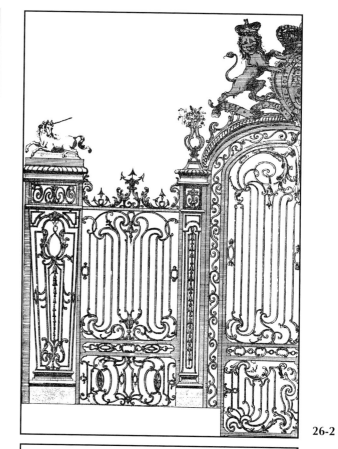

26-2

26/33: Gateways.
Grilles d'entrée.
Eingangstore.
Cancelas.
Ограды.

J. Jores, *A New Book of Iron Work containing a great variety of Designs*, London, 1759.

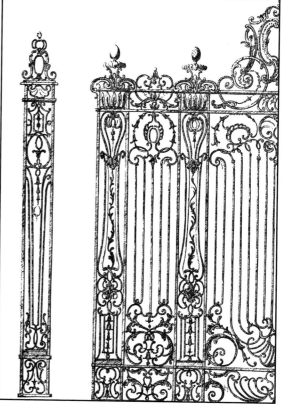

26-3

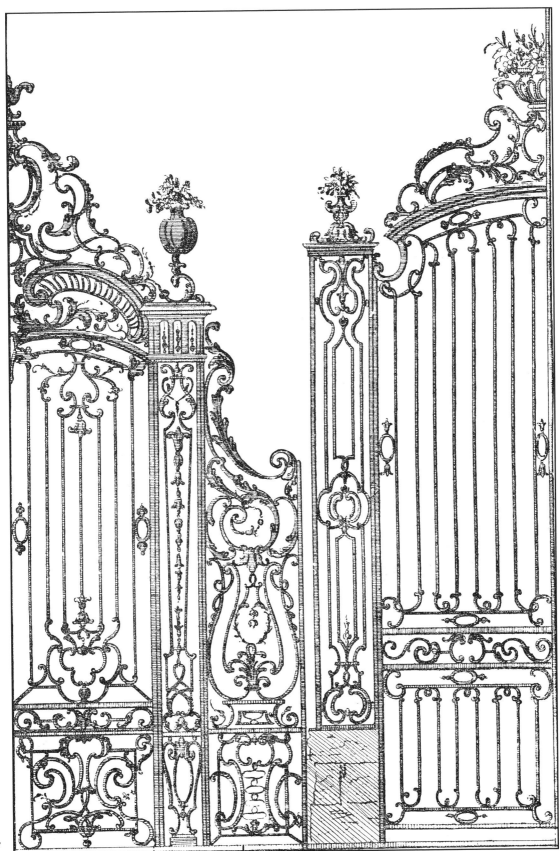

27

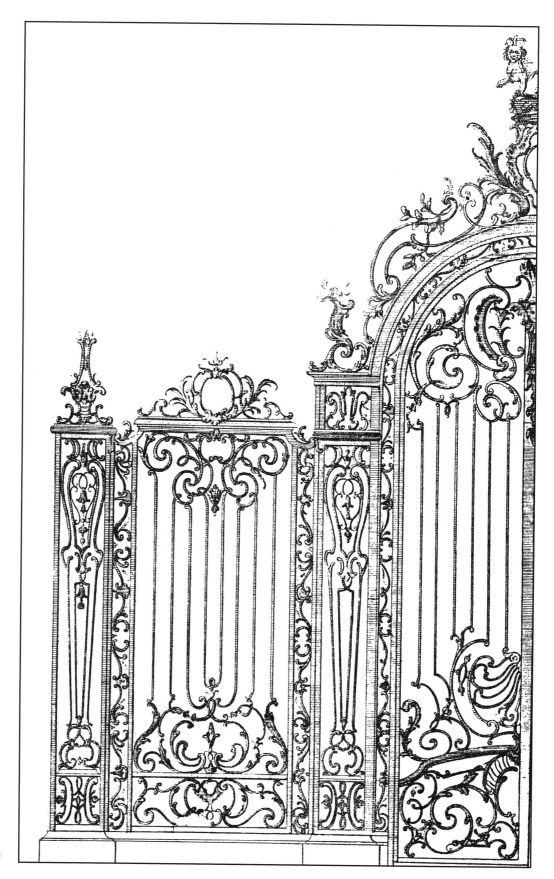

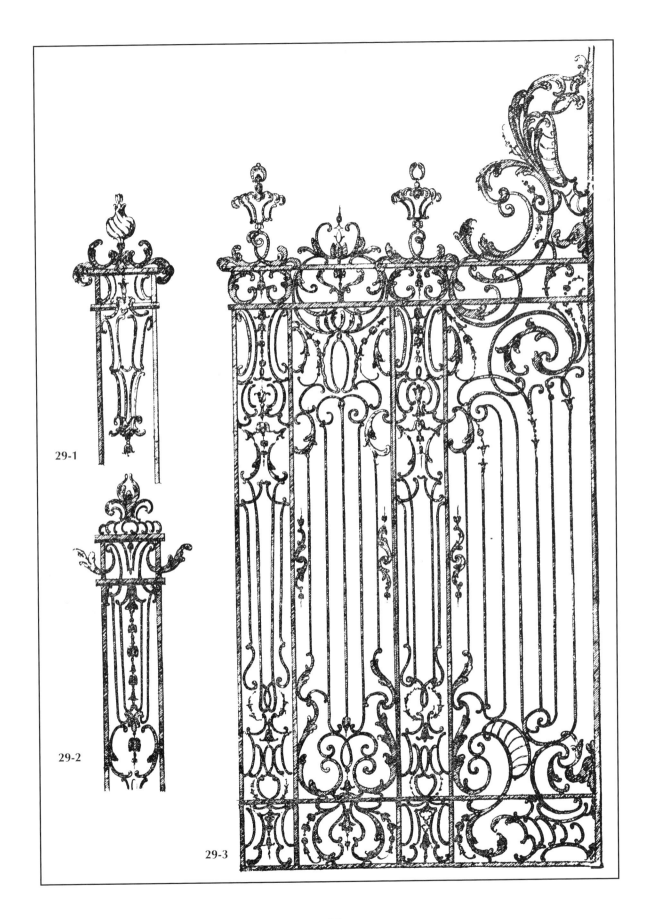

29-1

29-2

29-3

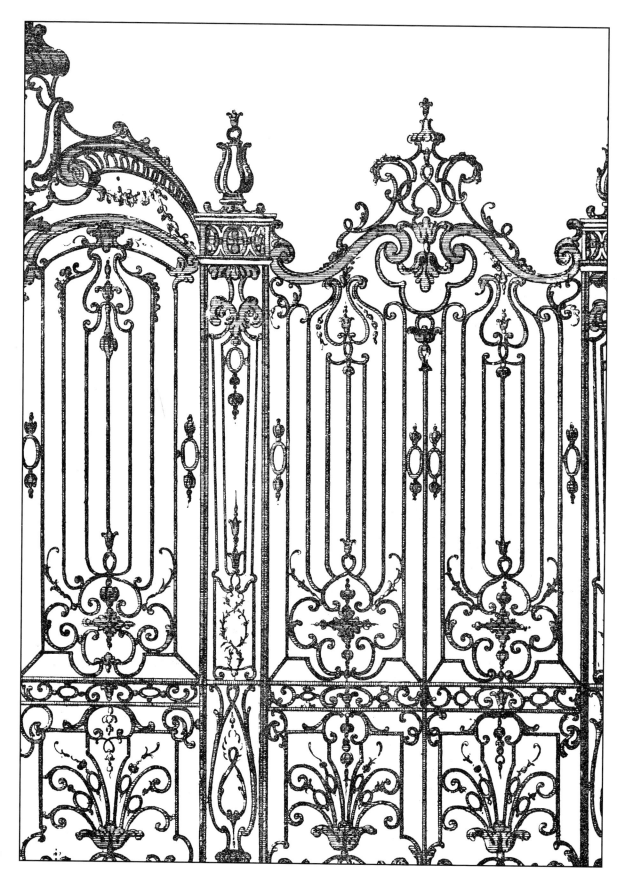

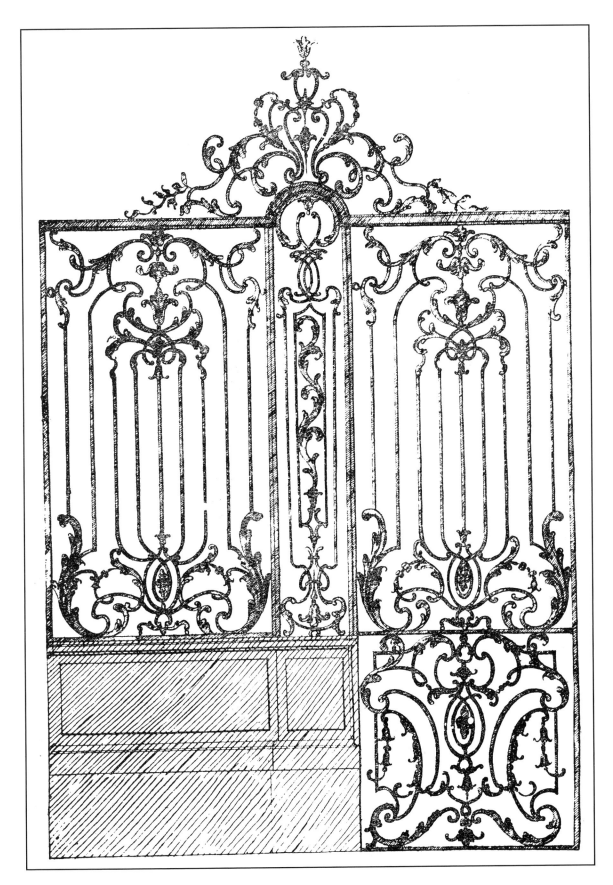

31

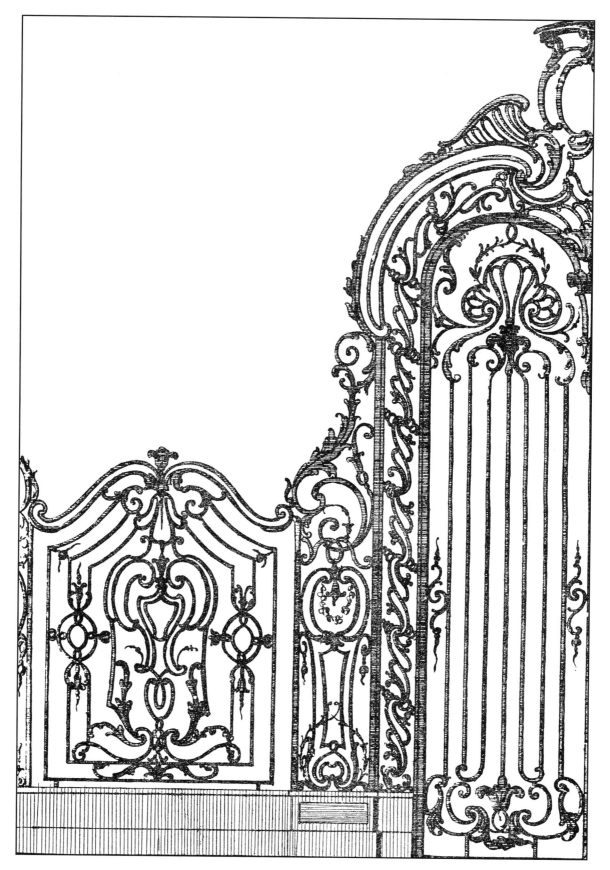

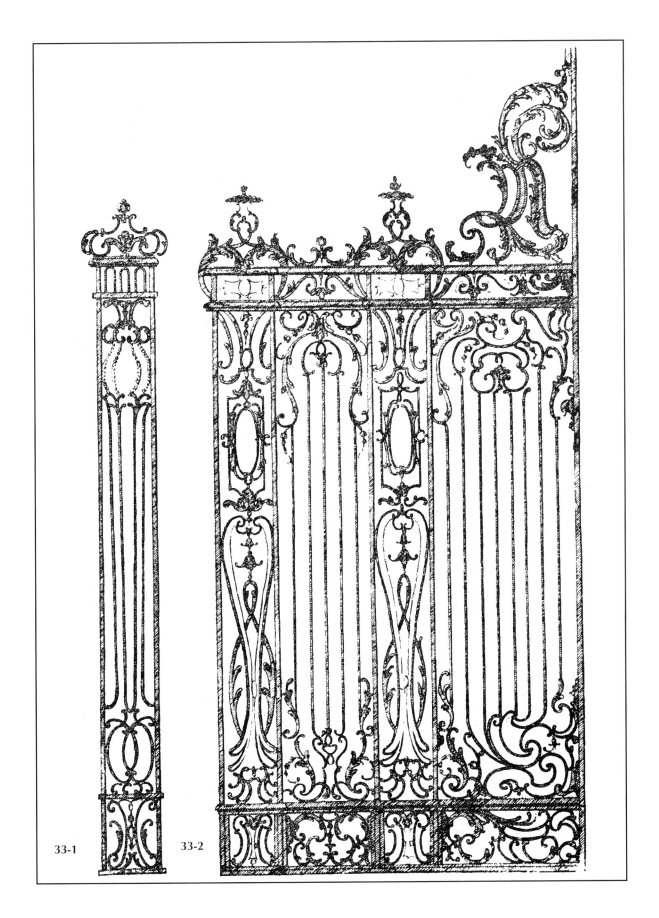

33-1 33-2

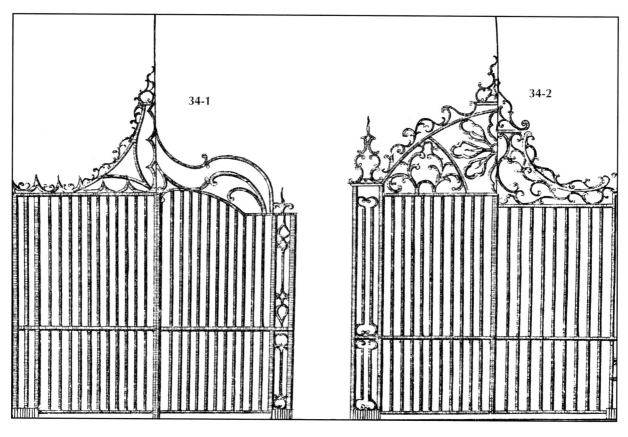

34-1

34-2

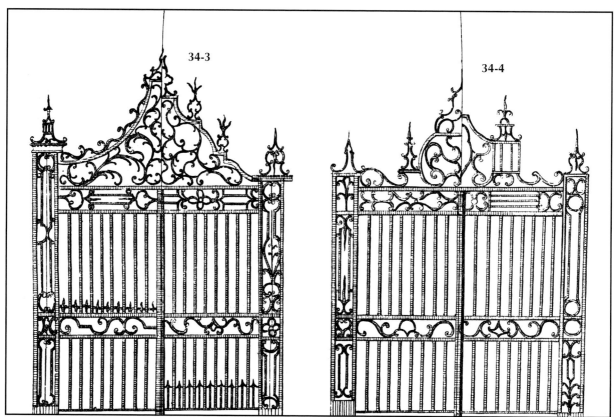

34-3

34-4

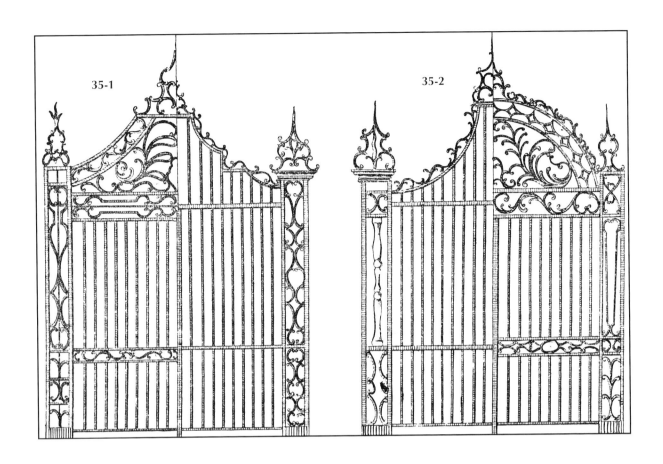

35-1

35-2

35-3

34/36: Gateways.
Grilles d'entrée.
Eingangstore.
Cancelas.
Ограды.

W. and J. Welldon, *The Smith's Right Hand*,
London, 1765.

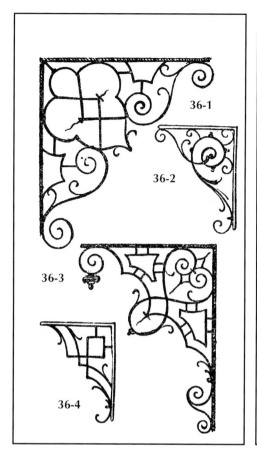

36-1

36-2

36-3

36-4

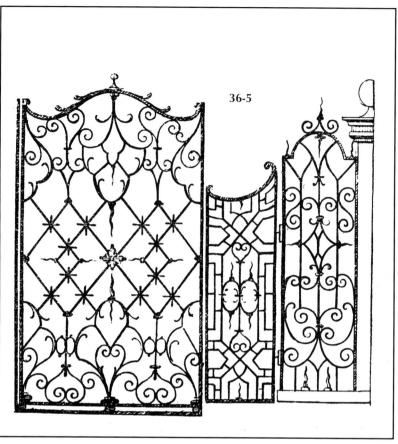

36-5

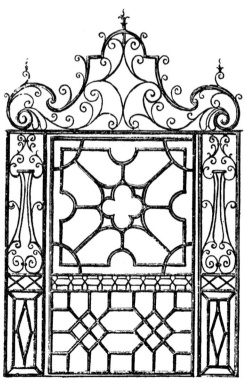

36-6

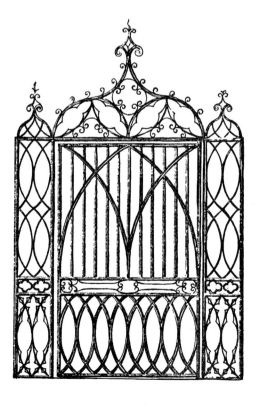

36-7

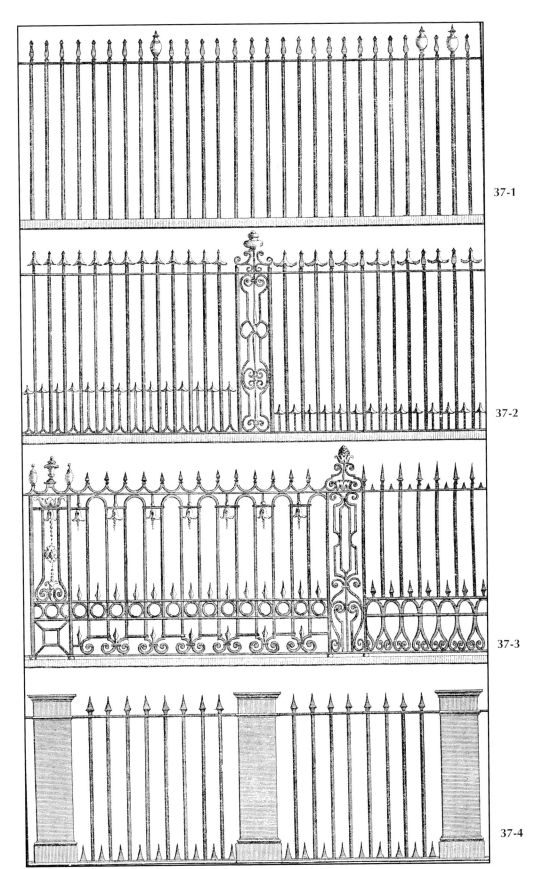

37-1

37-2

37-3

37: Railings.
Grilles.
Zaungitter.
Verjas.
Ограды.

Isaac Ware, *A Complete Body of Architecture*, London, 1726.

37-4

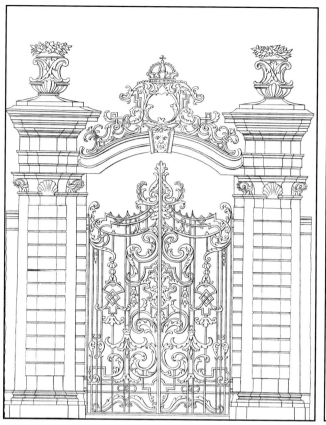

38-1

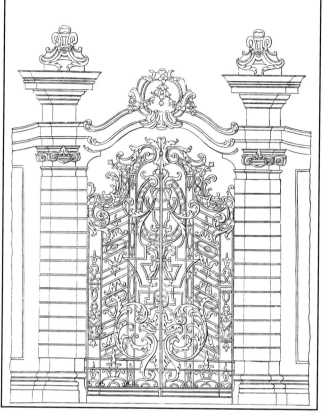

38-2

38/42: Gateways.
Grilles d'entrée.
Eingangstore.
Cancelas.
Ограды ворот.

Batty Langley, *Ancient Masonry both in the Theory
and the Practice*, London, 1736.

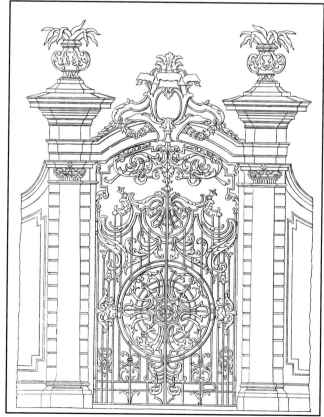

38-3

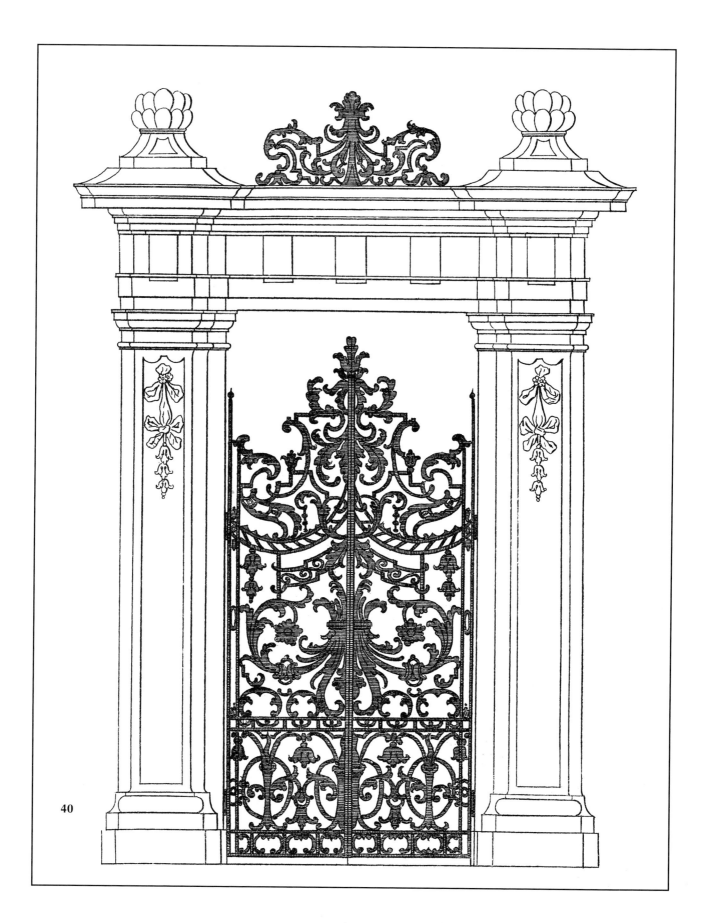

40

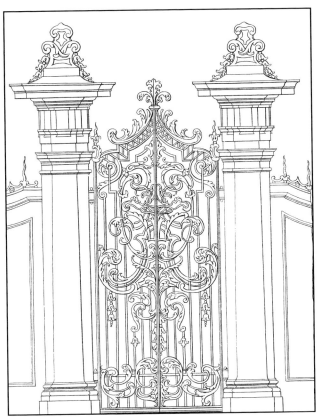

41-1

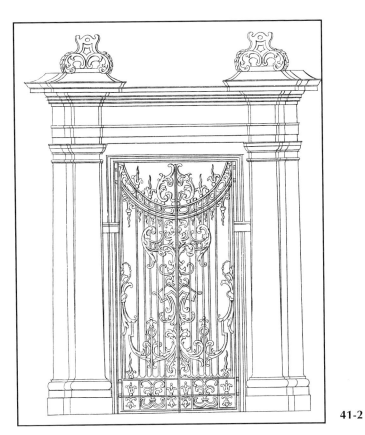

41-2

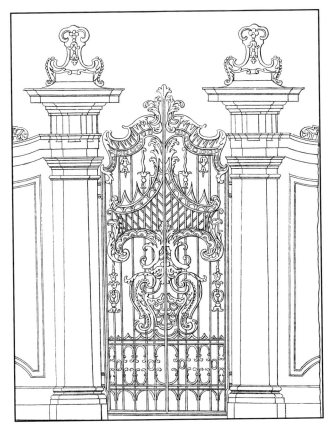

41-3

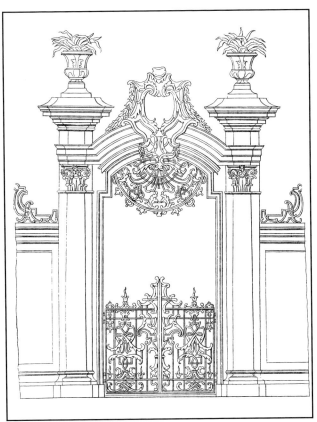

41-4

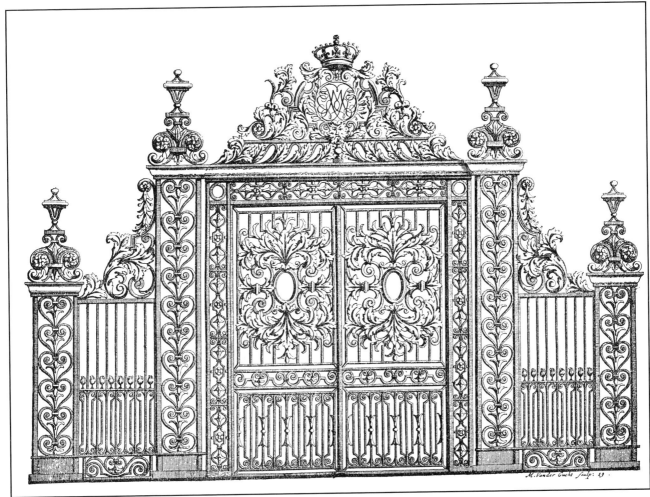

43-1

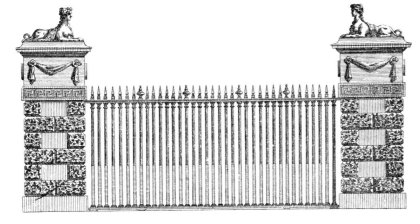

43-2

43-1: Gateway at Hampton Court.
Grille d'entrée de Hampton Court.
Eingangstor des Hampton Court.
Cancela de Hampton Court.
Ограда Хэмптон Корт.

Jean Tijou, *A New Book of Drawings Invented and Designed by Jean Tijou*, London, 1690.

43-2: Railings.
Grilles.
Zaungitter.
Verjas.
Решетка.

Isaac Ware, *Designs of Inigo Jones and Others*, London, 1756.

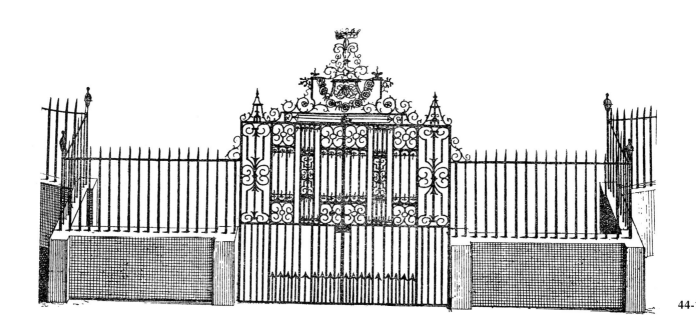

44-1

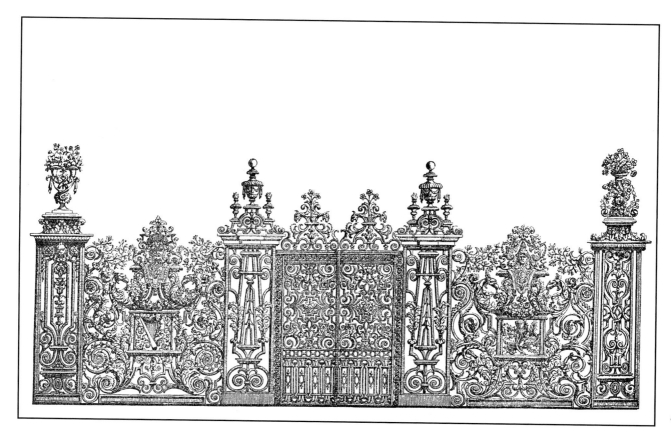

44-2

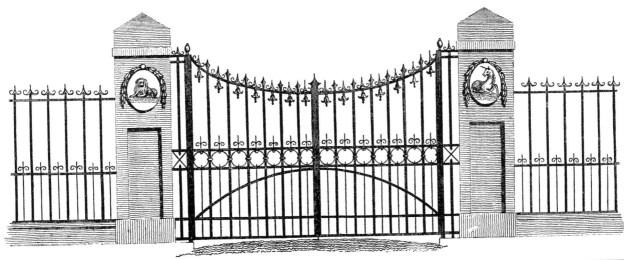

45-1

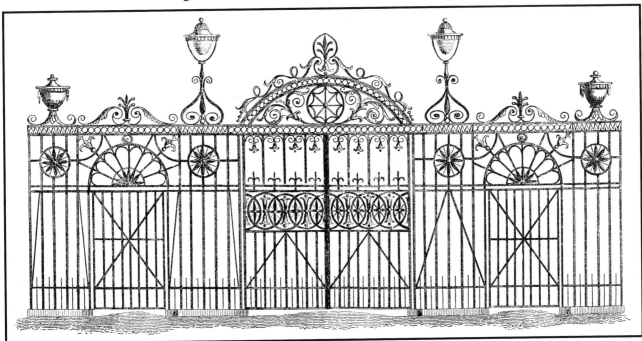

45-2

44-1: Gateway at Buckingham House.
Grille d'entrée de Buckingham House.
Eingangstor des Buckingham House.
Cancela de Buckingham House.
Ограда Букингемского дворца.

44-2: Gateway at Hampton Court.
Grille d'entrée de Hampton Court.
Eingangstor des Hampton Court.
Cancela de Hampton Court.
Ограда Хэмптон Корт.

Jean Tijou, *A New Book of Drawings Invented and Designed by Jean Tijou*, London, 1690.

45: Gateways.
Grilles d'entrées.
Eingangstore.
Cancelas.
Ограды.

I. and J. Taylor, *Ornamental Iron Work or Designs in the Present Taste*, London, *c.* 1795.

46-1

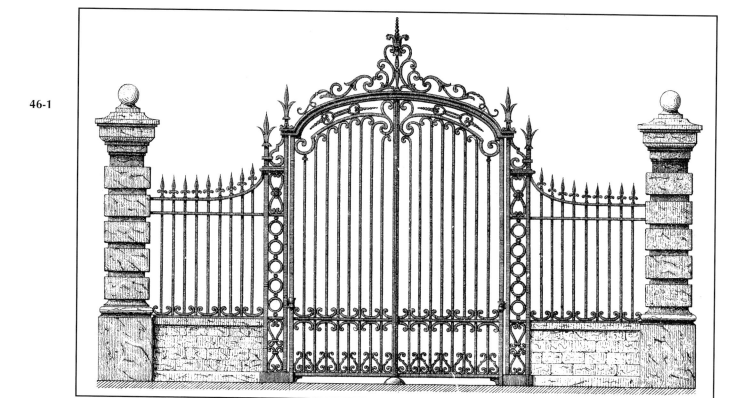

46-2

46-1: Gateway in the Louis XIII style.
Grille d'entrée dans le style Louis XIII.
Eingangstor im Stil von Louis XIII.
Cancela de estilo Luis XIII.
Ограда ворот в стиле Людовика XIII.

46-2: Gateway in the Greek style, France,
19th century.
Grille d'entrée dans le style grec, France,
XIXᵉ siècle.
Eingangstor im griechischen Stil, Frankreich, 19. Jh.
Cancela de estilo griego, Francia, siglo XIX.
Ограда ворот в греческом стиле, Франция,
XIX век.

Établissement J. Roy.

47-1, 47-2, 47-3, 47-4: Details of gates.
Détails de grilles.
Detail eines Gitterzauns.
Detalles de cancelas.
Детали оград.

E. Barberot, *Traité pratique de serrurerie*,
Paris & Liège, 1925.

47-5: Gateway in the Renaissance style,
19th century.
Grille d'entrée dans le style Renaissance,
XIXᵉ siècle.
Eingangstor im Stil der Renaissance, Frankreich,
19. Jh.
Cancela de estilo renacentista, Francia, siglo XIX.
Ограда в стиле Ренессанс, Франция,
XIX век.

Établissements J. Roy, France.

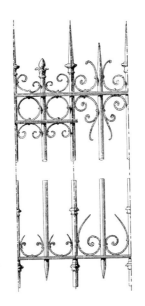

47-1

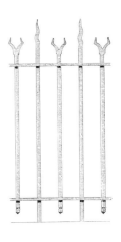

47-2

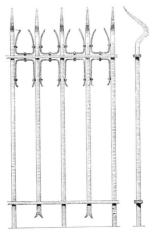

47-3

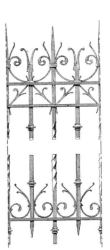

47-4

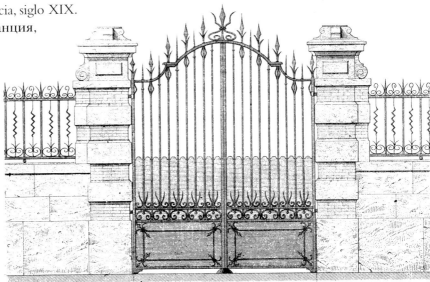

47-5

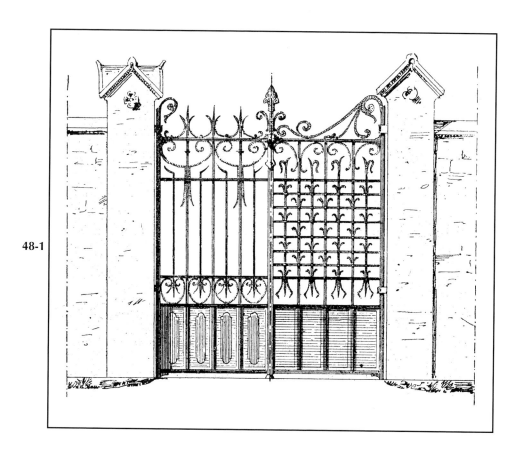

48-1

48-2

48/49: Gateways.
Grilles d'entrée.
Eingangstore.
Cancelas.
Ограды.

E. Barberot, *Traité pratique de serrurerie*, Paris & Liège, 1925.

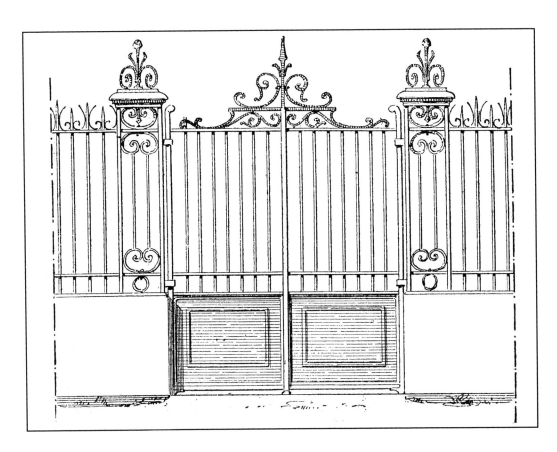

49-1

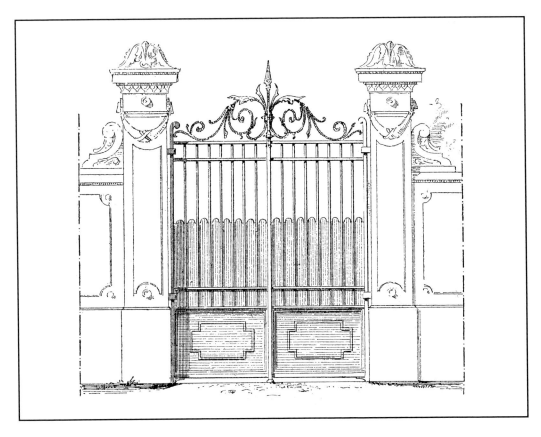

49-2

49

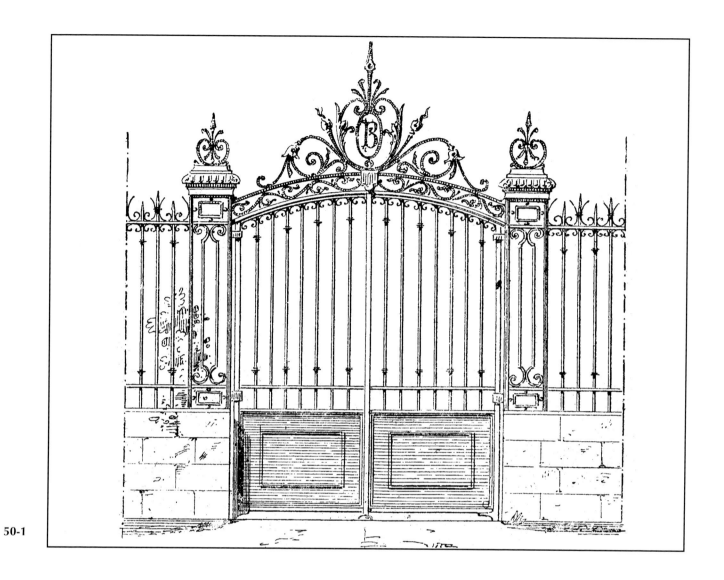

50-1

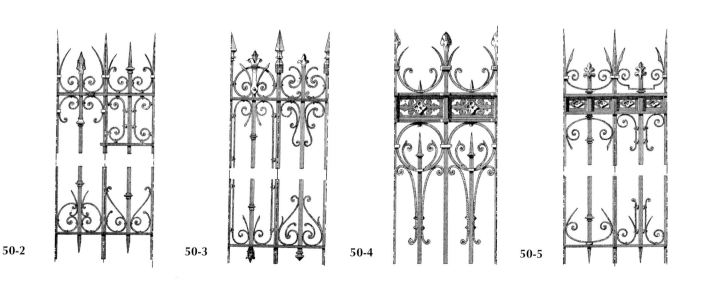

50-2　　　　　　50-3　　　　　　50-4　　　　　　50-5

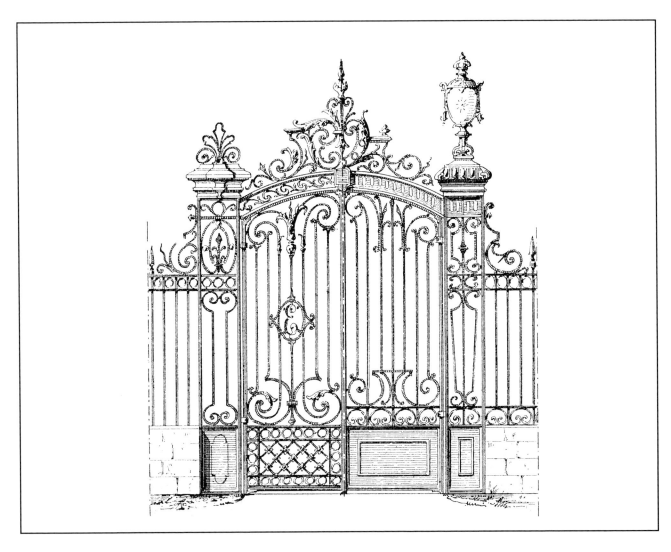

50-1: Gateway.
Grille d'entrée.
Eingangstor.
Cancela.
Ограда.

50-2, 50-3, 50-4, 50-5: Details of gates.
Détails de grilles.
Detail eines Gitterzauns.
Detalles de cancelas.
Детали оград.

E. Barberot, *Traité pratique de serrurerie*, Paris & Liège, 1925.

51: Gateway.
Grille d'entrée.
Eingangstor.
Cancela.
Ограда.

E. Barberot, *Traité pratique de serrurerie*, Paris & Liège, 1925.

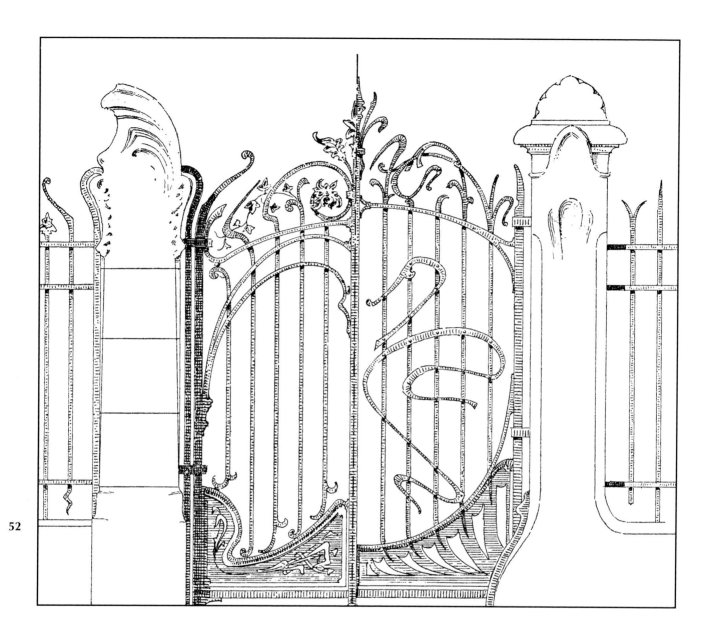

52: Gateway in the Art Nouveau style.
Grille d'entrée dans le style 1900.
Eingangstor um 1900.
Cancela de estilo 1900.
Ограда в стиле Арт Нуво.

E. Barberot, *Traité pratique de serrurerie*,
Paris & Liège, 1925.

53/56: Gate copings.
Détails de frontons de grille.
Details von Torkronen.
Detalles de frontones de cancela.
Детали фронтонов ограды.

E. Barberot, *Traité pratique de serrurerie*, Paris & Liège,
1925.

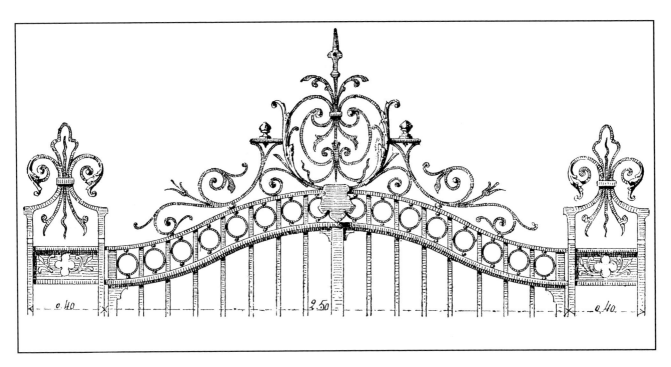

53-1

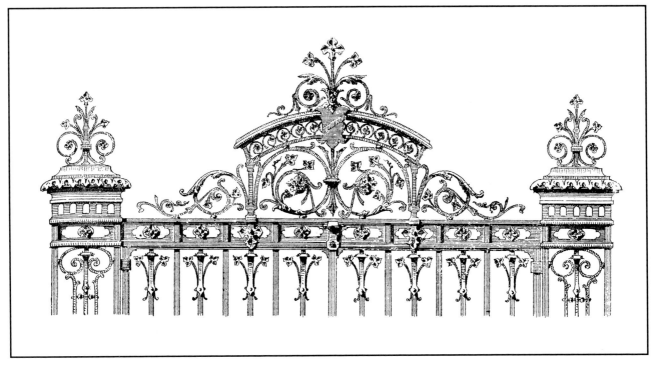

53-2

54-1

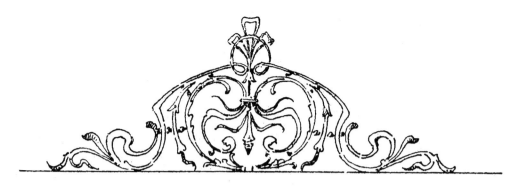

54-2

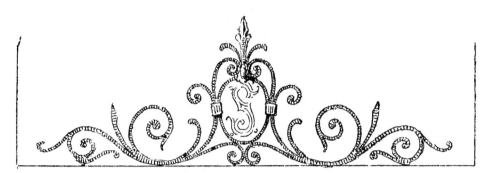

54-3

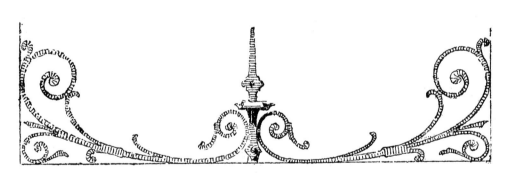

54-4

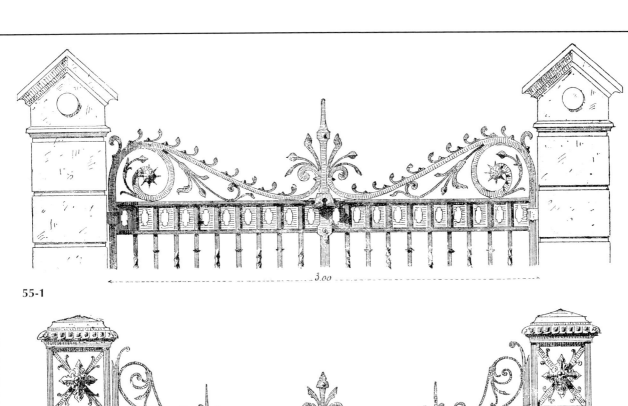

55-1

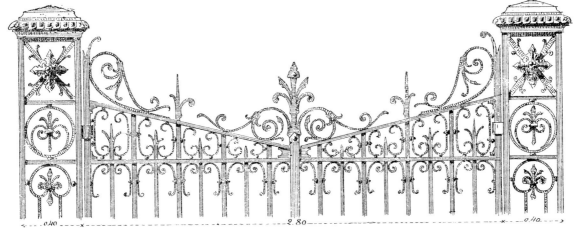

55-2

55-3   **55-4**   **55-5**

      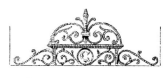

55-6   **55-7**   **55-8**

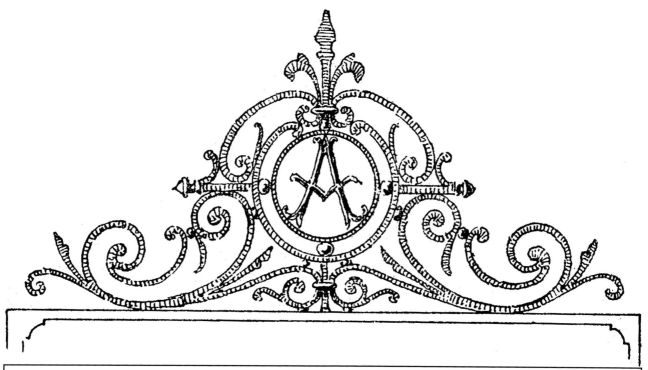

56-1

56-2

57-1: Grille uprights.
Montants de grilles.
Gitterverzierungen.
Largueros de cancelas.
Стойки оград.

57-2: Balcony partition.
Chardon.
Eisenspitze.
Barda de hierro.
Балконное ограждение.

E. Barberot, *Traité pratique de serrurerie*, Paris & Liège, 1925.

57-3:
Balcony partition, France, 19th century.
Chardon, France, XIXᵉ siècle.
Eisenspitze, Frankreich, 19. Jh.
Barda de hierro, Francia, siglo XIX.
Балконное ограждение, Франция, XIX век.

Établissement métallurgique A. Durenne.

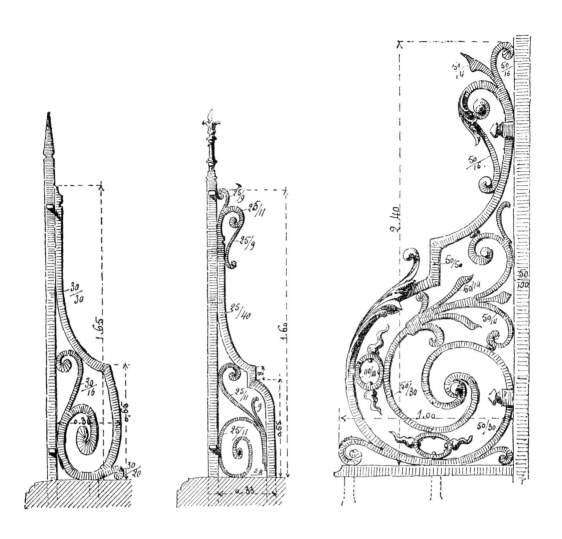

57-1

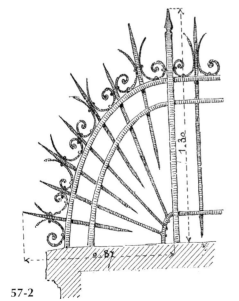

57-2

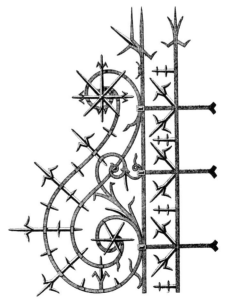

57-3

57

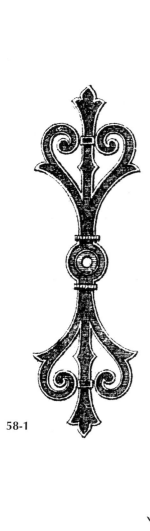

58-1

58-2

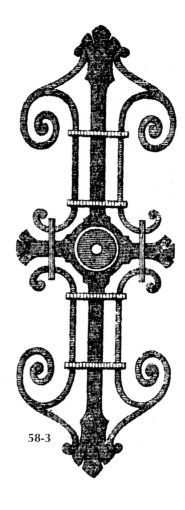

58-3

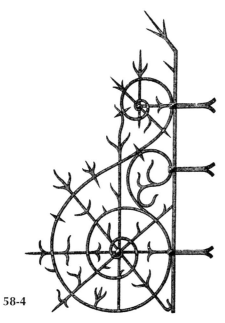

58-4

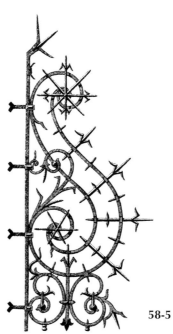

58-5

58/59: Balcony partitions,France, 19th century.
Chardons, France, XIXe siècle.
Eisenspitze, Frankreich, 19. Jh.
Bardas de hierro, Francia, siglo XIX.
Балконные ограждения, Франция, XIX век.

Établissement métallurgique A. Durenne.

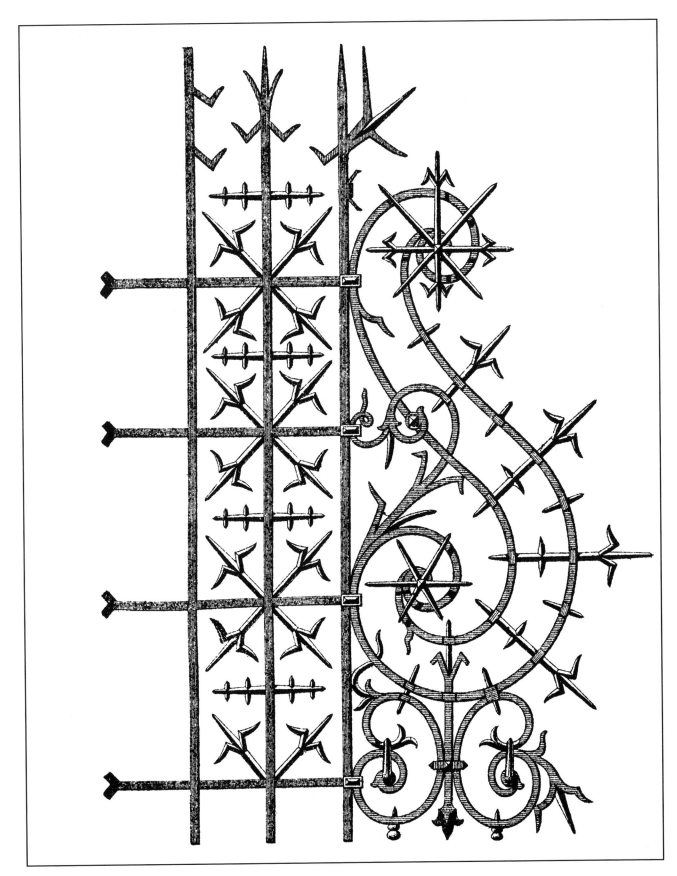

59

60: Balcony partitions.
Chardons.
Eisenspitze.
Bardas de hierro.
Балконные ограждения.

H. Grave, *Travaux en fer forgé*,
France, 1881.

61: Balcony partitions.
Chardons.
Eisenspitze.
Bardas de hierro.
Балконные ограждения.

E. Barberot, *Traité pratique de
serrurerie*, Paris & Liège,
1925.

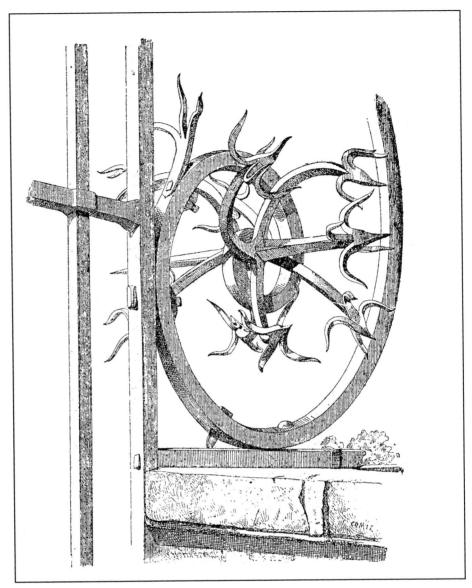

61-1

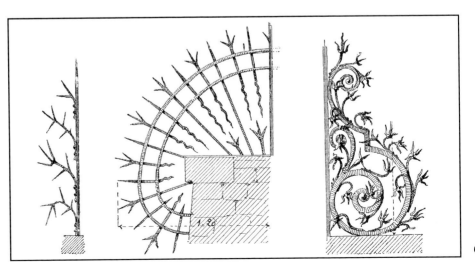

61-2

61

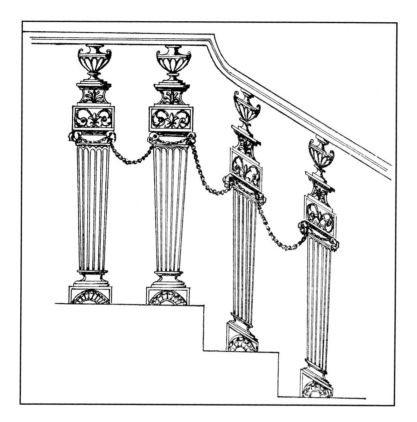

62

• Banisters • Rampes •
• Treppengeländer •
• Pasamanos •
• Перила •

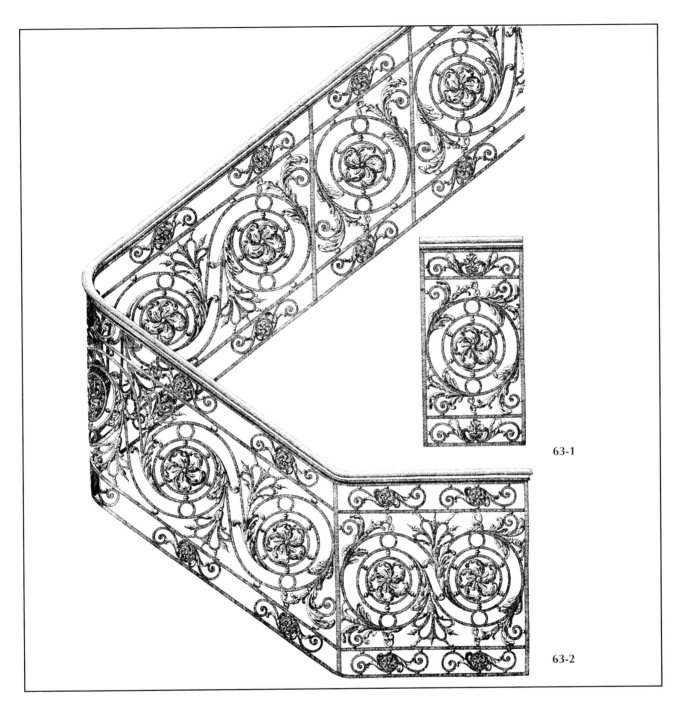

63-1

63-2

62: Robert Adam. Banister, England, second half of the 18th century.
Robert Adam. Rampe d'escalier, Angleterre, deuxième moirié du XVIIIe siècle.
Robert Adam. Treppengeländer, England, zweite Hälfte des 18. Jh.
Robert Adam. Pasamanos, Inglaterra, siglo XVIII.
Роберт Адам. Перила, Англия, вторая половина XVIII века.

63/67: Banisters, France, 19th century.

Rampes d'escalier, France, XIXe siècle.
Treppengeländer, Frankreich, 19. Jh.
Pasamanos, Francia, siglo XIX.
Перила, Франция, XIX век.

Établissement métallurgique A. Durenne.

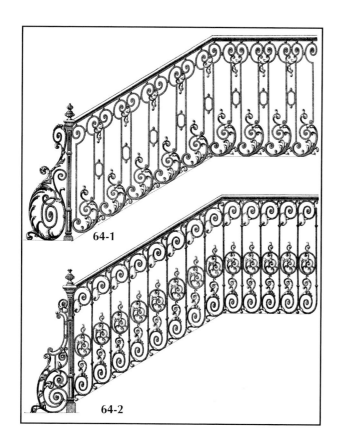

64-1

64-2

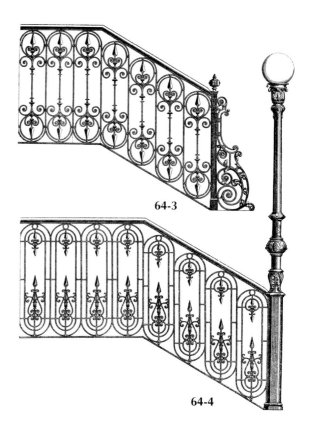

64-3

64-4

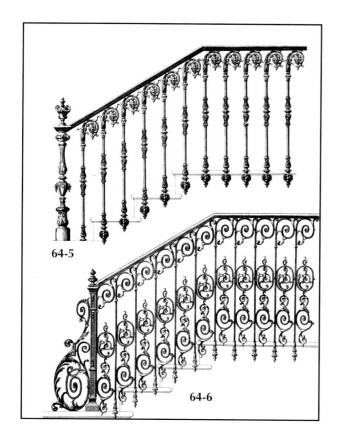

64-5

64-6

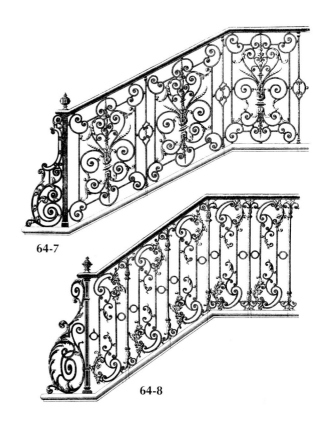

64-7

64-8

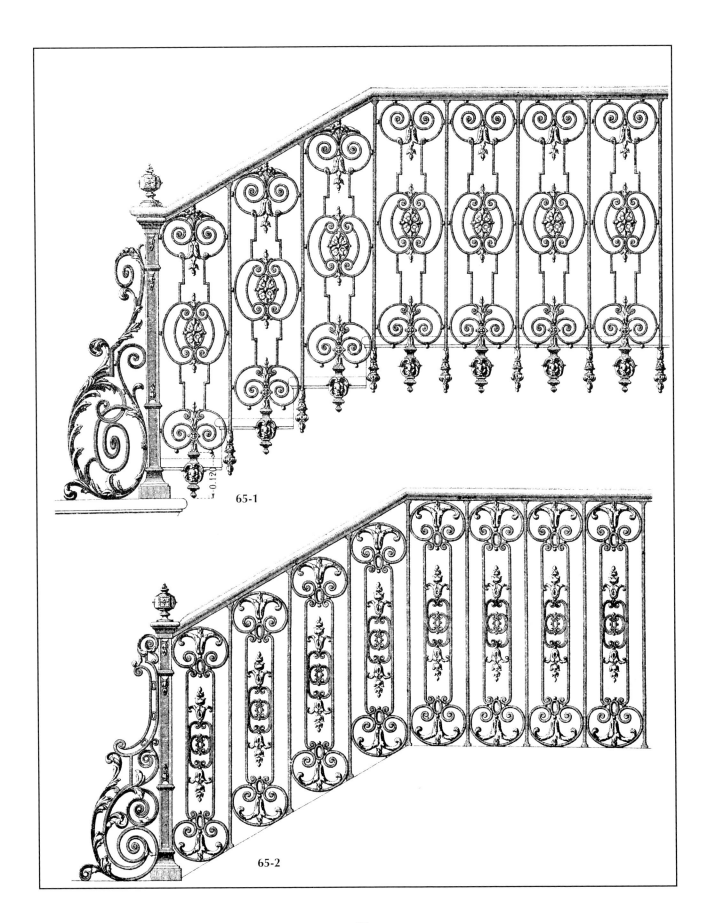

65-1

65-2

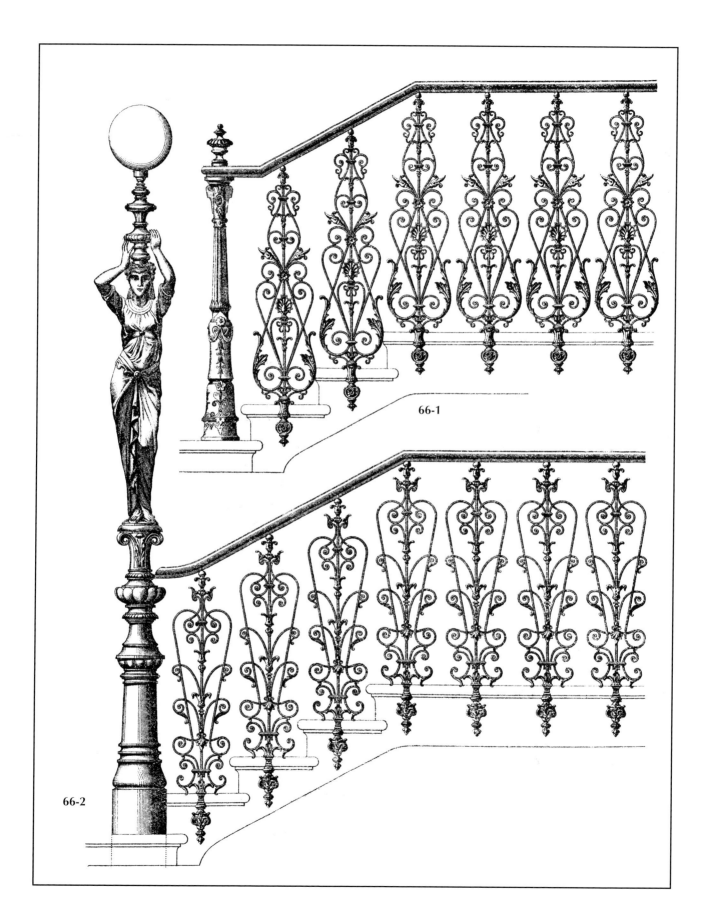

66-1

66-2

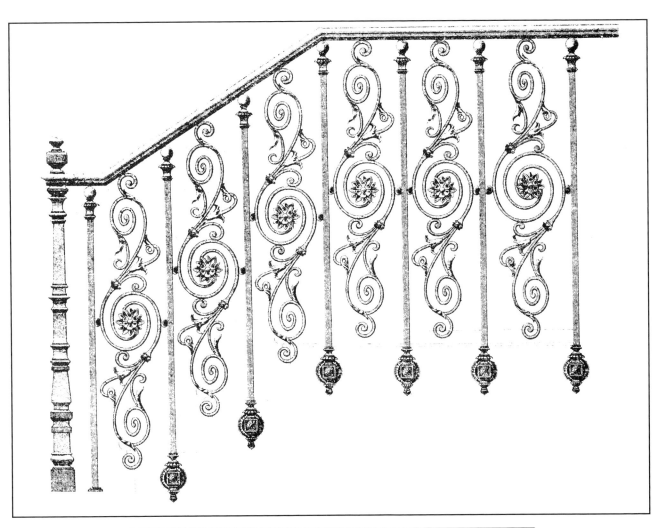

67-1

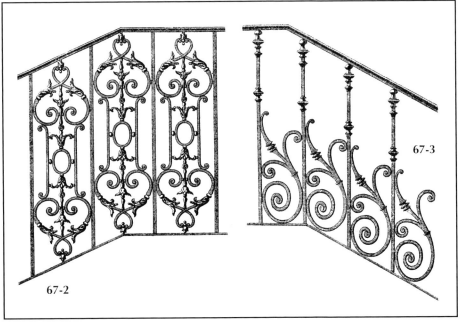

67-2

67-3

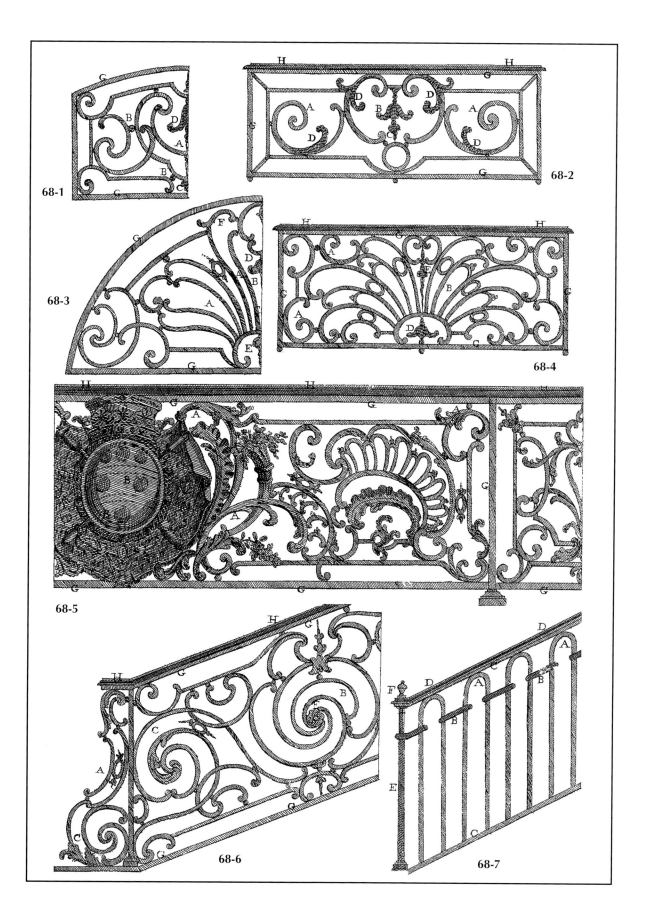

68-1

68-2

68-3

68-4

68-5

68-6

68-7

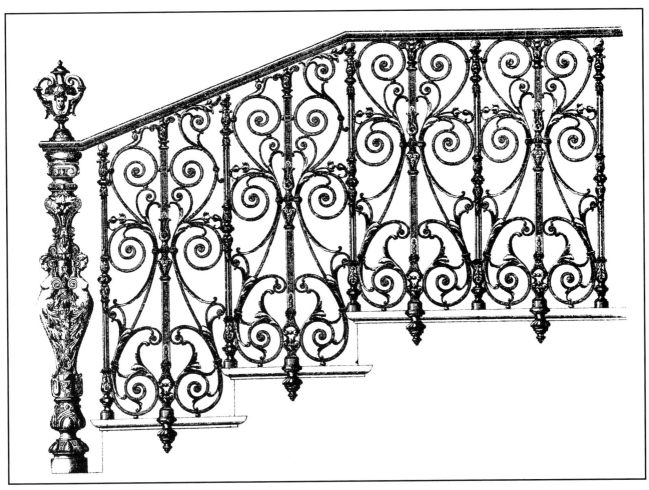

68: Fanlights, balconies, handrails and railings.
Dessus de portes, balcons, appuis et rampes.
Flächenverzierungen von Türen, Balcone, Untersetzungen
und Rampen.
Partes superiores de puertas, balcones, soportes
y pasamanos.
Фонари, балконы, перила и ограждения.

Diderot & D'Alembert, *L'Encyclopédie*, Paris,
1751–1772.

69-71: Banisters, France, 19th century.
Rampes d'escalier, France, XIXe siècle.
Treppengeländer, Frankreich, 19. Jh.
Pasamanos, Francia, siglo XIX.
Перила, Франция, XIX век.

Établissement métallurgique A. Durenne.

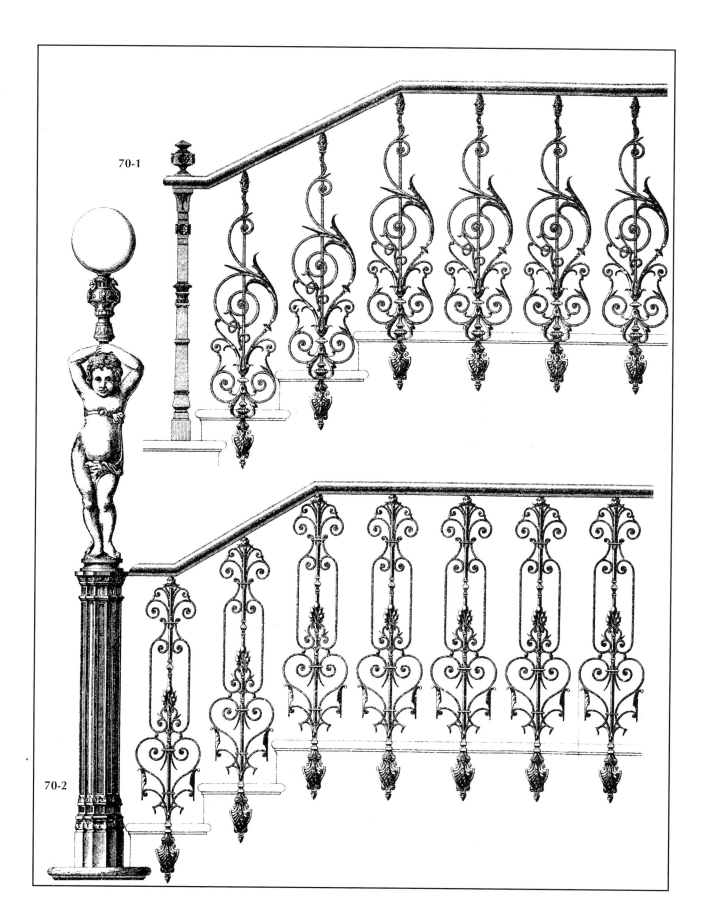

70-1

70-2

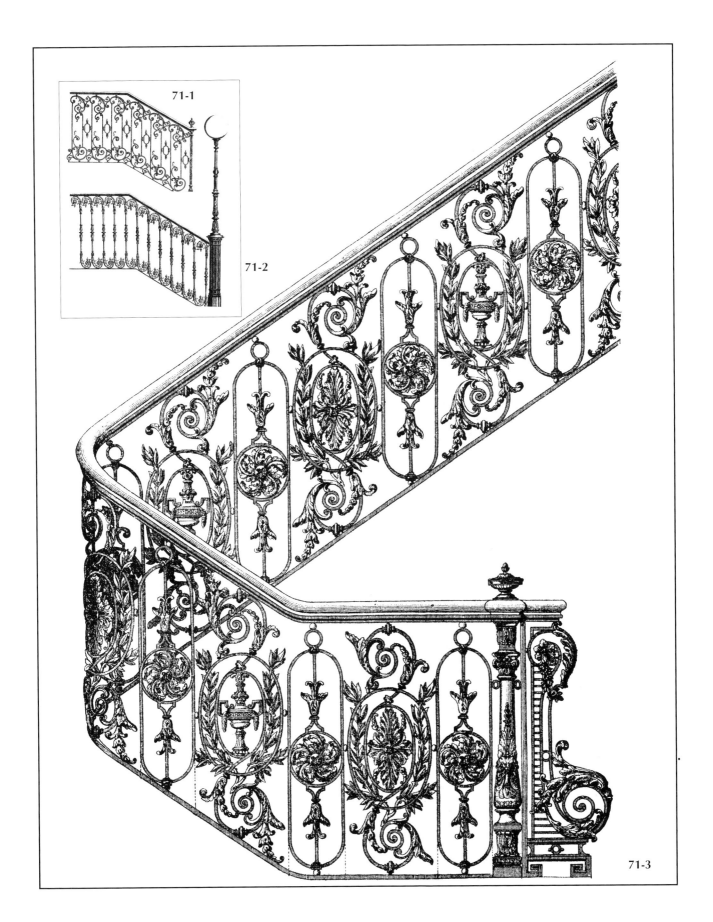

71-1

71-2

71-3

71

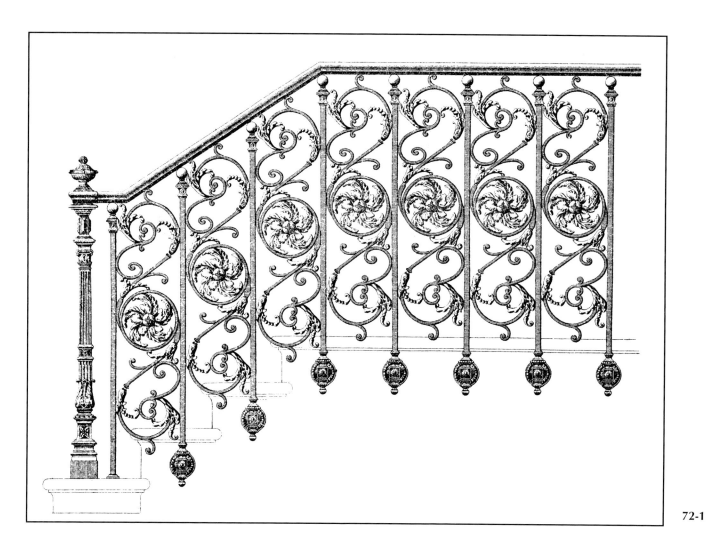

72-1

72: Banisters, England, 18th century.
Rampes d'escalier, Angleterre, XVIIIᵉ siècle.
Treppengeländer, England, 18. Jh.
Pasamanos, Inglaterra, siglo XVIII.
Перила, Англия, XVIII век.

73: Banisters, France, 19th century.
Rampes d'escalier, France, XIXᵉ siècle.
Treppengeländer, Frankreich, 19. Jh.
Pasamanos, Francia, siglo XIX.
Перила, Франция, XIX век.

Établissement métallurgique A. Durenne.

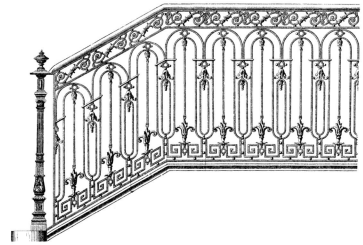

72-2

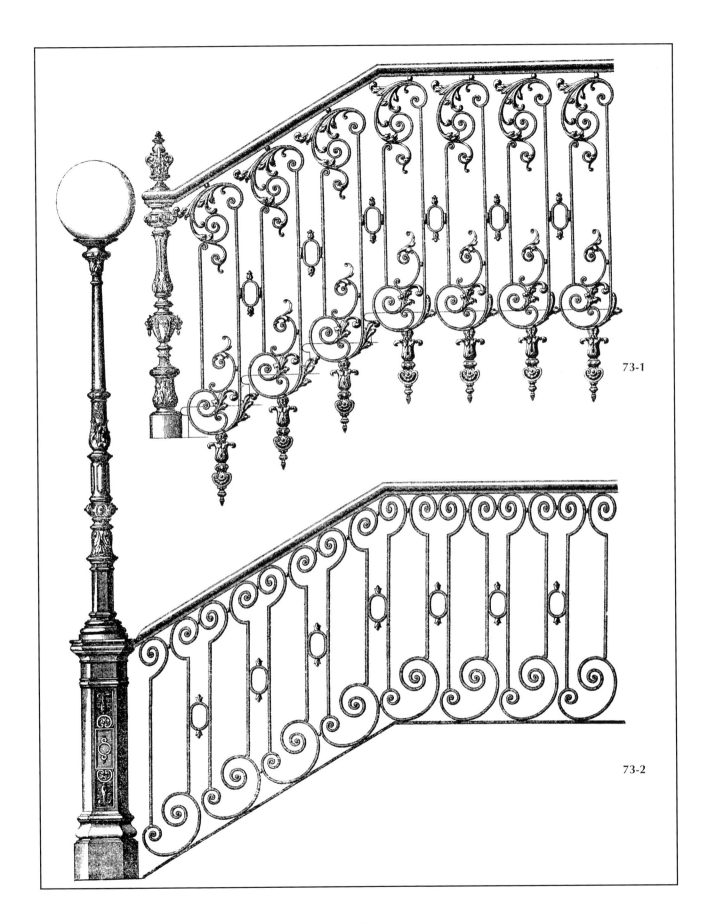

73-1

73-2

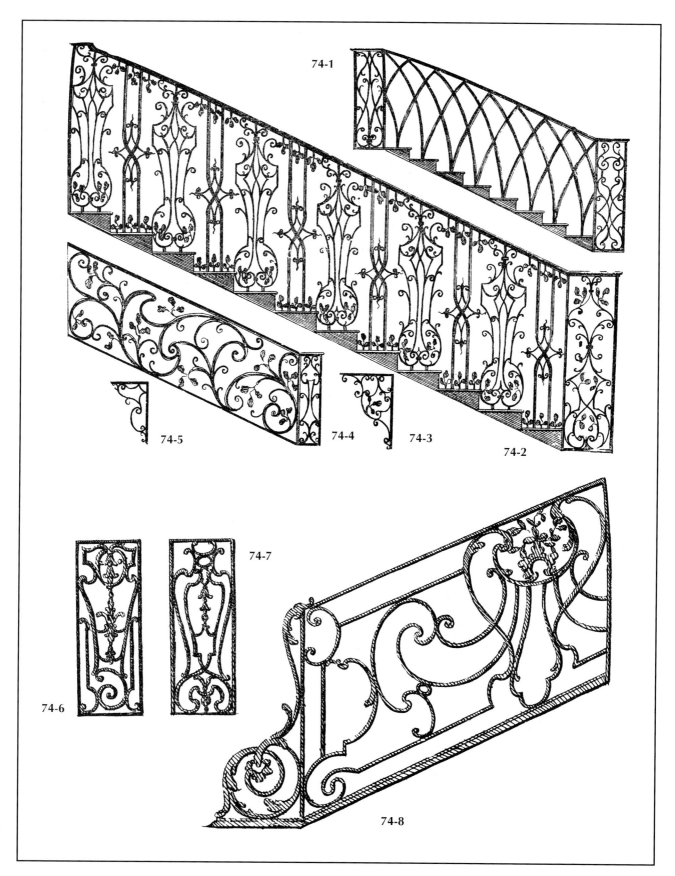

74-1

74-5

74-4

74-3

74-2

74-7

74-6

74-8

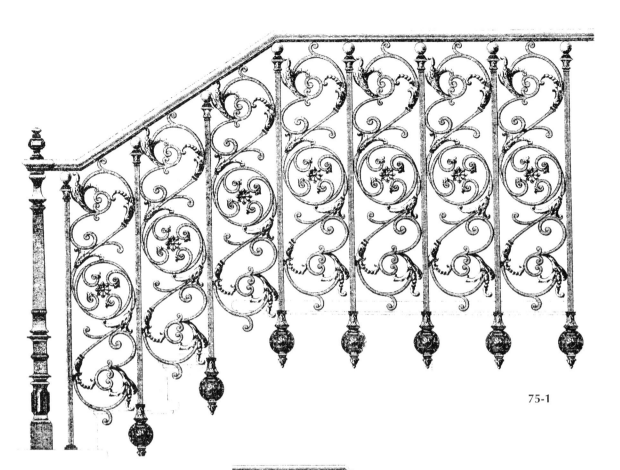

75-1

74: Banisters.
Rampes d'escalier.
Treppengeländer.
Pasamanos.
Перила.

W. and J Welldon, *The Smith's Right Hand,* London, 1765.

75: Banisters, France, 19th century.
Rampes d'escalier, France, XIXe siècle.
Treppengeländer, Frankreich, 19. Jh.
Pasamanos, Francia, siglo XIX.
Перила, Франция, XIX век.

Établissement métallurgique A. Durenne.

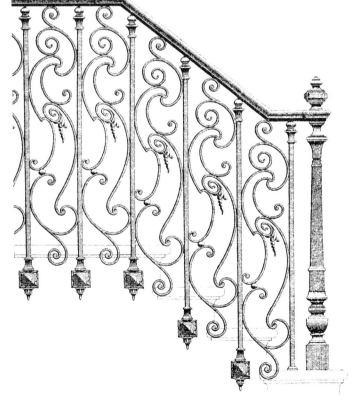

75-2

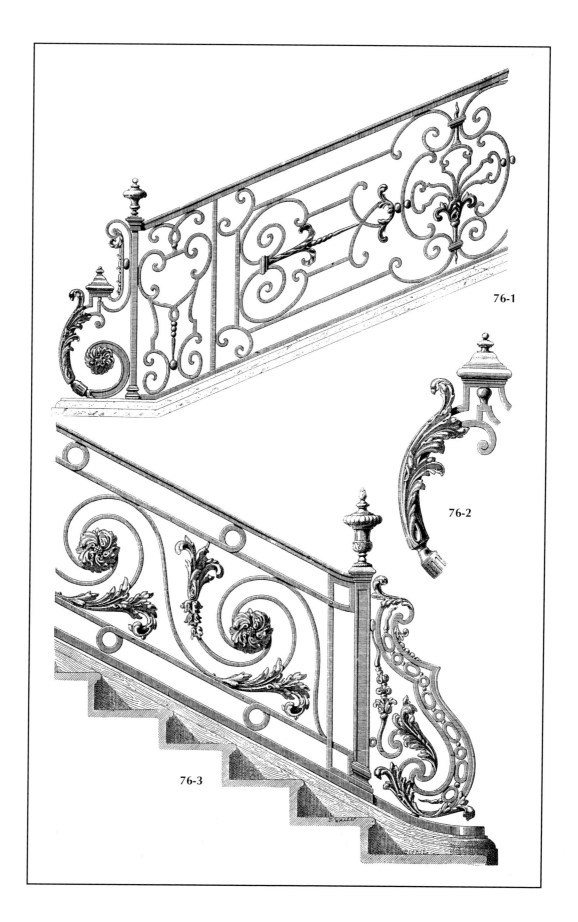

76-1

76-2

76-3

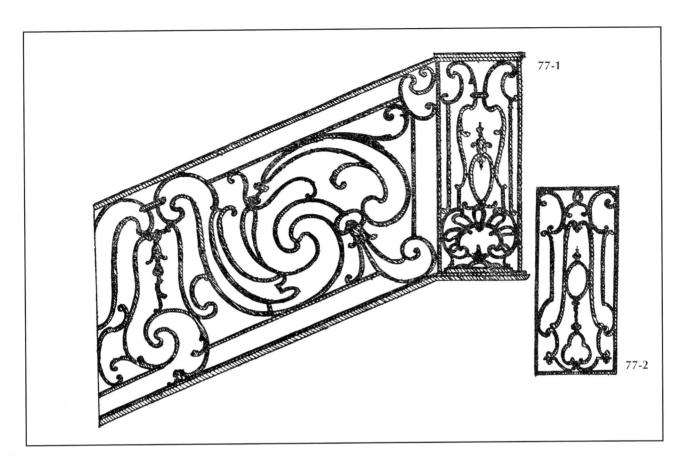

77-1

77-2

76: Banisters, France, 17th century.
Rampes d'escalier, France, XVIIᵉ siècle.
Treppengeländer, Frankreich, 17. Jh.
Pasamanos, Francia, siglo XVII.
Перила, Франция, XIX век.

77: Banisters.
Rampes d'escalier.
Treppengeländer.
Pasamanos.
Перила.

W. and J Welldon, *The Smith's Right Hand*,
London, 1765.

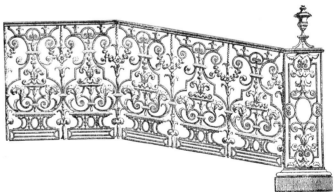

77-3

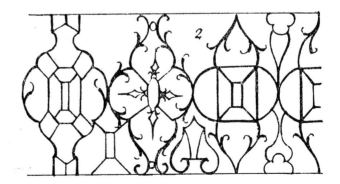

77-4

78-1

78-2

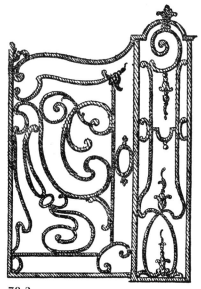

78-3

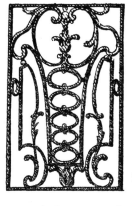

78-5

78-4

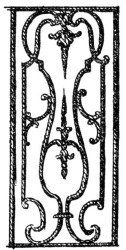

78-7

78-6

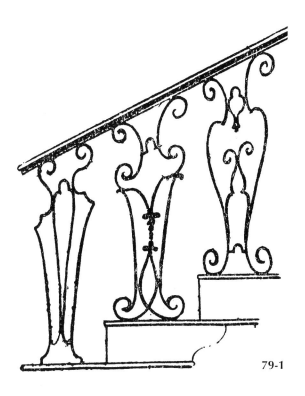

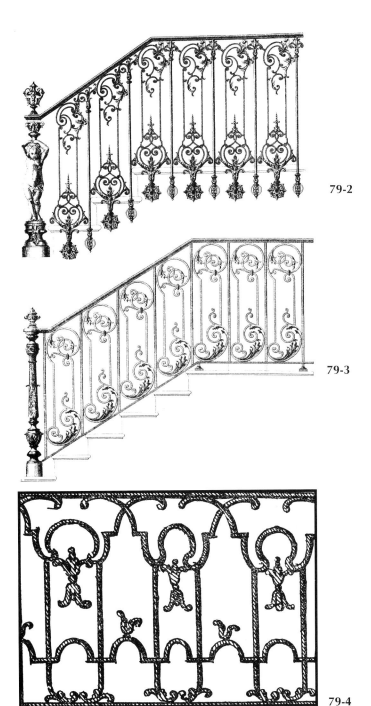

78: Handrails and railings.
Appuis et rampes.
Einsetzungen.
Pasamanos.
Перила и ограждения.

W. and J Welldon, *The Smith's Right Hand*,
London, 1765.

79-1: Banister.
Rampe d'escalier.
Treppengeländer.
Pasamano.
Перила.

W. Ince and J. Mayhew, *Universal System of Household
Furniture,* London, 1762.

79-2, 79-3: Banister, France, 19th century.
Rampe d'escalier, France, XIXᵉ siècle.
Treppengeländer, Frankreich, 19. Jh.
Pasamano, Francia, siglo XIX.
Перила, Франция, XIX век.

Établissement métallurgique A. Durenne.

79-4: Banisters.
Rampes d'escalier.
Treppengeländer.
Pasamanos.
Перила.

W. and J Welldon, *The Smith's Right Hand*,
London, 1765.

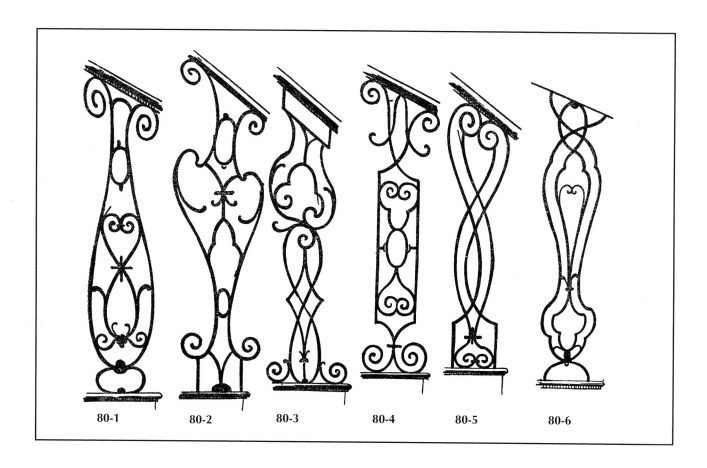

| 80-1 | 80-2 | 80-3 | 80-4 | 80-5 | 80-6 |

80: Details of balusters.
Détails de balustres.
Details von Balustraden.
Detalles de balaustres.
Деталь балясины.

W. and J. Welldon, *The Smith's Right Hand,* London, 1765.

81: Handrails and railings.
Appuis et rampes.
Einsetzungen und Rampen.
Pasamanos.
Псрила и ограждения.

Diderot & D'Alembert, *L'Encyclopédie*, Paris, 1751–1772.

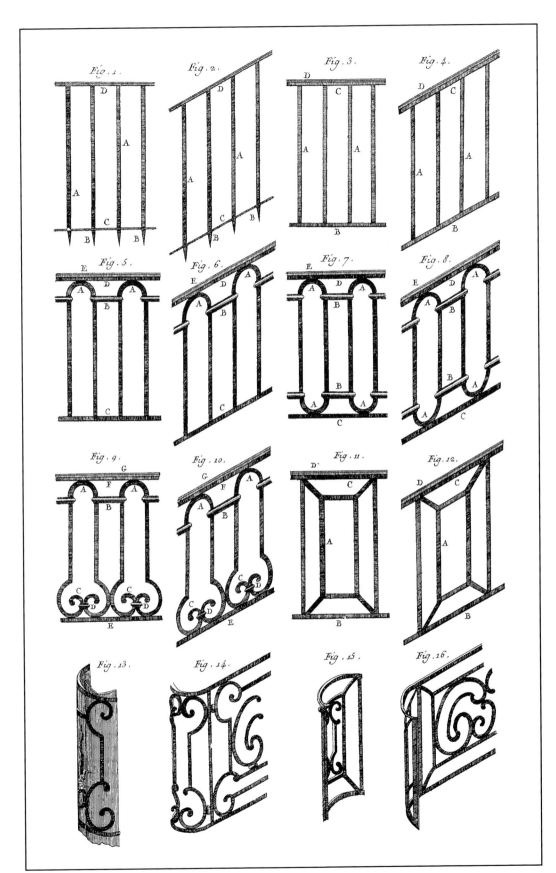

81

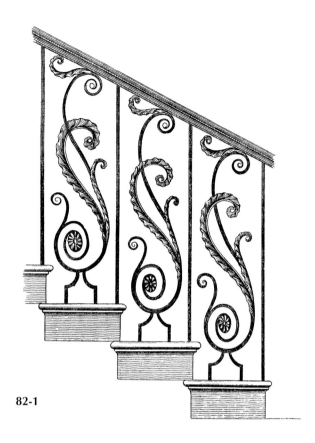

82-1

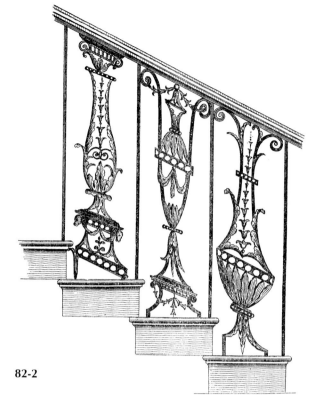

82-2

82 : Banisters.
Rampes d'escalier.
Treppengeländer.
Pasamanos.
Перила.

I. and J. Taylor, *Ornamental Iron Work or Designs in the Present Taste*, London, *c.* 1795.

83: Banisters.
Rampes d'escalier.
Treppengeländer.
Pasamanos.
Перила.

E. Barberot, *Traité pratique de serrurerie*, Paris & Liège, 1925.

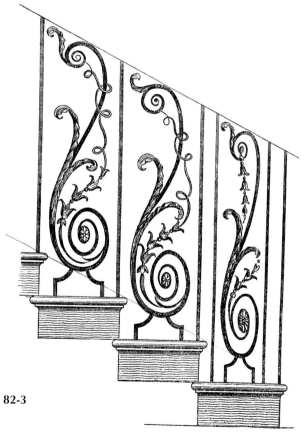

82-3

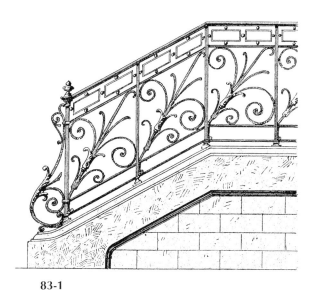

83-1

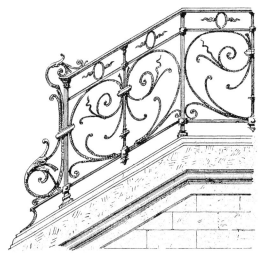

83-2

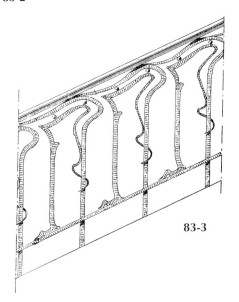

83-3

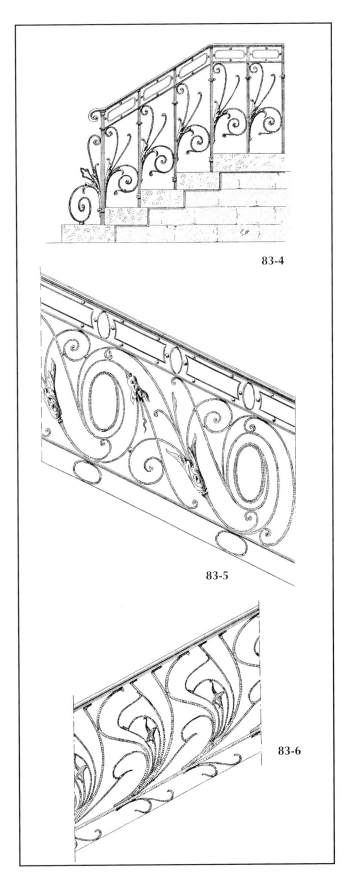

83-4

83-5

83-6

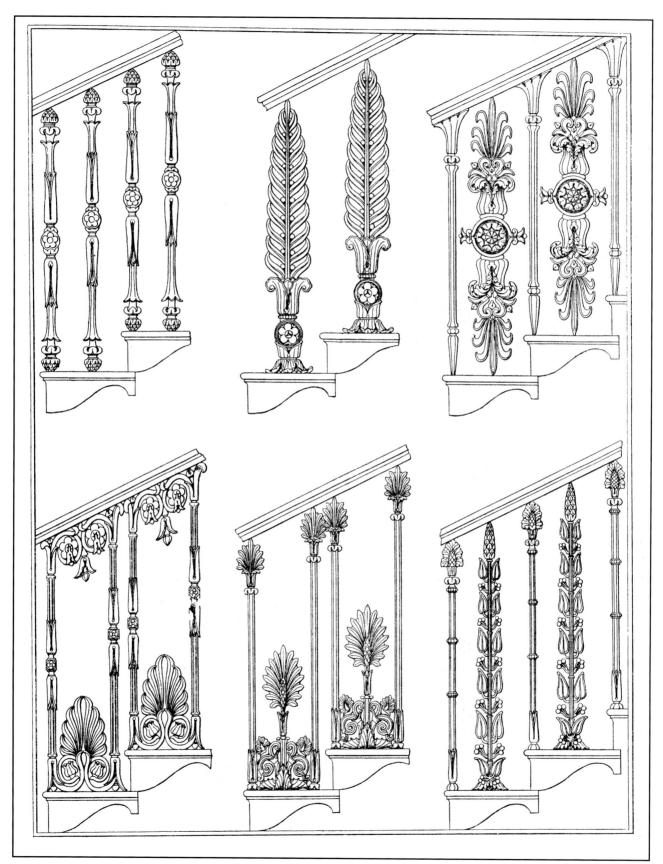

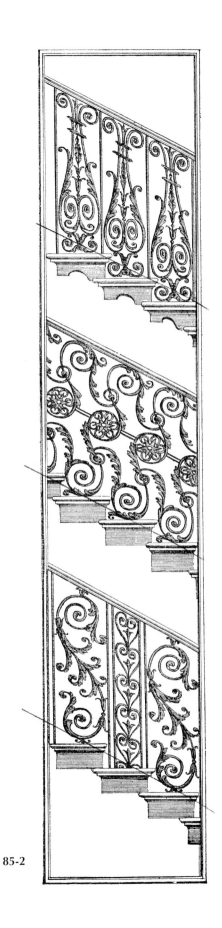

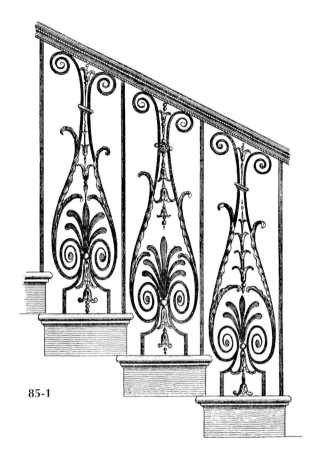

85-1

84: Banisters.
Rampes d'escalier.
Treppengeländer.
Pasamanos.
Перила.

Henry Shaw, *Examples of Ornamental Metal Work,* London, 1836.

85-1: Michelangelo Pergolesi, Banister, England, 1792.
Michelangelo Pergolesi, Rampe d'escalier, Angleterre, 1792.
Michelangelo Pergolesi, Treppengeländer, England, 1792.
Michelangelo Pergolesi, Pasamanos, Inglaterra, 1792.
Микеланджело Перголези. Перила, Англия, 1792.

85-2: Banisters.
Rampes d'escalier.
Treppengeländer.
Pasamanos.
Перила.

I. and J. Taylor, *Ornamental Iron Work or Designs in the Present Taste,* London, *c.* 1795.

85-2

86: Banisters, France, 19th century.
Rampes d'escalier, France, XIXe siècle.
Treppengeländer, Frankreich, 19. Jh.
Pasamanos, Francia, siglo XIX.
Перила, Франция, XIX век.

Établissement Le Val d'Osne.

87: Consoles.
Consoles de départ.
Eingangskonsolen.
Consolas.
Консоли.

E. Barberot, *Traité pratique de serrurerie*, Paris & Liège, 1925.

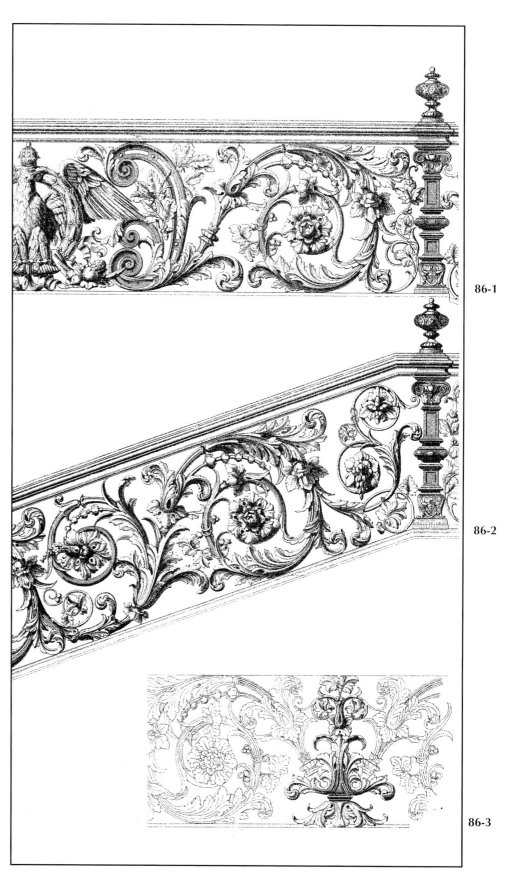

86-1

86-2

86-3

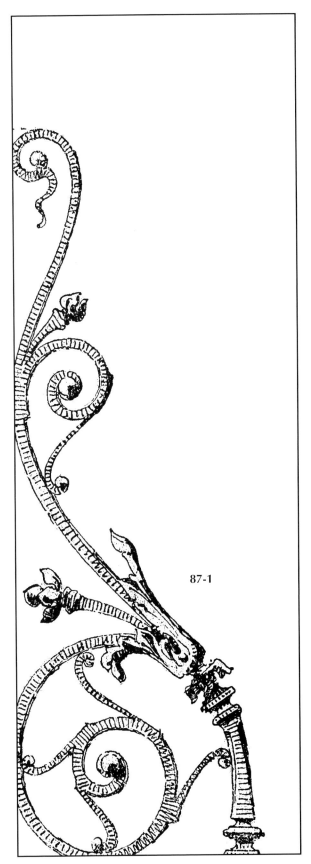

87-1

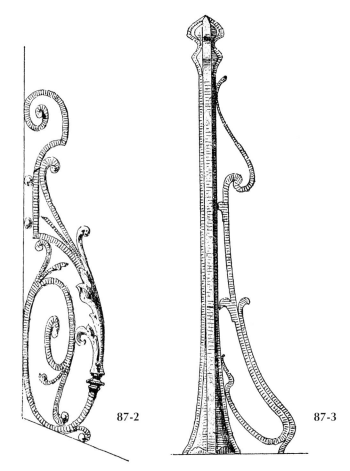

87-2

87-3

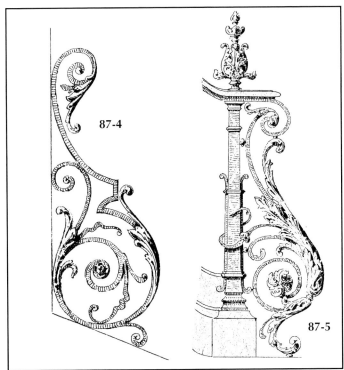

87-4

87-5

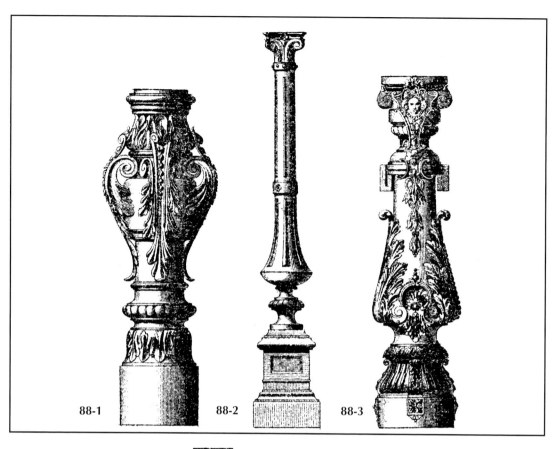

88-1   88-2   88-3

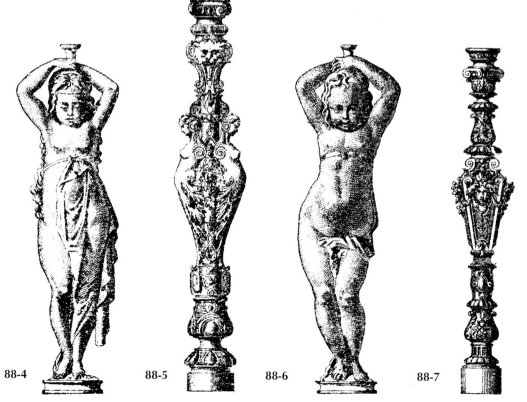

88-4   88-5   88-6   88-7

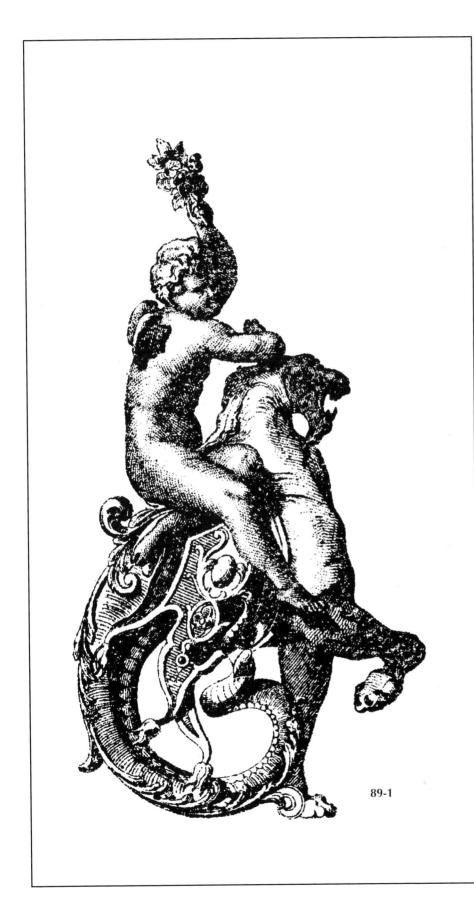

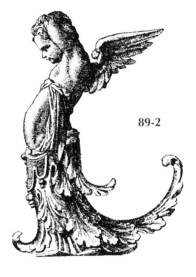

89-2

89-1

88-89: Stairway pilasters,
France, 19th century.
Pilastres d'escalier, France,
XIXe siècle.
Pilaster von Treppengeländern,
Frankreich, 19. Jh.
Pilastras de escaleras, Francia,
siglo XIX.
Пилястры лестниц,
Франция, XIX век.

Établissement métallurgique
A. Durenne.

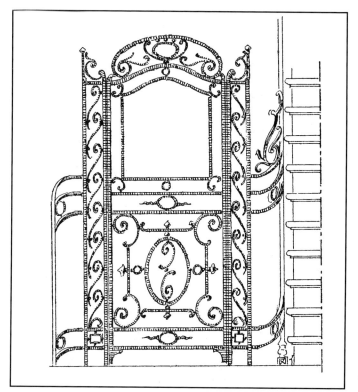

90

• Doors and windows •
• Portes et fenêtres • Türen
und Fenster • Puertas y
ventanas • Двери и
окна •

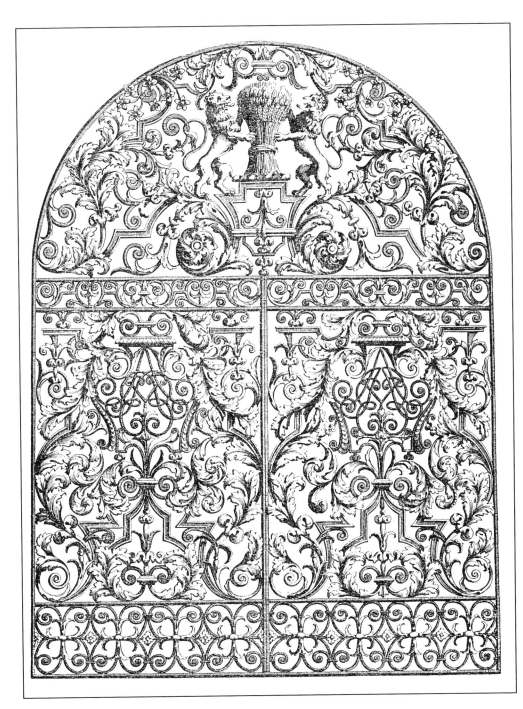

91

90: Elevator grille.
Grille d'ascenseur.
Tür eines Fahrstuhles.
Reja de ascensor.
Решетка лифта.

E. Barberot, *Traité pratique de serrurerie*,
Paris & Liège, 1925.

91: Entrance grille.
Grille d'entrée.
Eingangstor.
Cancela.
Решетка входа.

Jean Tijou, *A New Book of Drawings
Invented and Designed by Jean Tijou*,
London, 1690.

92: Window grille, Switzerland, 17th century.
Clôture de fenêtre, Suisse, XVIIᵉ siècle.
Fenstergitter, Schweiz, 17. Jh.
Reja de ventana, Suiza, siglo XVII.
Оконная решетка, Швейцария, XVII век.

93: Entrance grille at Hampton Court.
Grille d'entrée à Hampton Court.
Eingangstor in Hampton Court.
Cancela en Hampton Court.
Дверь Хэмптон Корт.

Jean Tijou, *A New Book of Drawings Invented and Designed by Jean Tijou*, London, 1690.

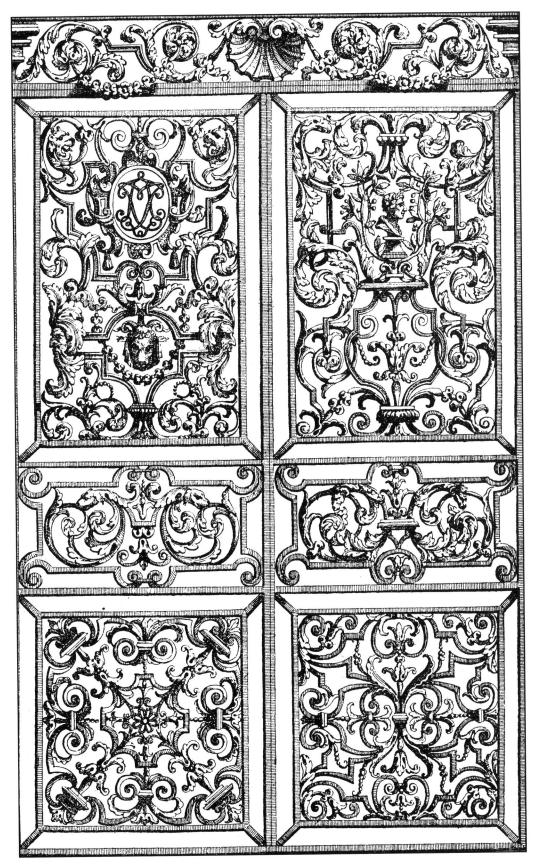

93

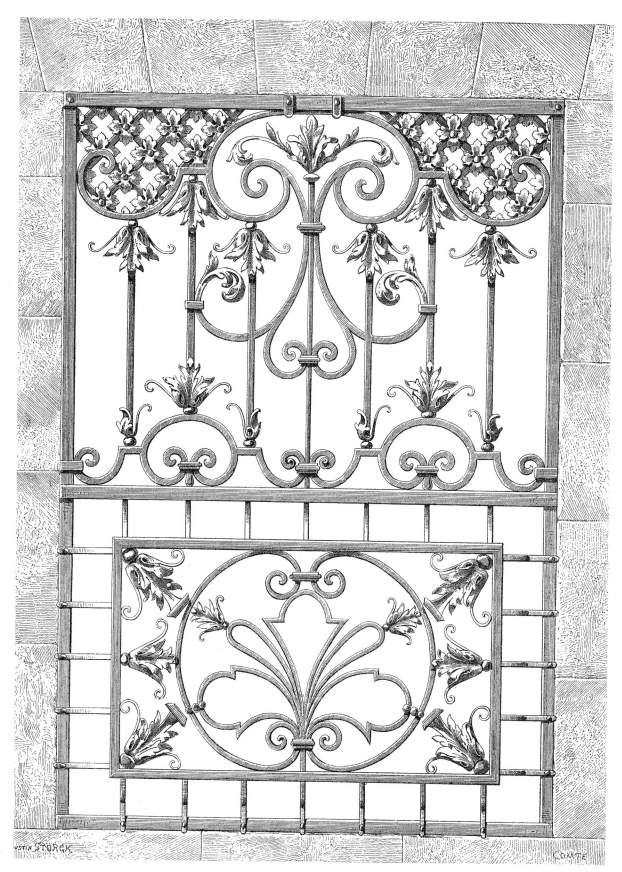

94 VSTIN STORCK

COMTE

94: Window grille, Switzerland,
17th century.
Clôture de fenêtre, Suisse,
XVIIᵉ siècle.
Fenstergitter, Schweiz, 17. Jh.
Reja de ventana, Suiza,
siglo XVII.
Оконная решетка,
Швейцария, XVII век.

95: Entrance at Queen's
College, Oxford.
Porte d'entrée à Queen's
College, Oxford.
Eingangstür vom Queen's
College, Oxford.
Puerta en Queen's College,
Oxford.
Входная дверь в Куинс
Колледж, Оксфорд.

Kip and Kynff, *Nouveau Théâtre
de la Grande Bretagne*,
London, 1714.

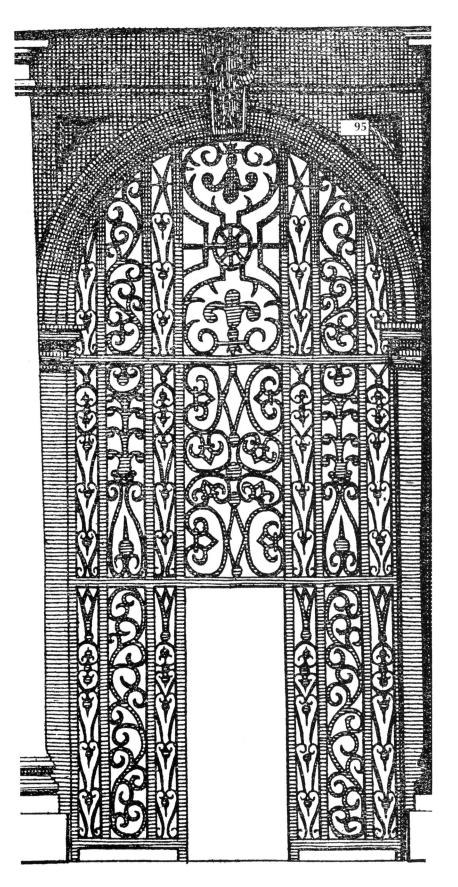

95

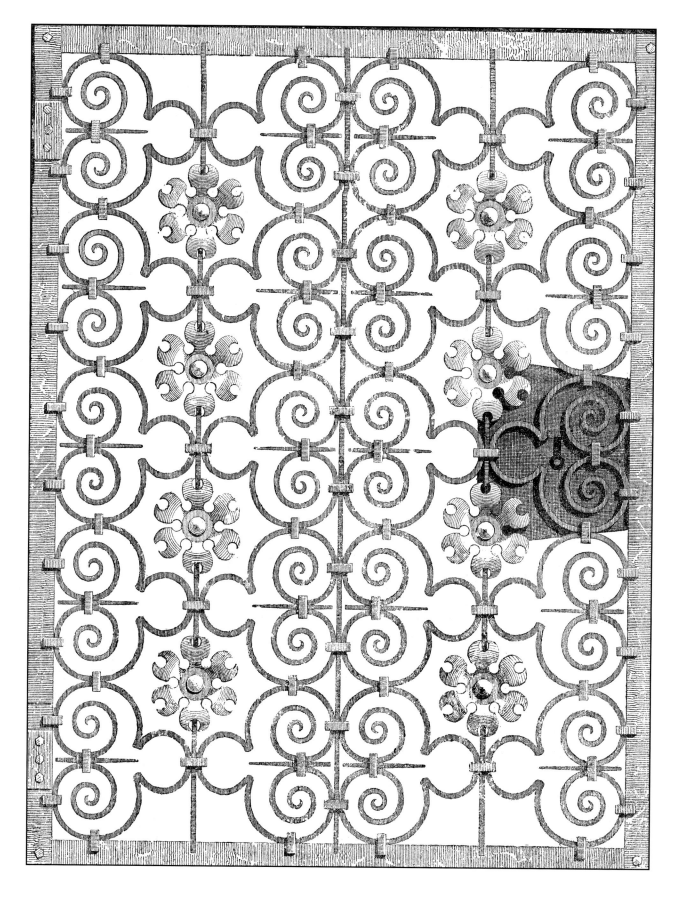

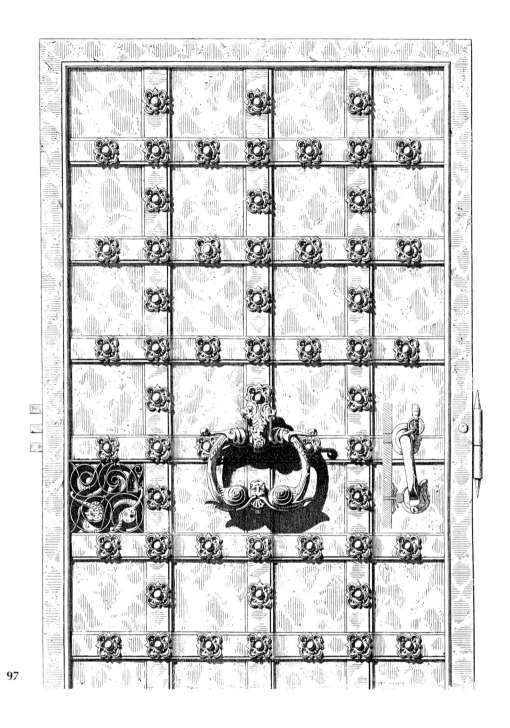

97

96: Wrought iron and gilt grille, France, 14th century.
Grille en fer forgé et doré, France, XIVᵉ siècle.
Vergoldetes Schmiedeeiserntor, Frankreich, 14. Jh.
Reja de hierro forjado y dorado, Francia, siglo XIV.
Позолоченная решетка из кованого железа,
Франция, XIV век.

97: Wrought iron and sheet metal door, Germany,
16th century.
Porte en tôle et fer forgé, Allemagne, XVIᵉ siècle.
Tür aus Emailleblech und geschmiedetem Eisen,
Deutschland, 16. Jh.
Puerta de chapa y hierro forjado, Alemania, siglo XVI.
Дверь из листового и кованого железа.
Германия, XVI век.

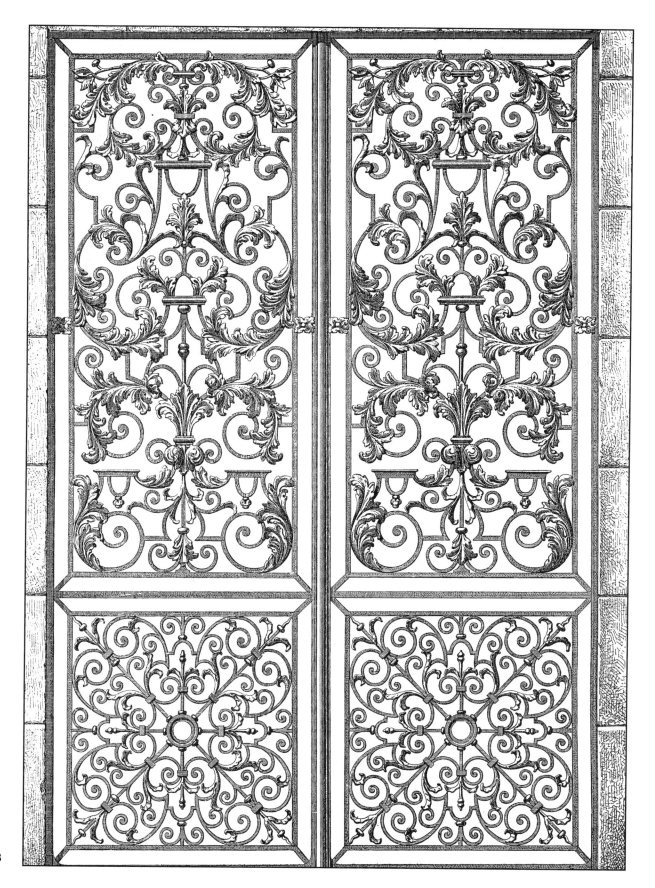

98

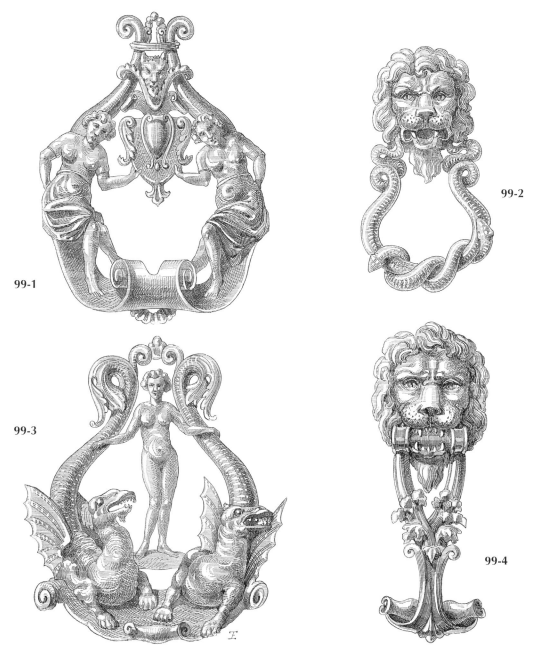

99-1

99-2

99-3

99-4

98: Door, England, 18th century.
Porte, Angleterre, XVIIIᵉ siècle.
Tor, England, 18. Jh.
Puerta, Inglaterra, siglo XVIII.
Дверь, Англия, XVIII век.

99: Wrought iron and bronze door-knockers, Venice,
17th century.
Heurtoirs en fer forgé et bronze, Venise, XVIIᵉ siècle.
Türklopfer aus geschmiedetem Eisen und Bronze,
Venedig, 17. Jh.
Albadas de hierro forjado y bronce, Venecia,
siglo XVII.
Дверной молоточек из кованого железа и
бронзы, Венеция, XVII век.

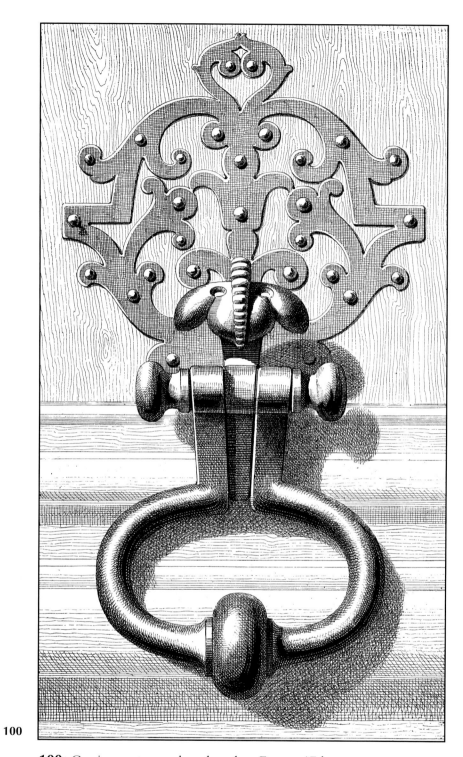

100

100: Carriage entrance door-knocker, France, 17th century.
Heurtoir de porte cochère, France, XVIIᵉ siècle.
Türklopfer eines Einfahrtstores, Frankreich, 17. Jh.
Albada, Francia, siglo XVII.
Дверной молоточек, Франция, XVII век.

101: Door-knocker,
Belgium, 15th century.
Heurtoir, Belgique,
XV^c siècle.
Türklopfer, Belgien, 15. Jh.
Albada, Bélgica, siglo XV.
Дверной молоточек,
Бельгия, XV век.

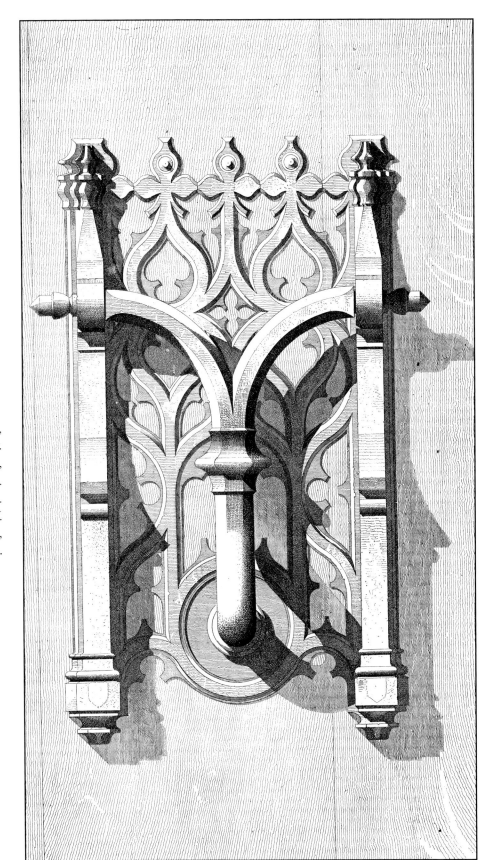

102: Carriage
entrance door-
knocker, France,
17th century.
Heurtoir de porte
cochère, France,
XVIIᵉ siècle.
Türklopfer eines
Einfahrtstores,
Frankreich, 17. Jh.
Albada, Francia,
siglo XVII.
Дверной
молоточек,
Франция, XVII век.

102

103 : Door-knocker, France,
16th century.
Heurtoir, France, XVIᵉ siècle.
Türklopfer, Frankreich, 16. Jh.
Albada, Francia, siglo XVI.
Дверной молоточек,
Франция, XVI век.

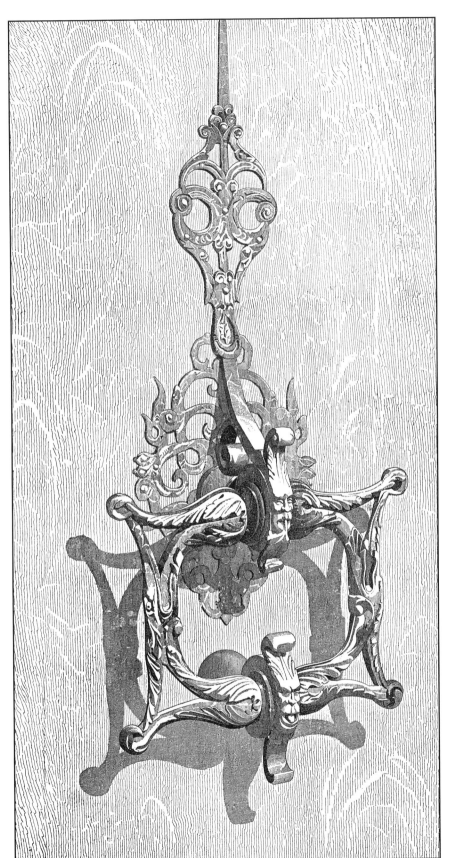

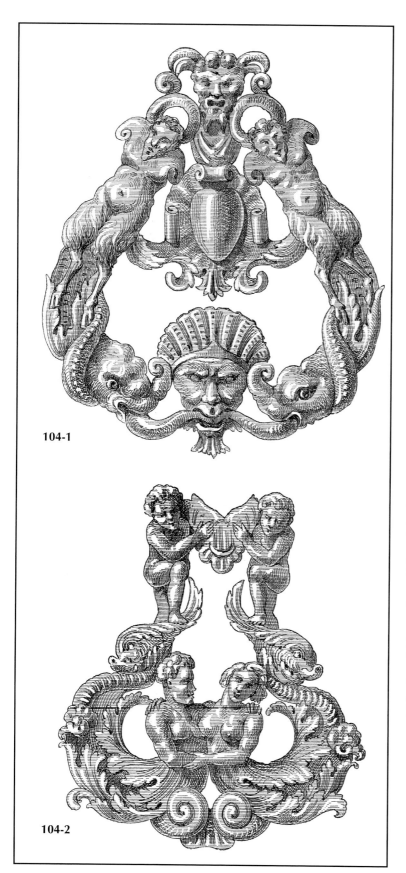

104-1

104-2

104: Wrought iron and bronze door-knockers, Venice, 17th century.
Heurtoirs en fer forgé et bronze, Venise, XVIIe siècle.
Türklopfer aus Schmiedeeisen und Bronze, Venedig, 17. Jh.
Albadas de hierro forjado y bronce, Venecia, siglo XVII.
Дверные молоточки из кованого железа и бронзы, Венеция, XVII век.

105: Door-knocker, Switzerland, 17th century.
Heurtoir, Suisse, XVIIe siècle.
Türklopfer, Schweiz, 17. Jh.
Albada, Suiza, siglo XVII.
Дверной молоточек, Швейцария, XVII век.

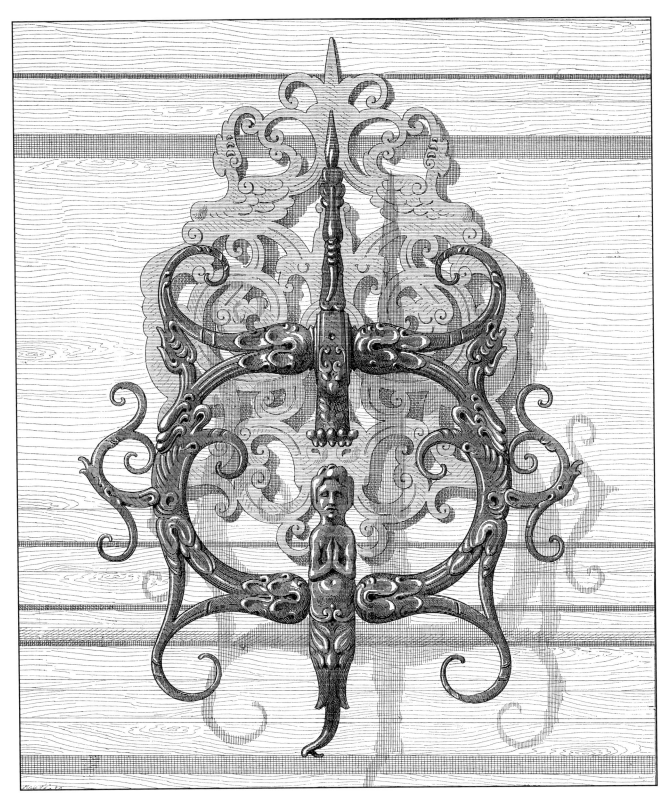

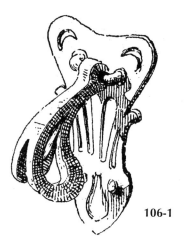

106-1

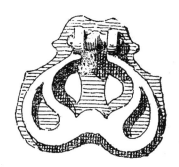

106-2

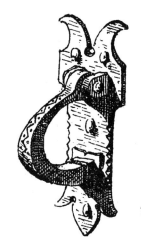

106-3

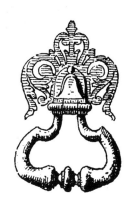

106-4

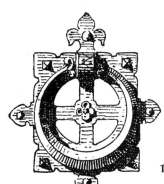

106-5

106: Door-knockers.
Heurtoirs.
Türklopfer.
Albadas.
Дверные молоточки.

E. Barberot, *Traité pratique de serrurerie*, Paris & Liège, 1925.

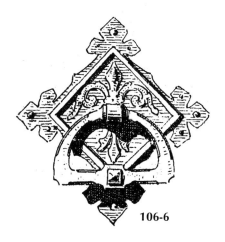

106-6

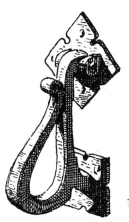

106-7

107-1: Elevator grille.
Grille d'ascenseur.
Gittertür eines Fahrstuhls.
Reja de ascensor.
Решетка лифта.

107-1

107-2: Window grilles.
Grilles de fenêtres.
Fenstergitter.
Rejas de ventanas.
Оконные решетки.

E. Barberot, *Traité pratique de serrurerie*,
Paris & Liège, 1925.

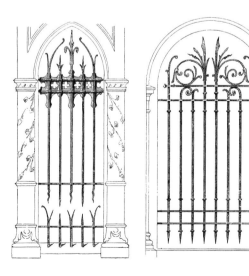

107-3

107-2

108-1

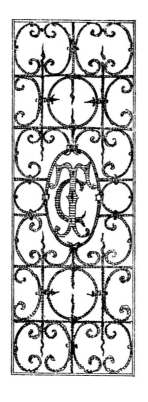

108-2

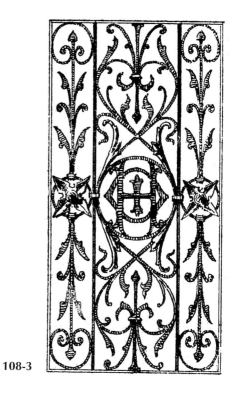

108-3

108-1, 108-2, 108-3: Door panels.
Panneaux de portes.
Türfüllung.
Cuarterones.
Дверные панели.

E. Barberot, *Traité pratique de serrurerie*,
Paris & Liège, 1925.

108-4, 108-5: Door panels,France,
19th century.
Panneaux de portes, France, XIXe
siècle.
Türenpanneaux, Frankreich, 19. Jh.
Cuarterones, Francia, siglo XIX.
Дверные панели, Франция, XIX
век.

Établissement métallurgique
A. Durenne.

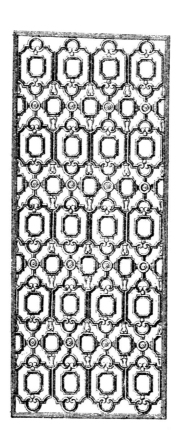

108-4

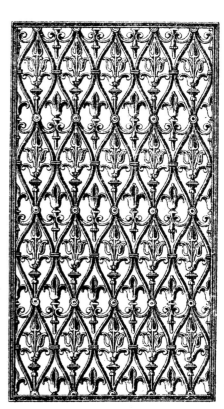

108-5

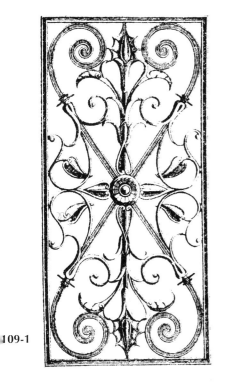

109-1

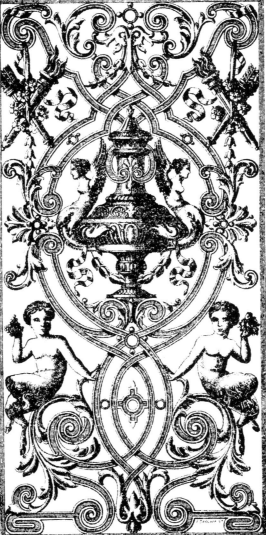

109-3

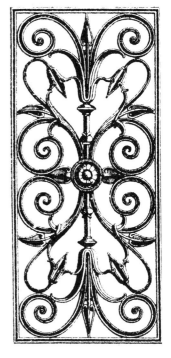

109-4

109-5

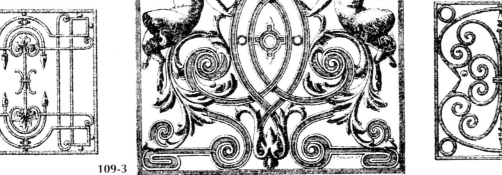

109-2

109-6

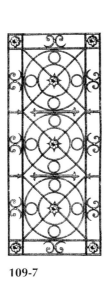

109-7

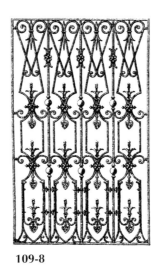

109-8

109/116: Door panels, France,
19th century.
Panneaux de portes, France,
XIXe siècle.
Türenpanneaux, Frankreich, 19. Jh.
Cuarterones, Francia, siglo XIX.
Дверные панели, Франция,
XIX век.

Établissement métallurgique
A. Durenne.

109

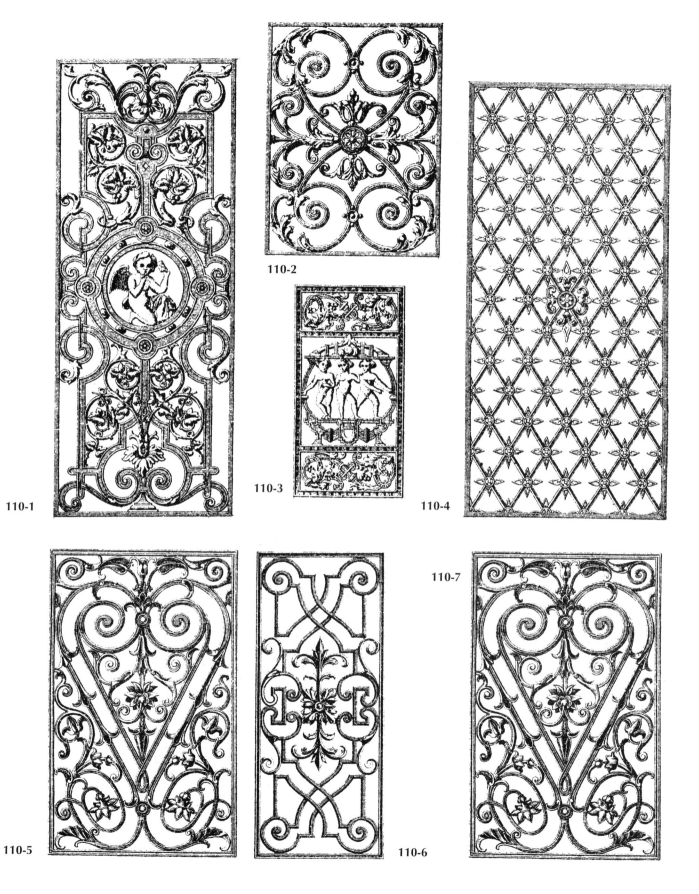

110-1

110-2

110-3

110-4

110-5

110-6

110-7

110

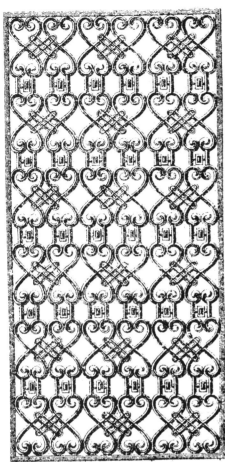

111-1

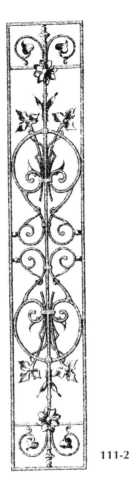

111-2

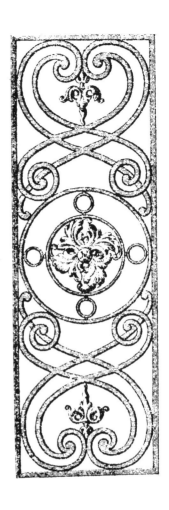

111-3

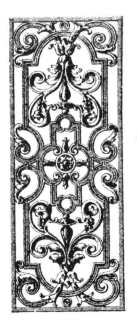

111-4

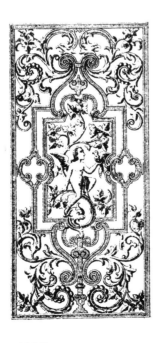

111-5

111-6

111-7

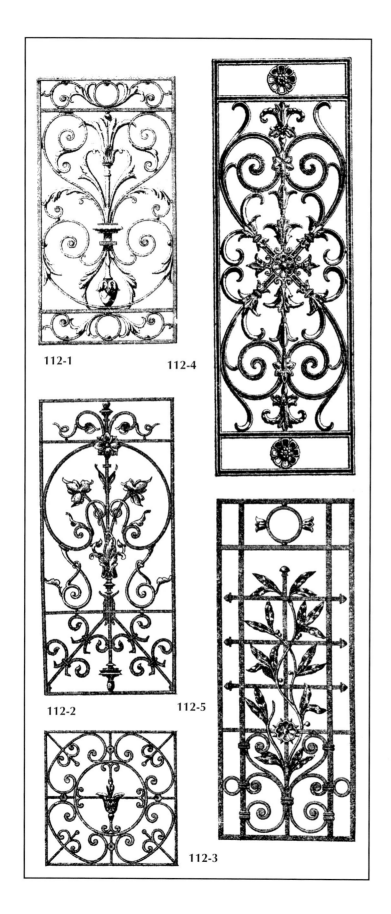

112-1

112-4

112-2

112-5

112-3

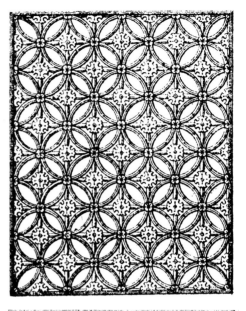

112-6

112-7

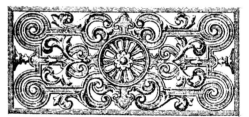

112-8

112-9

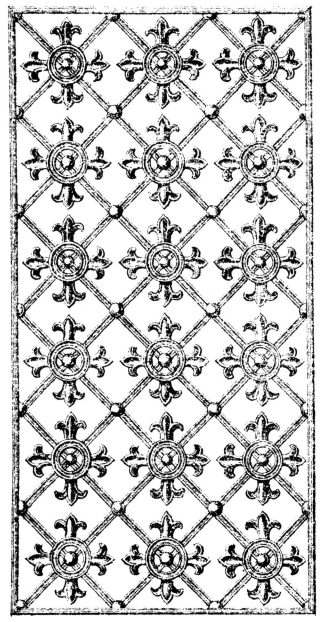

113-1

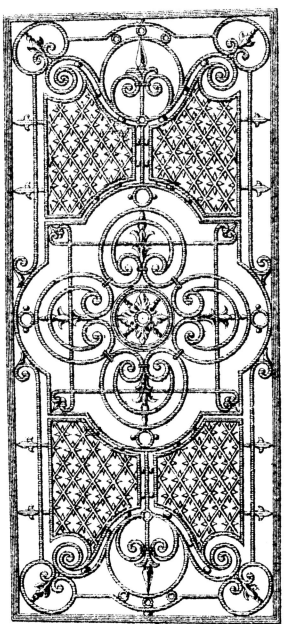

113-2

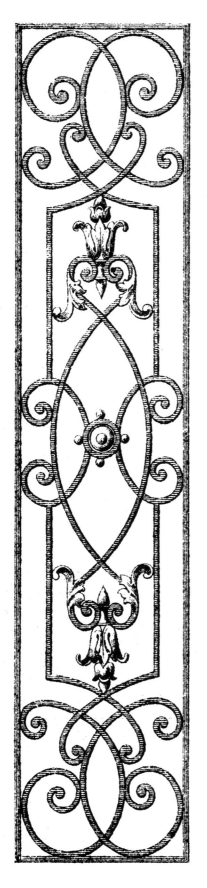

114-1

114-2

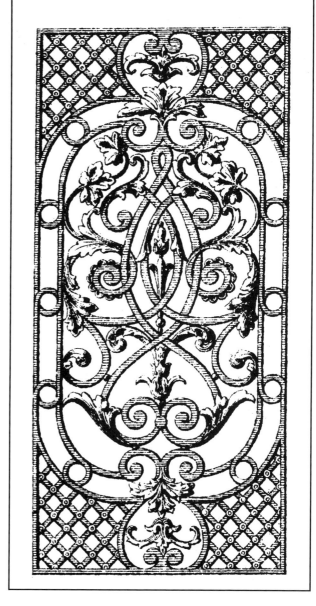

114-3

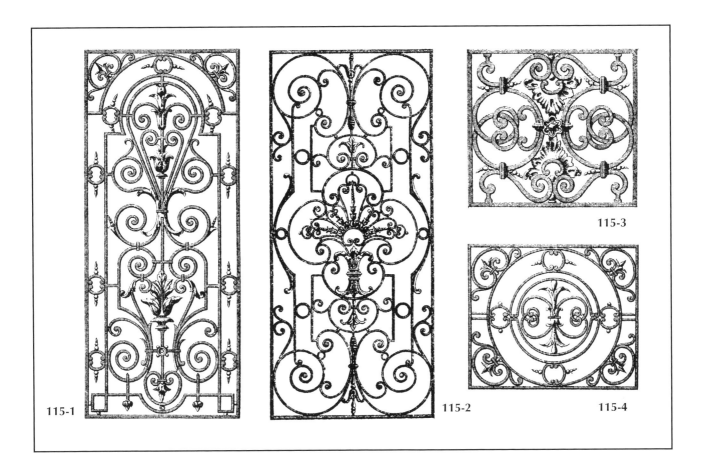

115-1

115-2

115-3

115-4

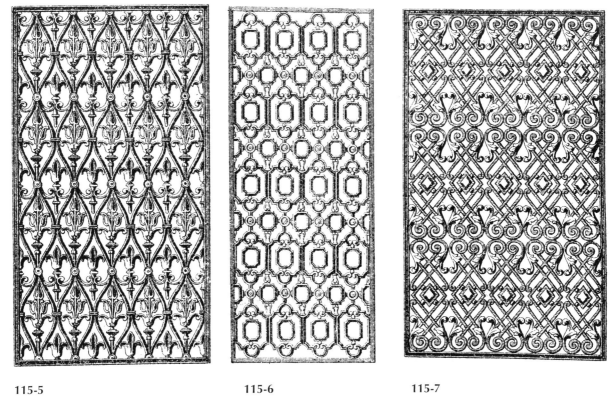

115-5

115-6

115-7

115

116-1

116-2

116-3

116-4

116-5

116-6

116-7

116-8

116-9

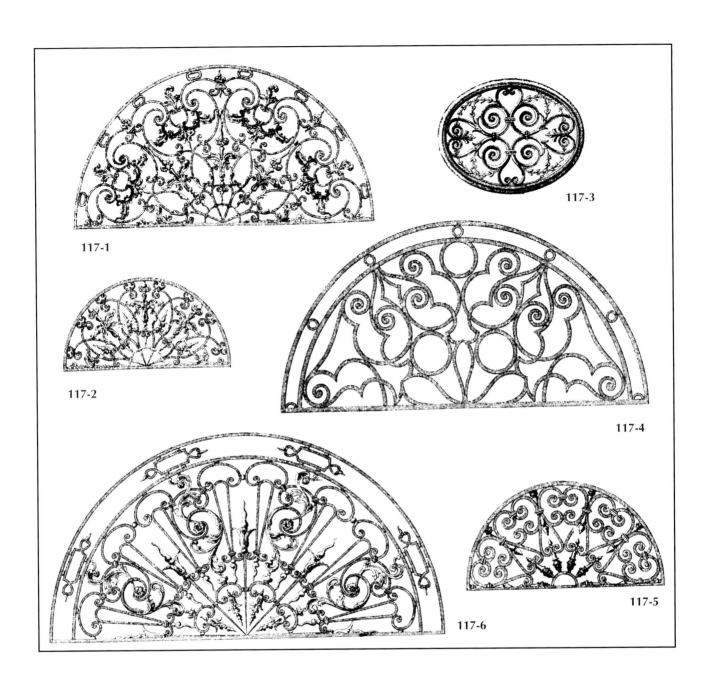

117: Fanlight grilles, France, 19th century.
Impostes, France, XIXe siècle.
Gitter von oberen Rundfenstern, Frankreich, 19. Jh.
Impostas, Francia, siglo XIX.
Импосты, Франция, XIX век.

Établissement métallurgique A. Durenne.

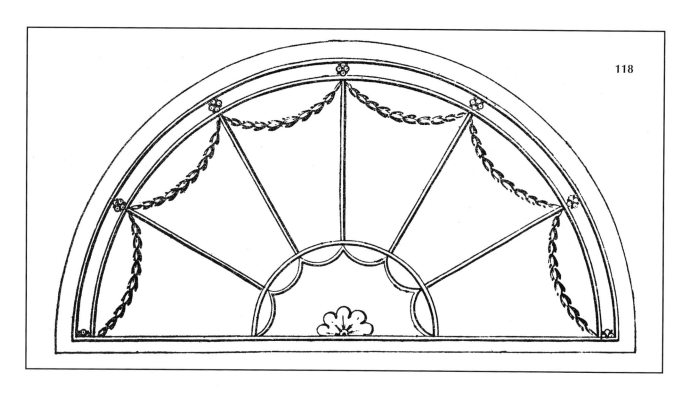

118: Fanlight grille.
Imposte.
Gitter von oberen Rundfenster.
Imposta.
Импост.

J. Bottomley, *A Book of Designs,* London, 1793.

119: Fanlight grilles.
Impostes.
Gitter von oberen Rundfenstern.
Impostas.
Импосты

W. and J. Welldon, *The Smith's Right Hand,* London, 1765.

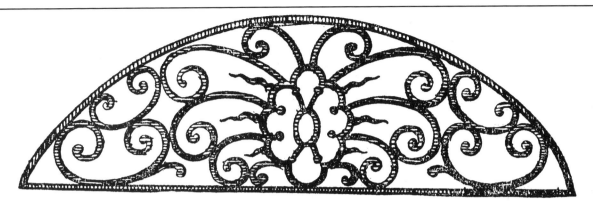

119-1

119-2

119-3

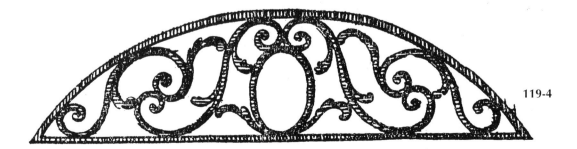

119-4

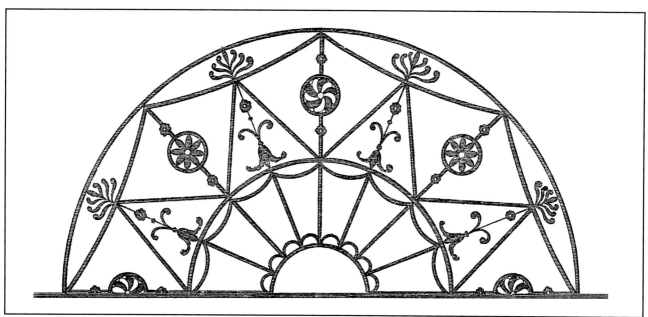

120-1

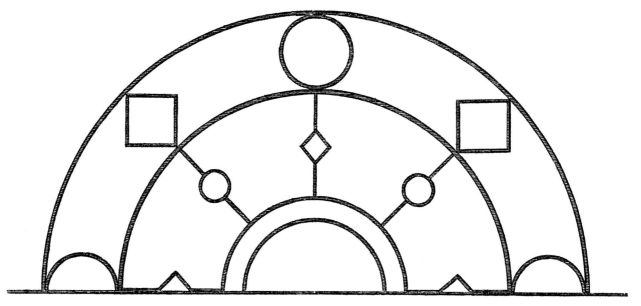

120-2

120/121 : Fanlight grilles.
Impostes.
Gitter von oberen Rundfenstern.
Impostas.
Импосты.

J. Bottomley, *A Book of Designs*, London, 1793.

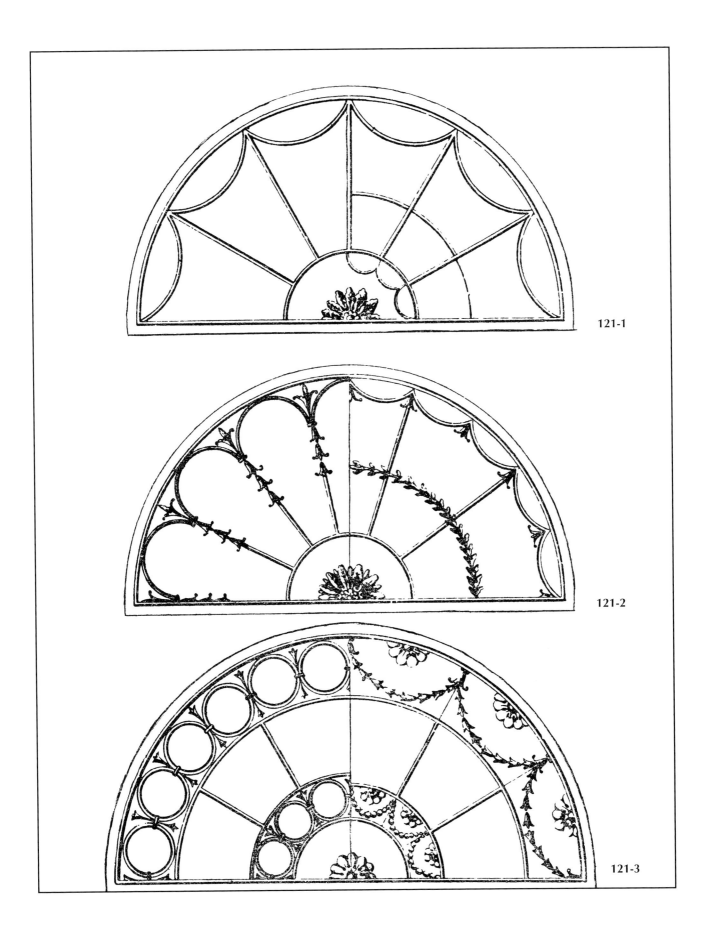

121-1

121-2

121-3

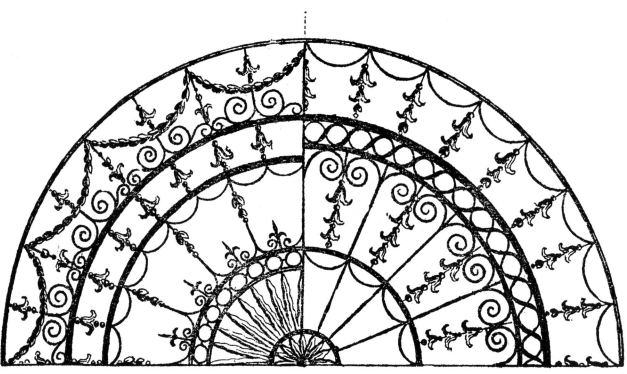

122-1

122-2

122/123: Fanlight grilles.
Impostes.
Gitter von oberen Rundfenstern.
Impostas.
Импосты.

I. and J. Taylor, *Ornamental Iron Work or Designs in the Present Taste*, London, *circa* 1795.

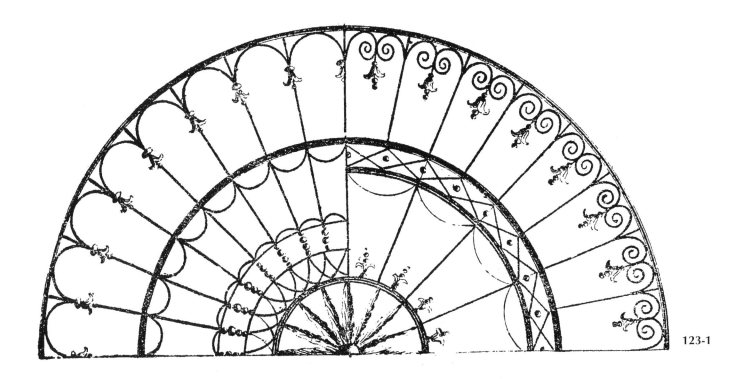

123-1

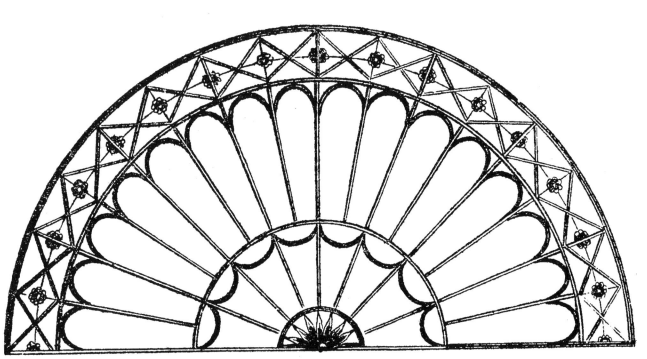

123-2

123

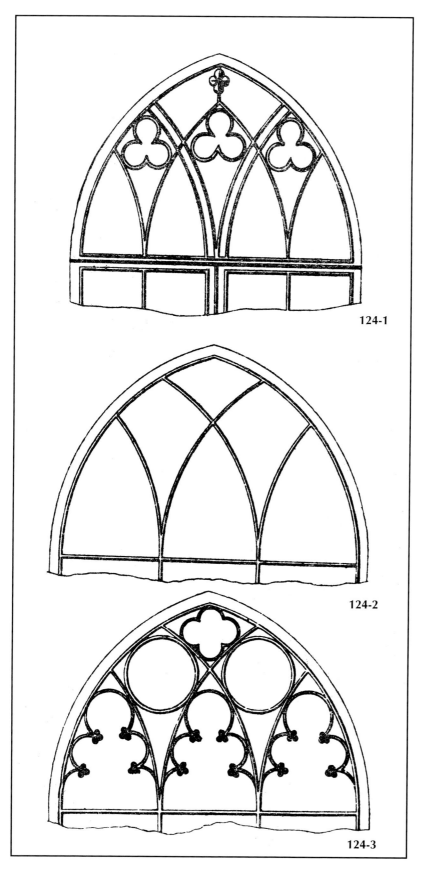

124-1

124-2

124-3

124/127: Fanlight grilles.
Impostes.
Rundgitter und andere Fenstergitter.
Impostas.
Импосты.

J. Bottomley, *A Book of Designs,*
London, 1793.

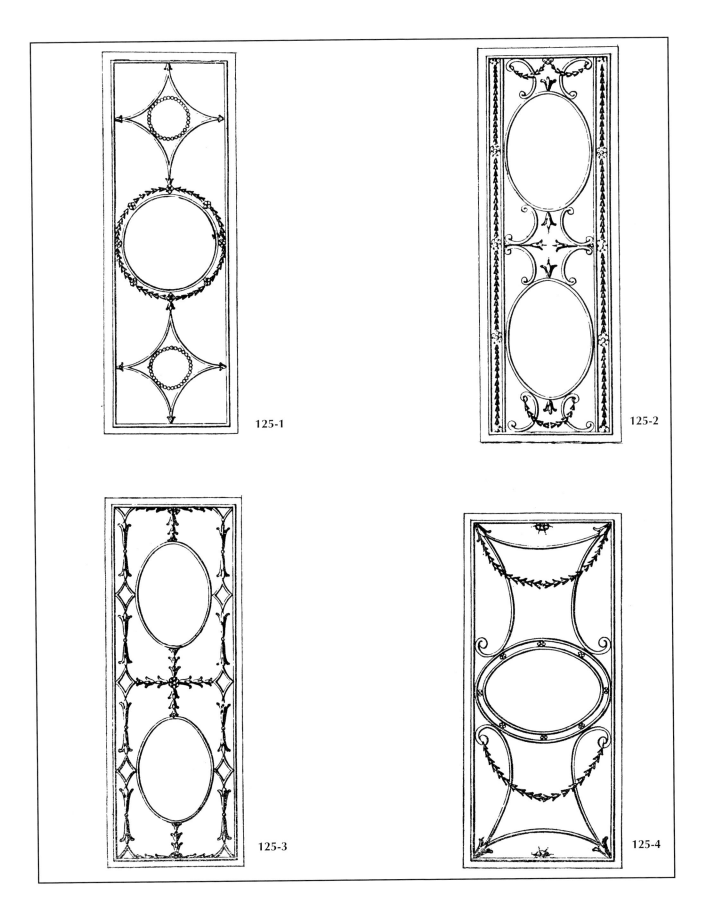

125-1

125-2

125-3

125-4

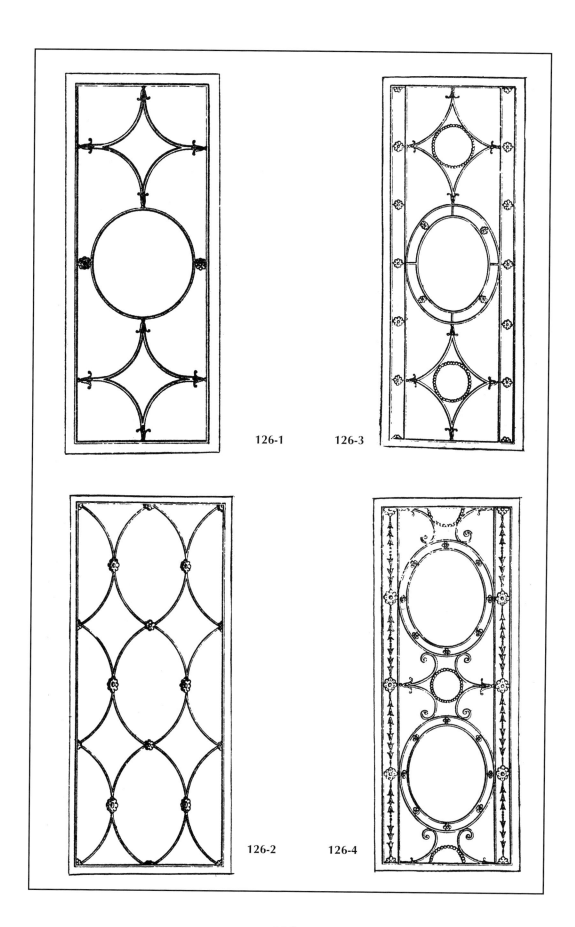

126-1

126-3

126-2

126-4

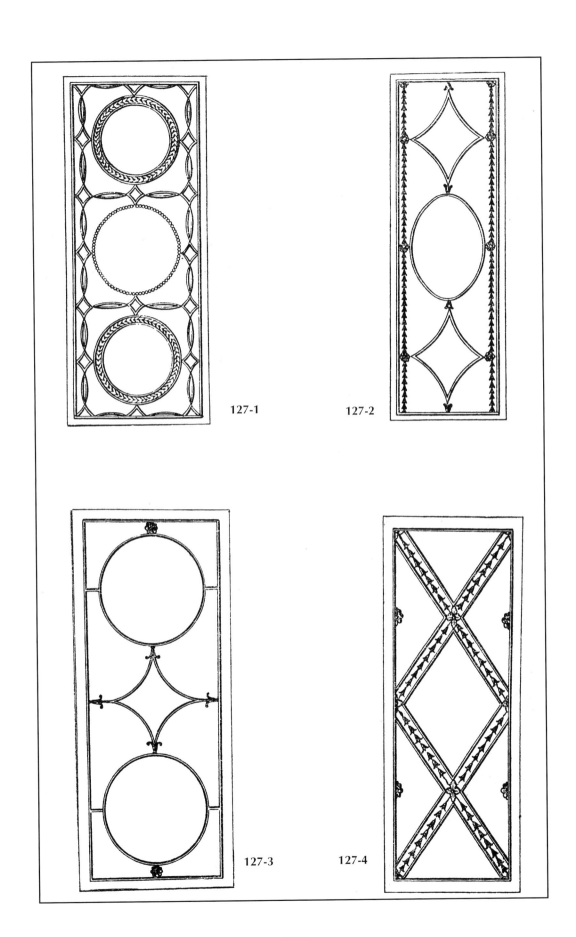

127-1

127-2

127-3

127-4

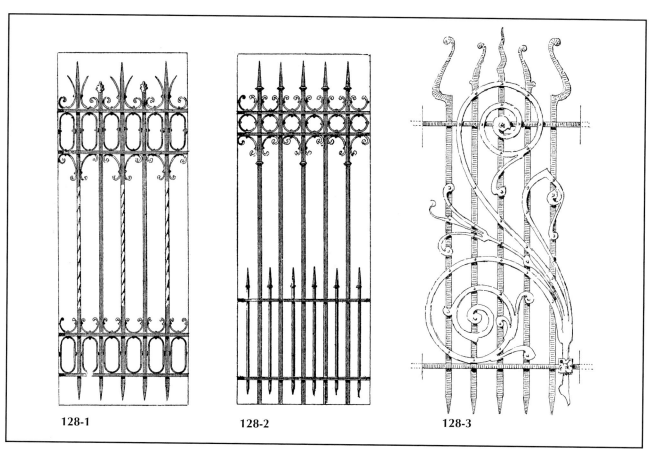

128-1

128-2

128-3

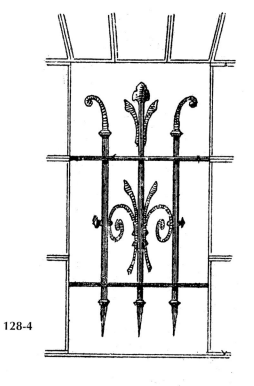

128-4

128: Window bars.
Défenses de fenêtres.
Fenstergitter.
Rejas de ventanas.
Оконные решетки.

E. Barberot, *Traité pratique de serrurerie*, Paris & Liège, 1925.

129: Door panels.
Panneaux de portes.
Türenpanneaux.
Cuarterones.
Дверные панели.

E. Barberot, *Traité pratique de serrurerie*, Paris & Liège, 1925.

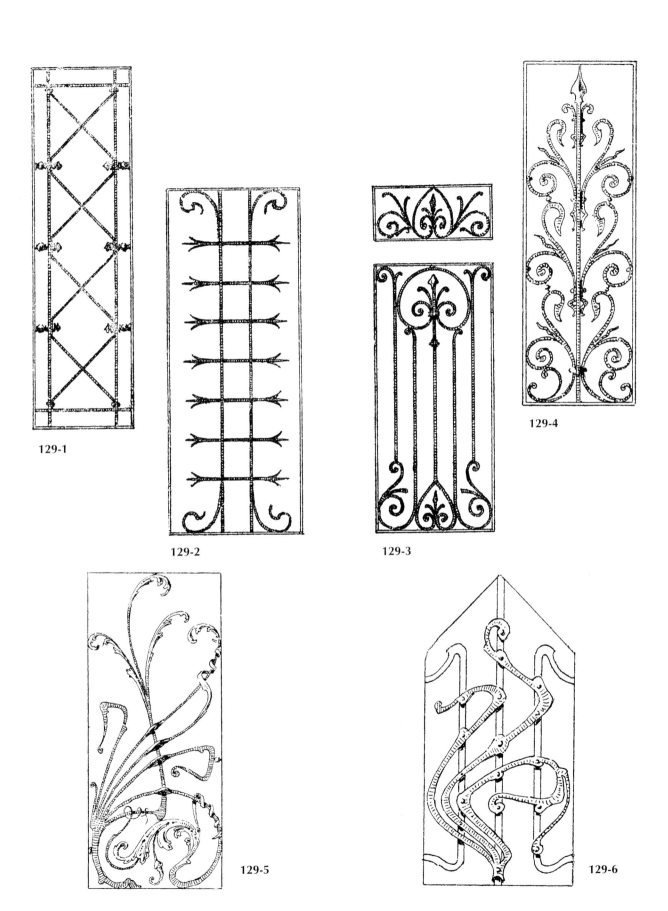

129-1

129-2

129-3

129-4

129-5

129-6

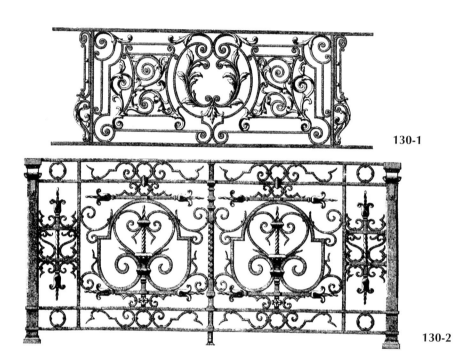

130-1

130-2

• Balconies and railings •
• Balcons et balustrades •
• Balkone und Balustraden •
• Balcones y balaustradas •

131-1

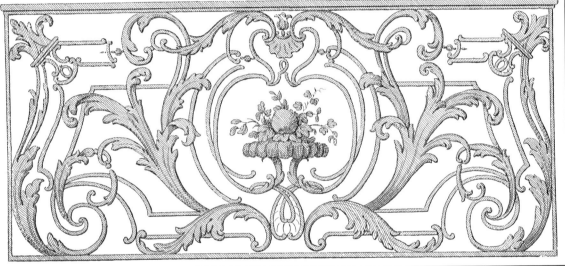

131-2

130: Balconies, France, 19th century.
Balcons, France, XIXᵉ siècle.
Balkone, Frankreich, 19. Jh.
Balcones, Francia, siglo XIX.
Балконы, Франция, XIX век.

Établissement métallurgique A. Durenne.

131: Wrought iron and sheet metal balconies, Florence, 17th century
Balcons en tôle et fer forgé, Florence, XVIIᵉ siècle.
Balkone aus geschmiedetem Eisen und Emaille, Florenz, 17. Jh.
Balcones de chapa y hierro forjado, Florencia, siglo XVII.
Балконы из листового и кованого железа, Флоренция, XVII век.

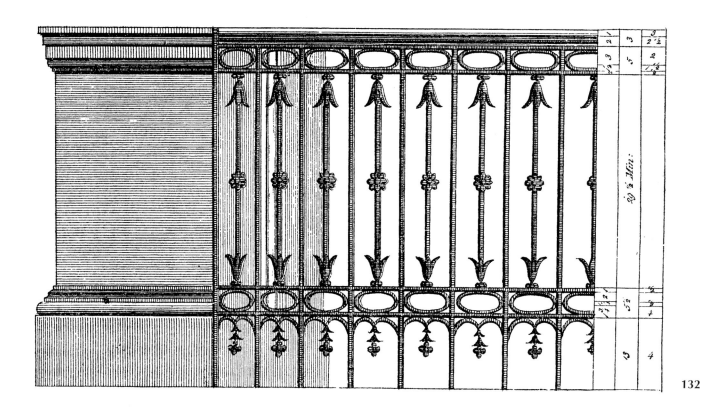

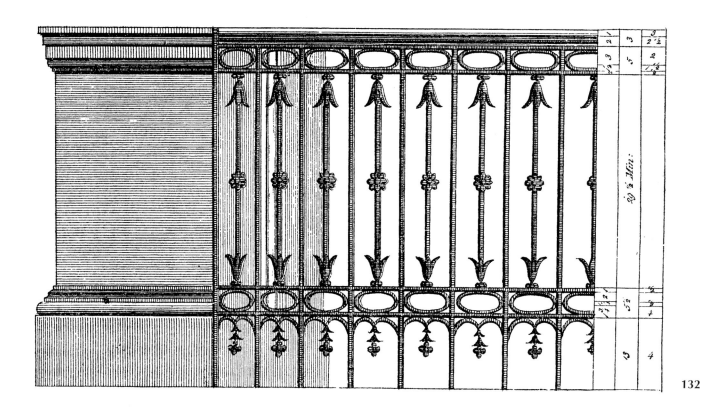

132

132: Balcony.
Balcon.
Balkon.
Balcón.
Балкон.

W. Thomas, *Original Designs in Architecture,* London, 1783.

133/135: Balconies, France, 19th century.
Balcons, France, XIXe siècle.
Balkone, Frankreich, 19. Jh.
Balcones, Francia, siglo XIX.
Балконы, Франция, XIX век.

Établissement métallurgique A. Durenne.

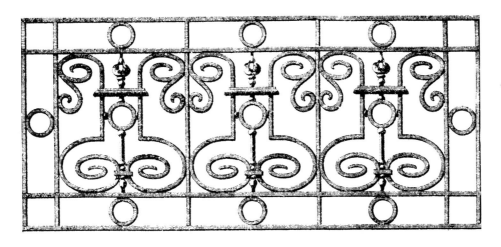

133-1

133-2

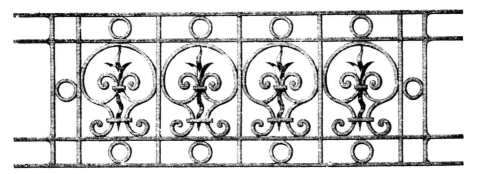

133-3

133-4

133

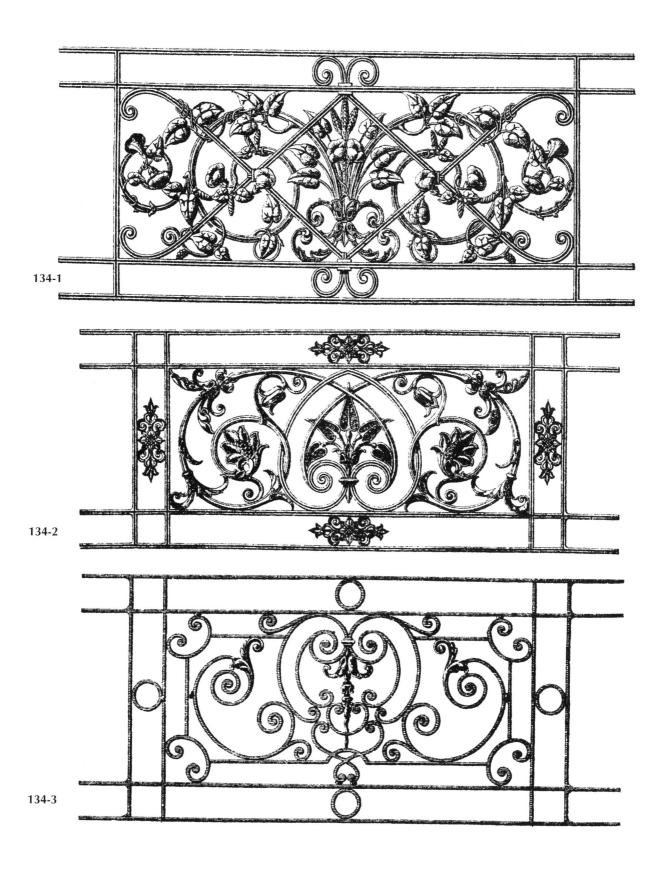

134-1

134-2

134-3

135-1

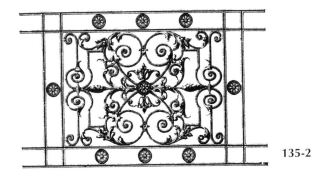

135-2

135-3

135-4

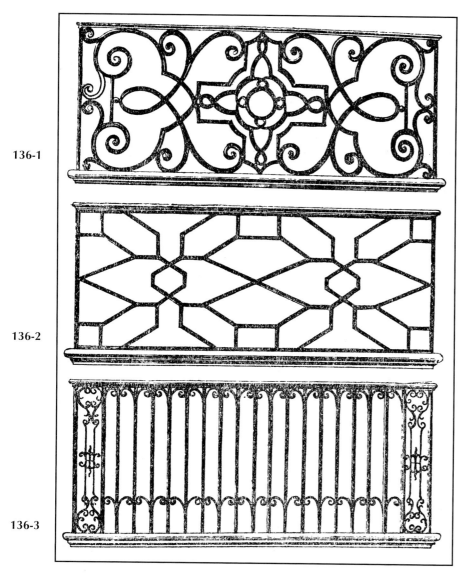

136-1

136-2

136-3

136: Balconies.
Balcons.
Balkone.
Balcones.
Балконы.

W. and J Welldon, *The Smith's Right Hand,* London, 1765.

137-1: Balcony.
Balcon.
Balkon.
Balcón.
Балкон.

W. Ince and J. Mayhew, *Universal System of Household Furniture,* London, 1762.

137-2: Details of balconies.
Détails de balcons.
Details eines Balkons.
Detalles de balcones.
Детали балконов.

Sébastien Le Clerc, *A Treatise of Architecture,* London, 1723-1724.

137-1

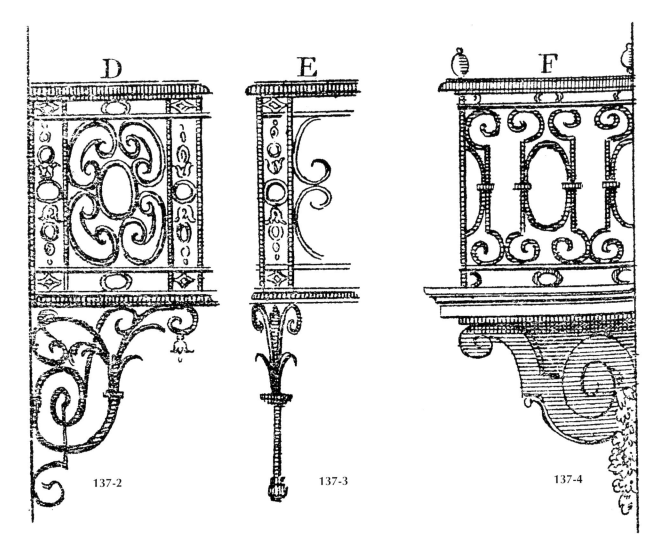

D

E

F

137-2

137-3

137-4

137

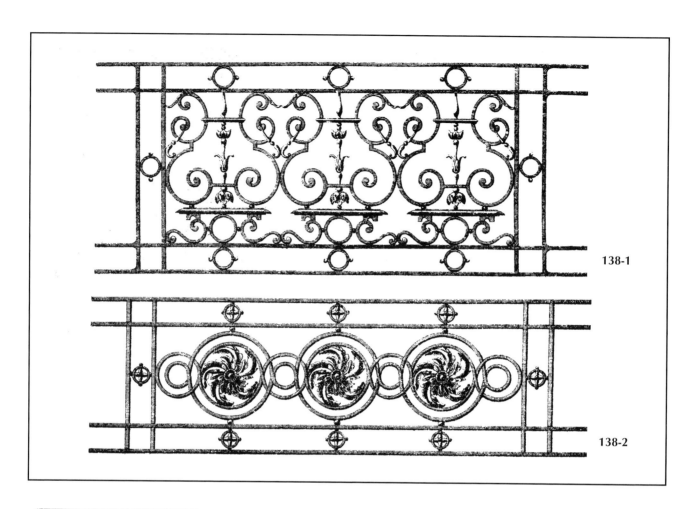

138-1

138-2

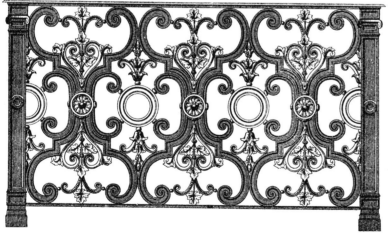

138-3

138,140 : Balconies, France,
19th century.
Balcons, France, XIXᵉ siècle.
Balkonen, Frankreich, 19. Jh.
Balcones, Francia, siglo XIX.
Балконы, Франция, XIX век.

Établissement métallurgique
A. Durenne.

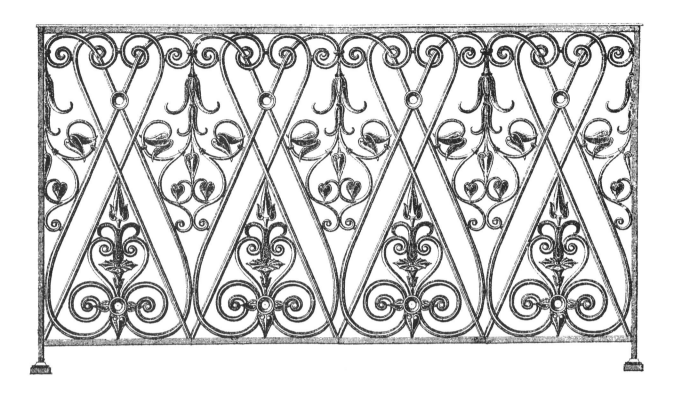

139-1

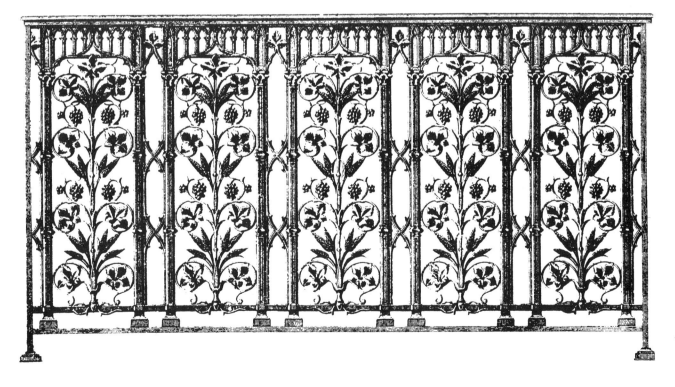

139-2

139

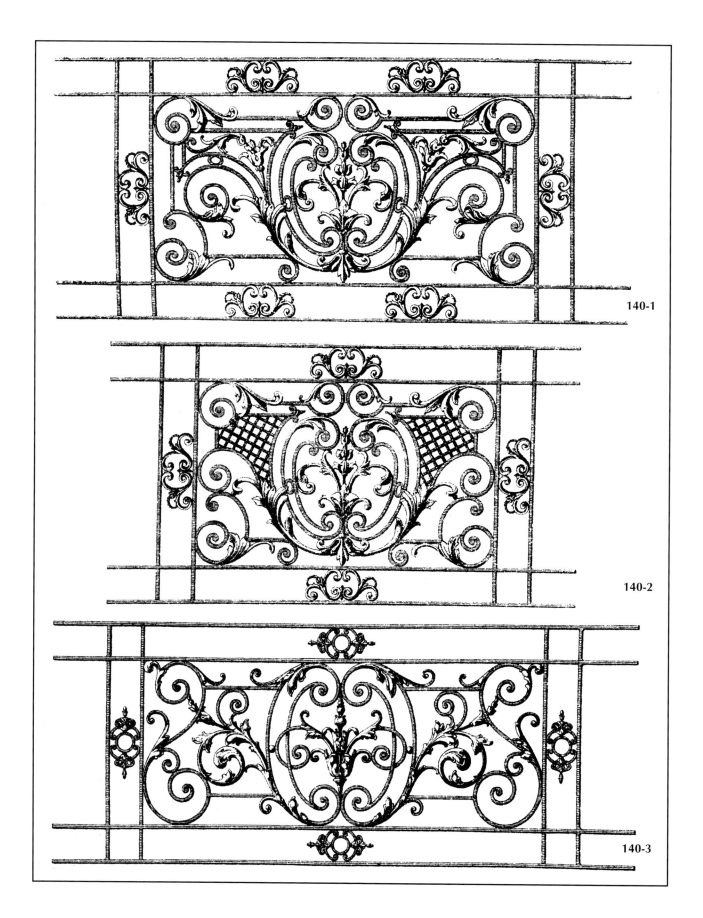

140-1

140-2

140-3

140

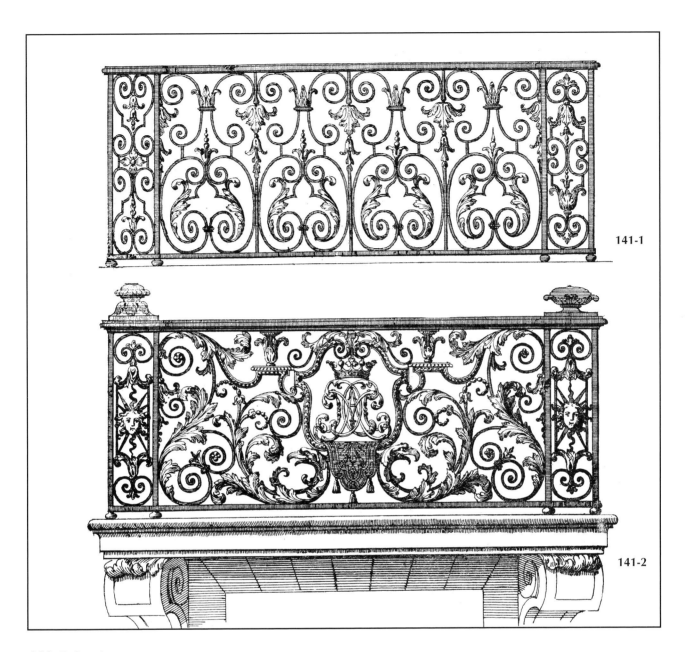

141 141-1

141-2

141: Balconies.
Balcons.
Balkonen.
Balcones.
Балконы.

Daniel Marot, *Nouveau Livre de Serrurerie*, The Hague, 1703.

142-1

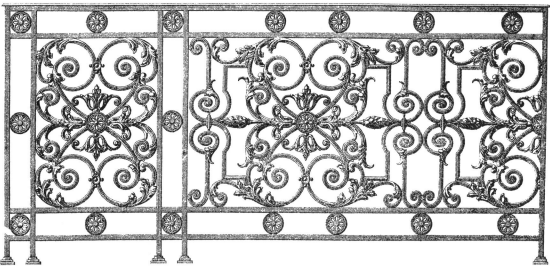

142-2

142/150: Balconies, France, 19th century.
Balcons, France, XIXe siècle.
Balkonen, Frankreich, 19. Jh.
Balcones, Francia, siglo XIX.
Балконы, Франция, XIX век.

Établissement métallurgique A. Durenne.

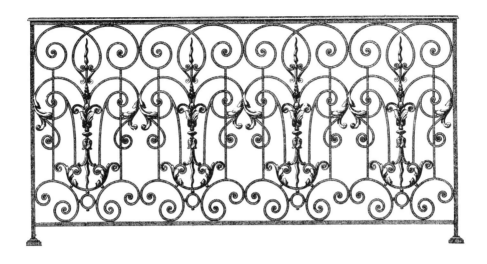

143-1

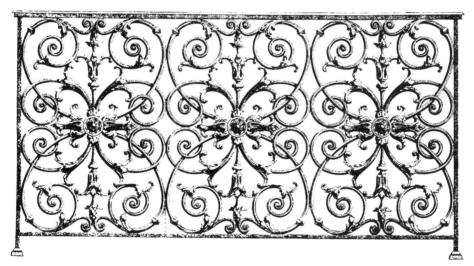

143-2

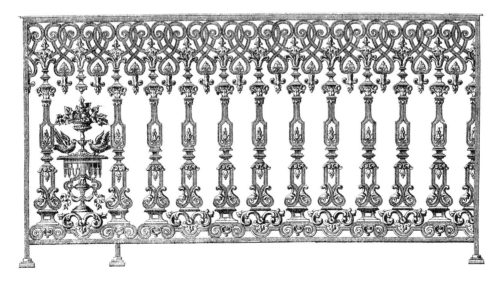

143-3

143

144-1

144-2

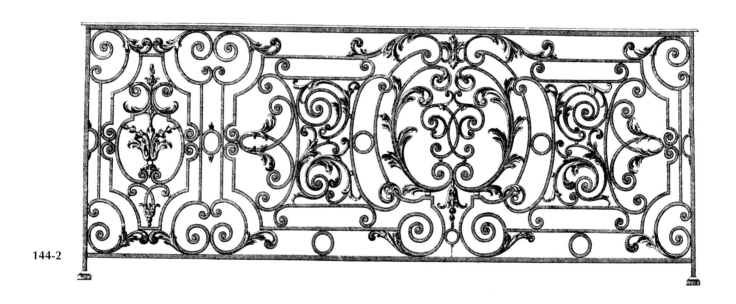

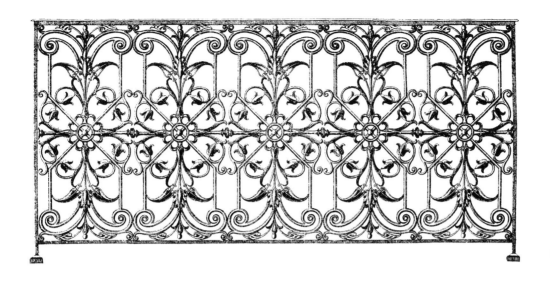

145-1

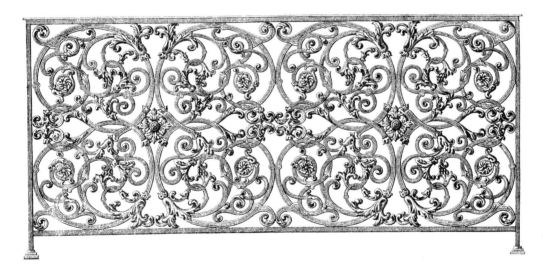

145-2

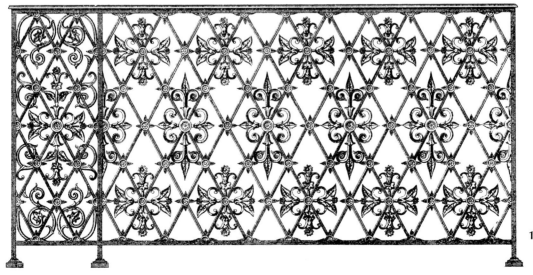

145-3

146-1

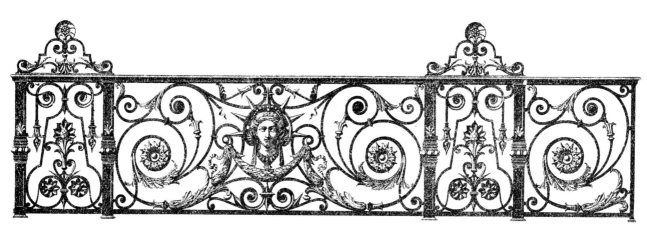

146-2

147-1

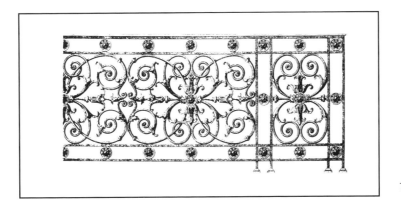

147-2

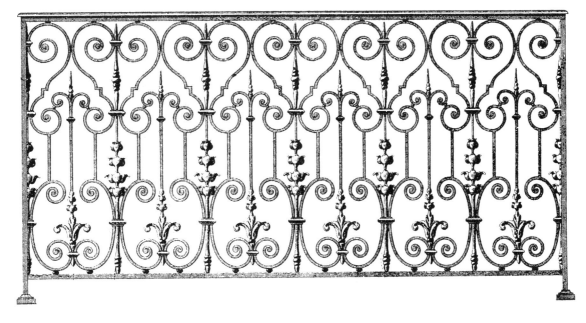

147-3

148-1

148-2

148-3

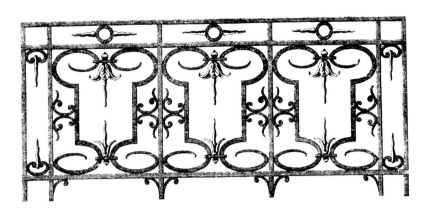

149-1

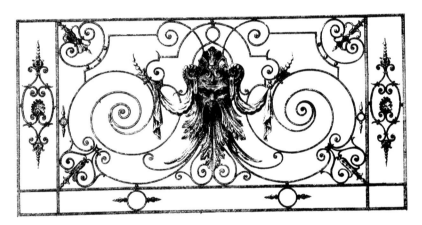

149-2

149-3

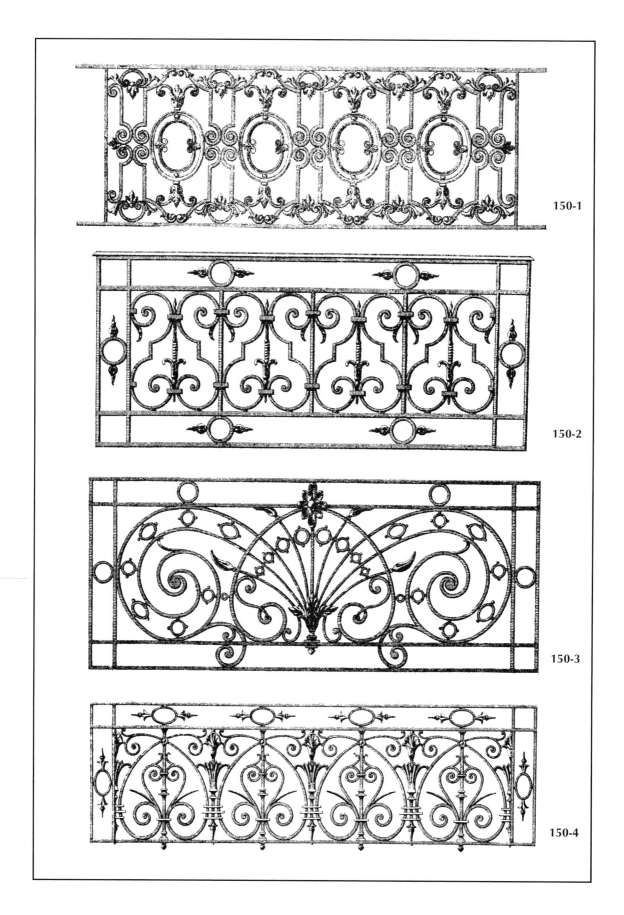

150-1

150-2

150-3

150-4

151-1

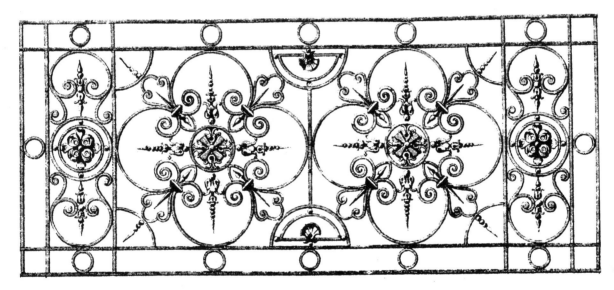

151-2

151/155 : Balconies, France, 19th century.
Balcons, France, XIXᵉ siècle.
Balkonen, Frankreich, 19. Jh.
Balcones, Francia, siglo XIX.
Балконы, Франция, XIX век.

Établissement métallurgique A. Durenne.

152-1

152-2

153-1

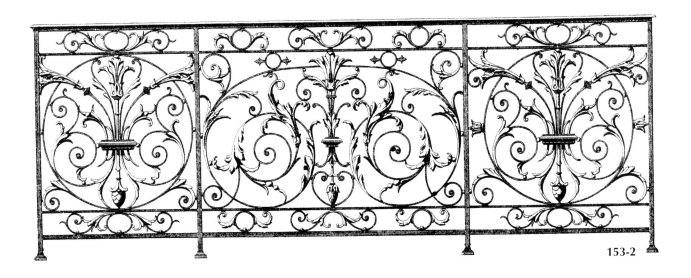

153-2

153

154-1

154-2

154

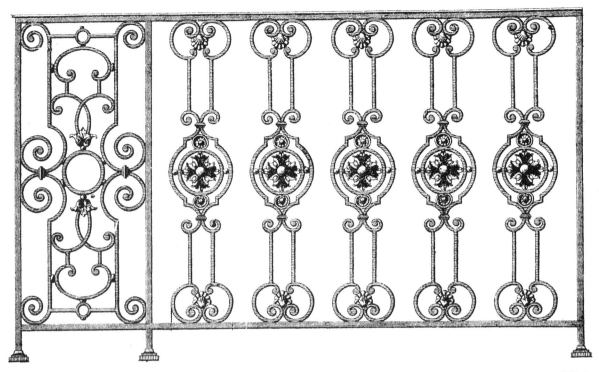

155-1

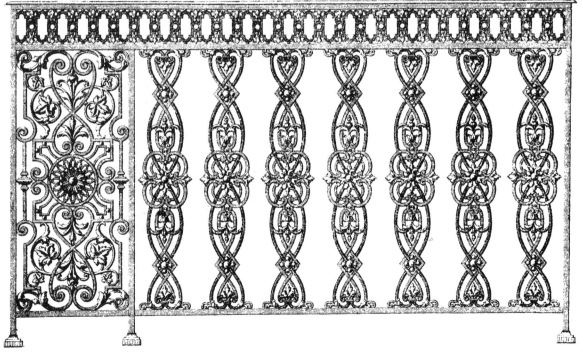

155-2

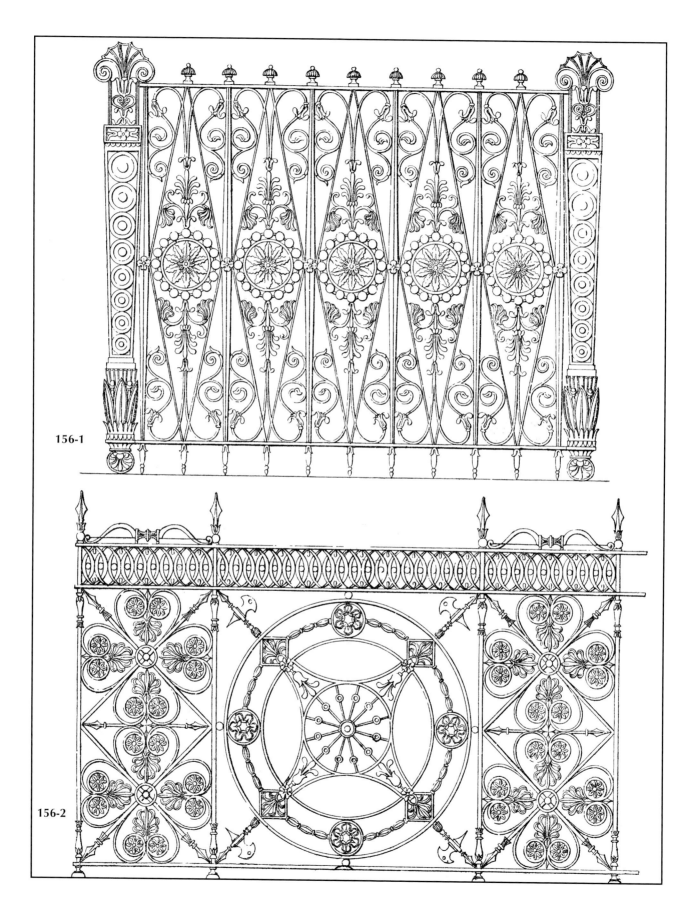

156-1

156-2

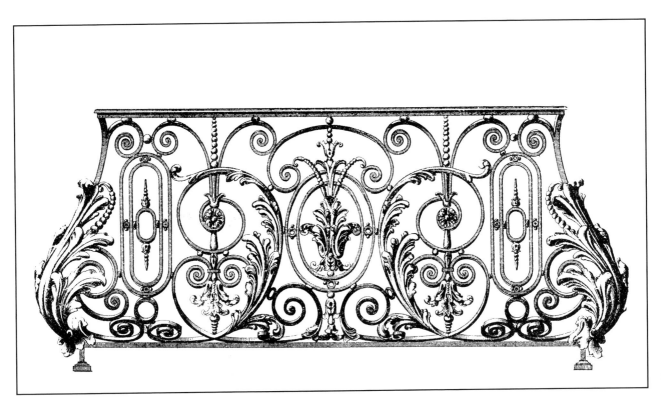

157-1

156: Balconies.
Balcons.
Balkonen.
Balcones
Балконы.

L.N. Cottingham, *The Smith and Founder's Director,* London, 1824.

157: Balconies, France,
19th century.
Balcons, France, XIXe siècle.
Balkonen, Frankreich, 19. Jh.
Balcón, Francia, siglo XIX.
Балконы, Франция, XIX век.

Établissement métallurgique
A. Durenne.

157-2

158

158: Balcony.
Balcon.
Balkon.
Balcón.
Балкон.

Jean Tijou, *A New Book of Drawings Invented and Designed by Jean Tijou*, London, 1690.

159/160: Balconies.
Balcons.
Balkonen.
Balcones.
Балконы.

L.N. Cottingham, *The Smith and Founder's Director*, London, 1824.

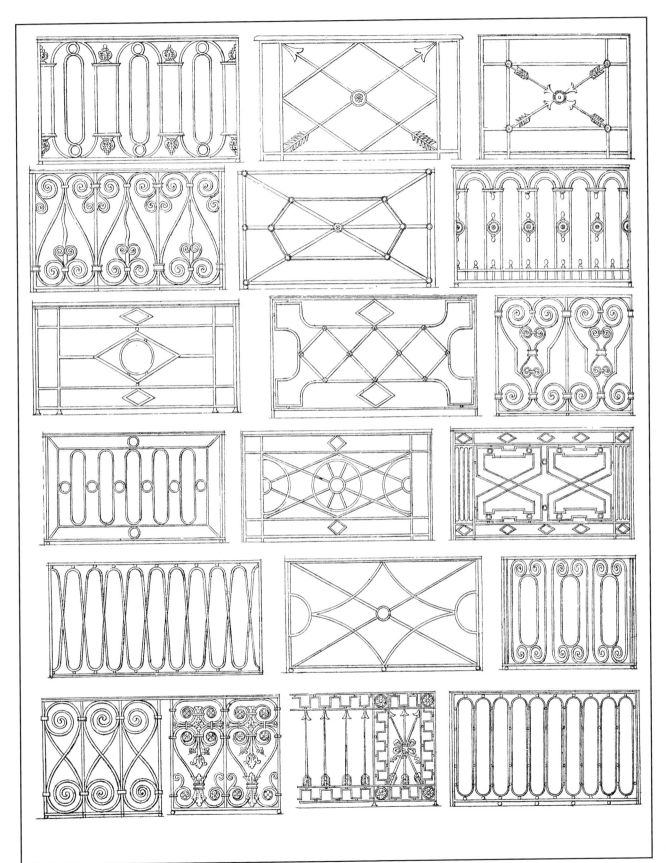

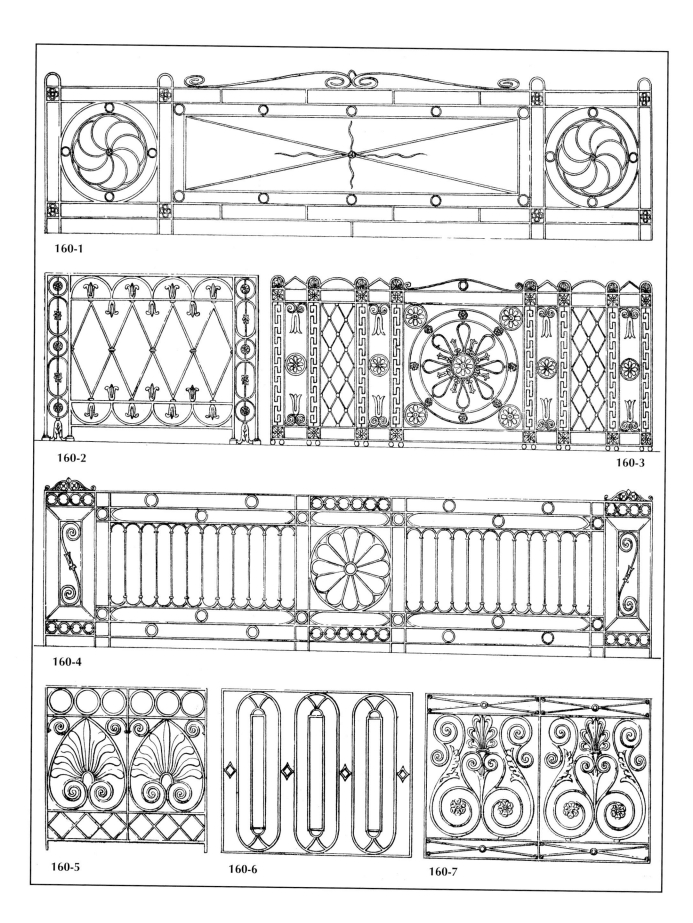

160-1

160-2

160-3

160-4

160-5

160-6

160-7

161-1

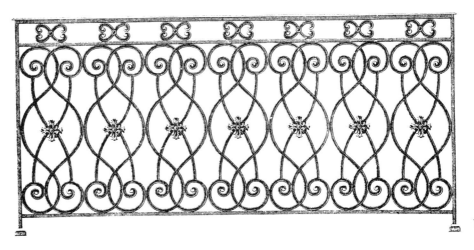

161-2

161: Balconies, France, 19th century.
Balcons, France, XIXᵉ siècle.
Balkonen, Frankreich, 19. Jh.
Balcones, Francia, siglo XIX.
Балконы, Франция, XIX век.

Établissement métallurgique A. Durenne.

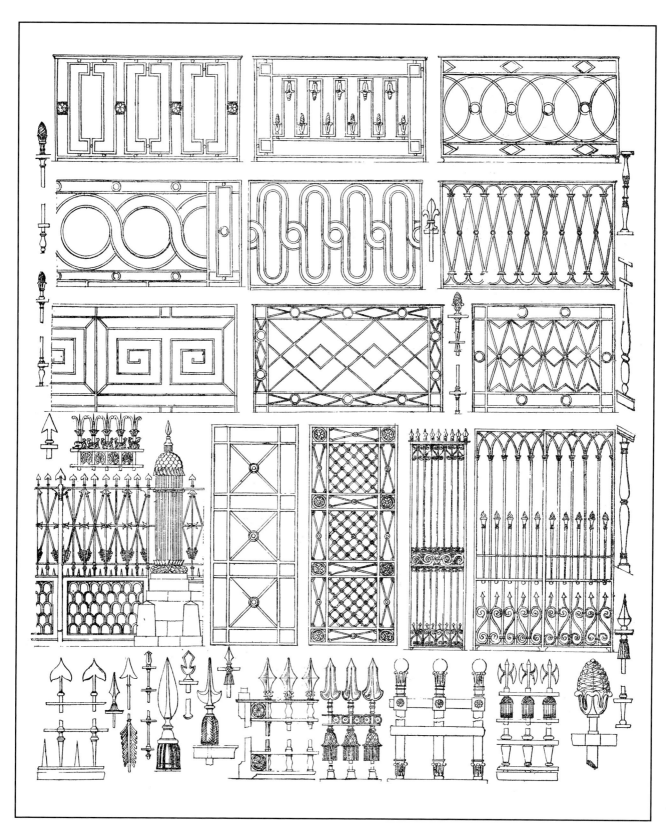

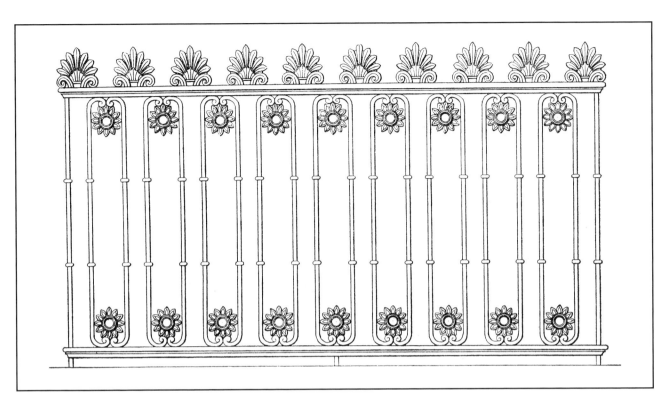

163-1

162: Balconies.
Balcons.
Balkonen.
Balcones.
Балконы.

L.N. Cottingham, *The Smith and Founder's Director,* London, 1824.

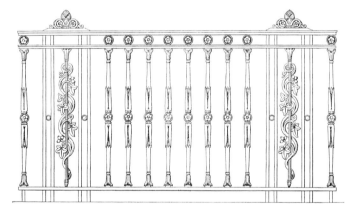

163-2

163: Balconies.
Balcons.
Balkonen.
Balcones.
Балконы.

H. Shaw, *Examples of Ornamental Iron Work,* London, 1836.

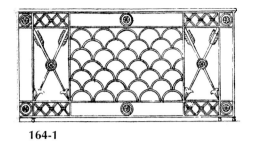

164-1

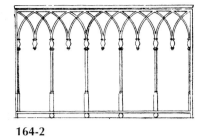

164-2

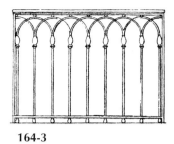

164-3

164-4

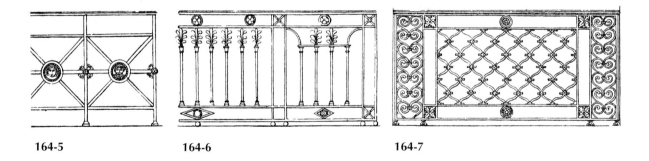

164-5   **164-6**   **164-7**

164-1, 164-7: Balconies.
Balcons.
Balkonen.
Balcones.
Балконы.

L.N. Cottingham, *The Smith and Founder's Director,*
London, 1824

164-4: Balcony, France, 19th century.
Balcon, France, XIXᵉ siècle.
Balkon, Frankreich, 19. Jh.
Balcón, Francia, siglo XIX.
Балконы, Франция, XIX век.

Établissement métallurgique A. Durenne.

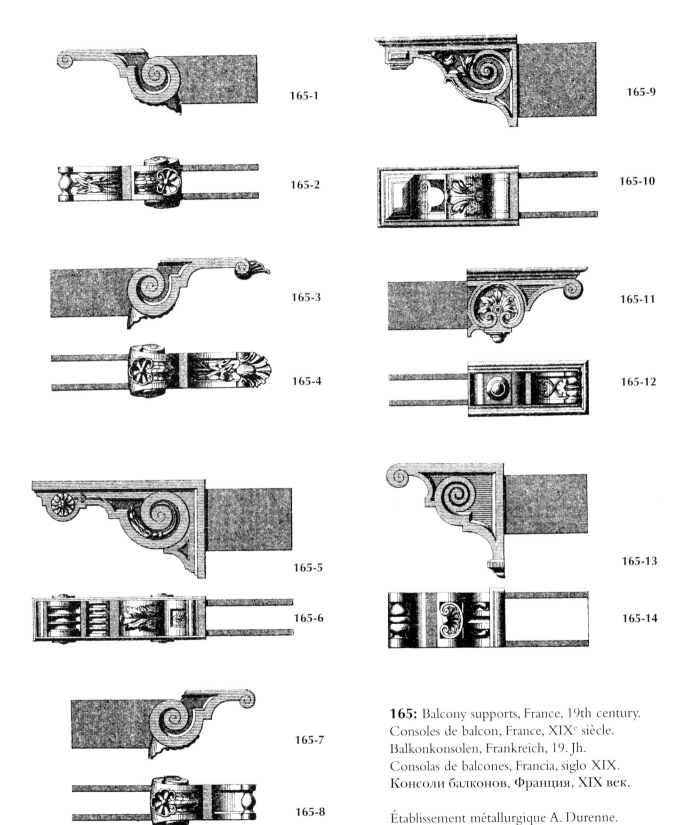

165-1

165-2

165-3

165-4

165-5

165-6

165-7

165-8

165-9

165-10

165-11

165-12

165-13

165-14

165: Balcony supports, France, 19th century.
Consoles de balcon, France, XIXe siècle.
Balkonkonsolen, Frankreich, 19. Jh.
Consolas de balcones, Francia, siglo XIX.
Консоли балконов, Франция, XIX век.

Établissement métallurgique A. Durenne.

166-1

166-2

166-3

166-4

166-5

166-6

166-7

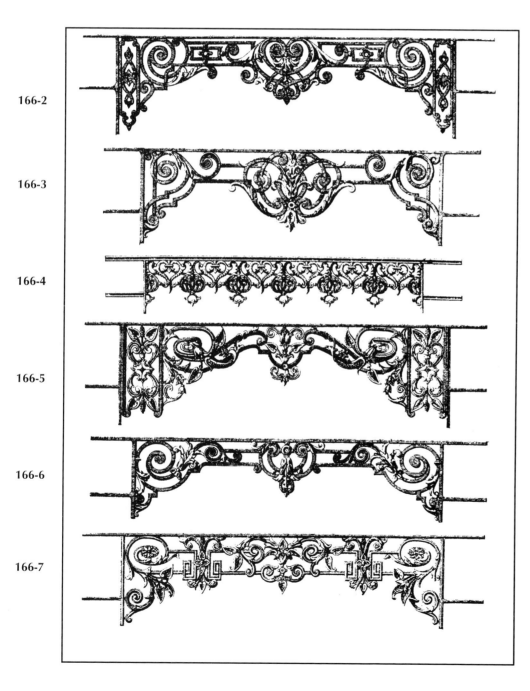

166/168:
Railings, France,
19th century.
Rampes, France,
XIXᵉ siècle.
Rampen, Frankreich,
19. Jh.
Pasamanos, Francia,
siglo XIX.
Перила, Франция,
XIX век.

Établissement
métallurgique A. Durenne.

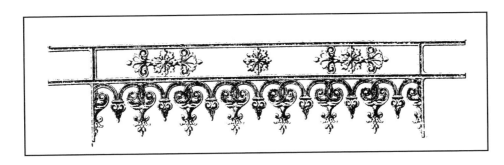

167-1

167-2

167-3

167-4

167-5

167-6

167-7

168-1

168-2

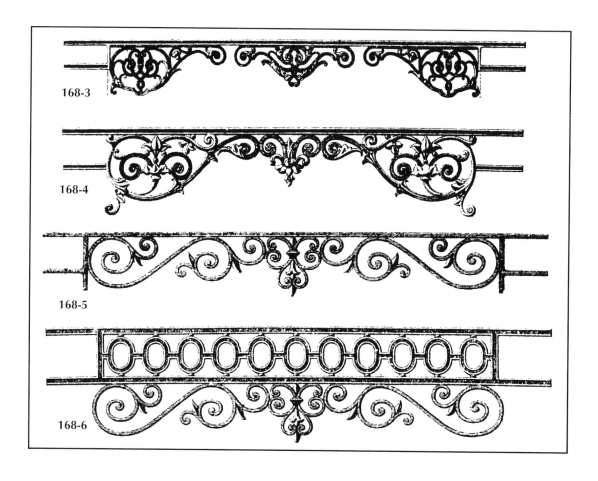

168-3

168-4

168-5

168-6

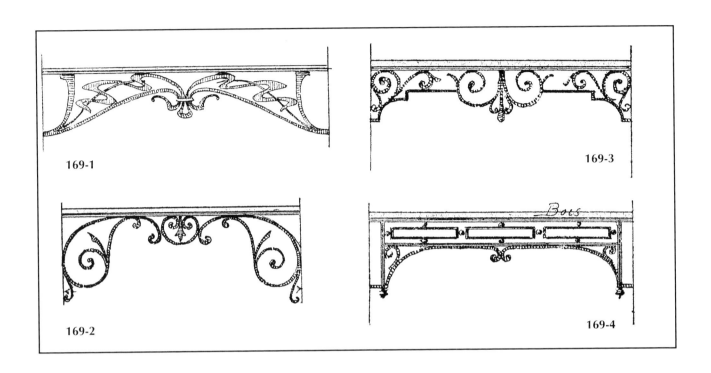

169-1

169-3

169-2

169-4

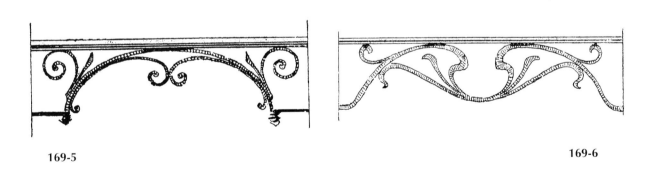

169-5

169-6

169: Railings.
Rampes.
Rampen.
Pasamanos.
Перила.

E. Barberot, *Traité pratique de serrurerie*, Paris & Liège,
1925.

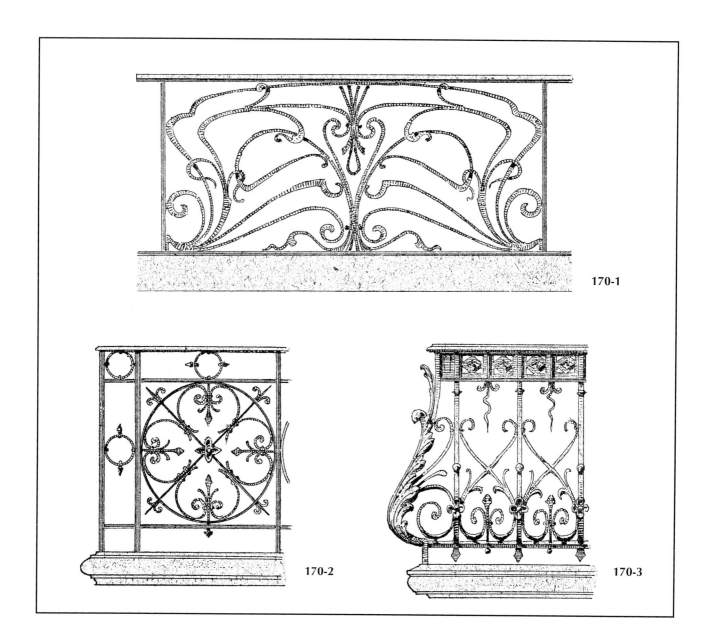

170-1

170-2

170-3

170: Balconies.
Balcons.
Balkonen.
Balcones.
Балконы.

E. Barberot, *Traité pratique de serrurerie*, Paris & Liège, 1925.

171: Canopies.
Marquises.
Vordächern.
Marquesinas.
Навесы.

E. Barberot, *Traité pratique de serrurerie*, Paris & Liège, 1925.

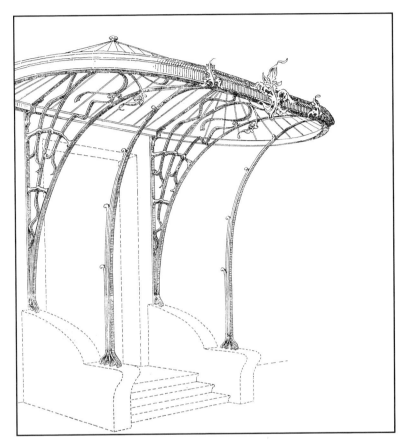

171

• Glass roofs, verandas, roofs • Auvents,
vérandas, toitures • Vördächer,
Veranden, Bedachnungen • Tejadillos,
verandas, tejados • Навесы •

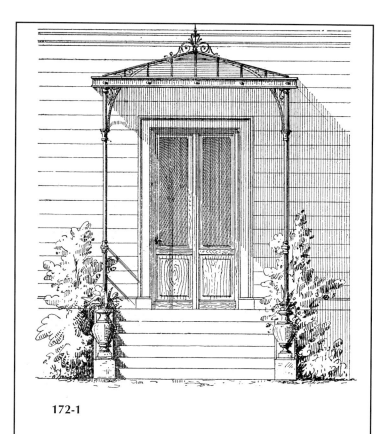

172-1

172-2

172: Canopies.
Marquises.
Vordächern.
Marquesinas.
Навесы.

E. Barberot, *Traité pratique de serrurerie*,
Paris & Liège, 1925.

173-1: Glass porch on columns.
Auvent sur colonnes.
Vordach.
Marquesina sobre columnas.
Навес над колонной.

173-2: Canopies.
Marquises.
Vordächern.
Marquesinas.
Навесы.

E. Barberot, *Traité pratique de serrurerie*, Paris
& Liège, 1925.

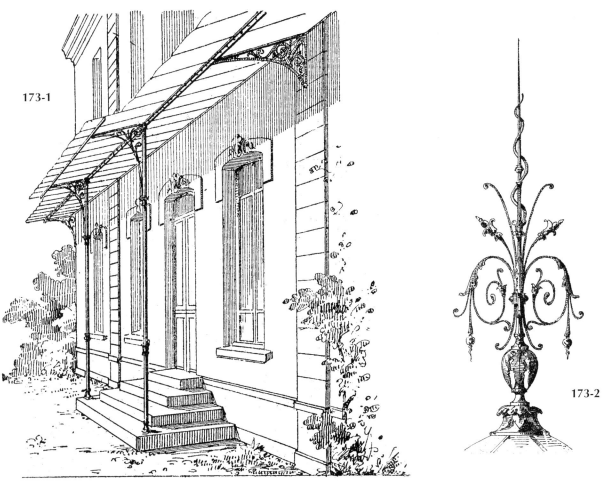

173-1

173-2

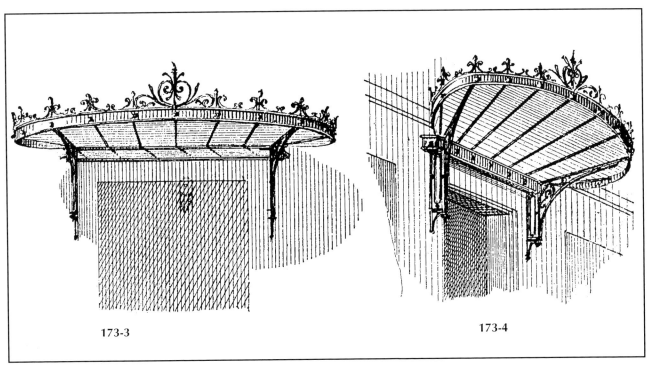

173-3

173-4

173

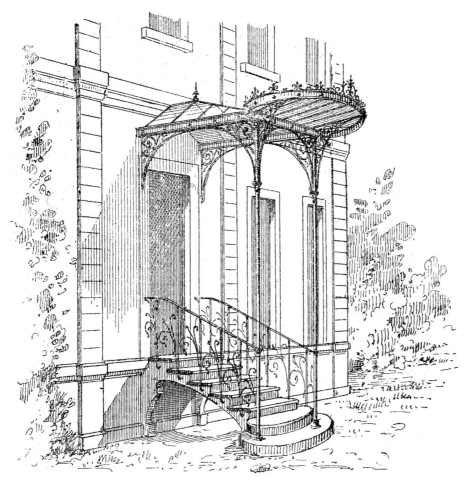

174: Canopies.
Marquises.
Vordächern.
Marquesinas.
Навесы.

E. Barberot, *Traité pratique de serrurerie*, Paris & Liège, 1925.

175 : Bow-windows.
Эркеры.

E. Barberot, *Traité pratique de serrurerie*, Paris & Liège, 1925.

174-1

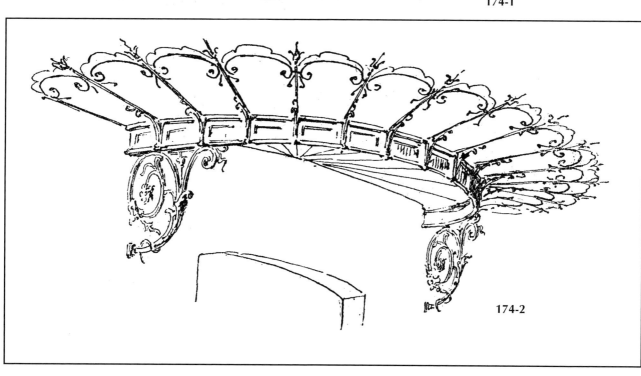

174-2

174

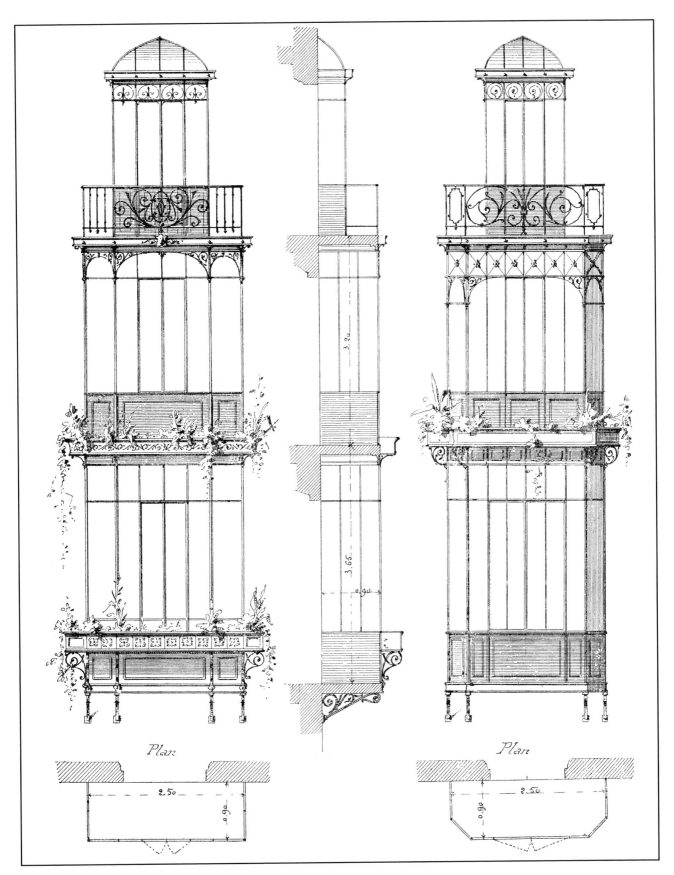

Plan

Plan

175

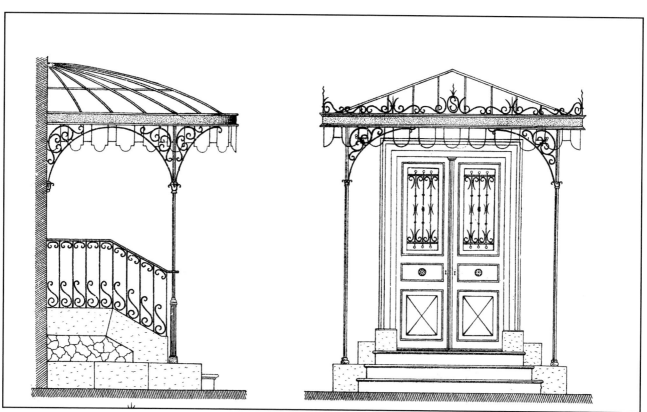

176-

176: Canopies.
Marquises.
Vordächern.
Marquesinas.
Навесы.

H. Grave, *Travaux en fer forgé,* France, 1881.

177:
Verandas.
Vérandas.
Veranden.
Verandas.
Веранды.

H. Grave, *Travaux en fer forgé,* France, 1881.

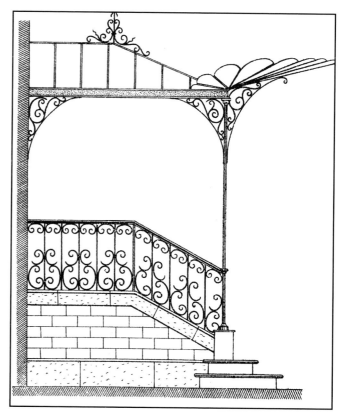

176-3

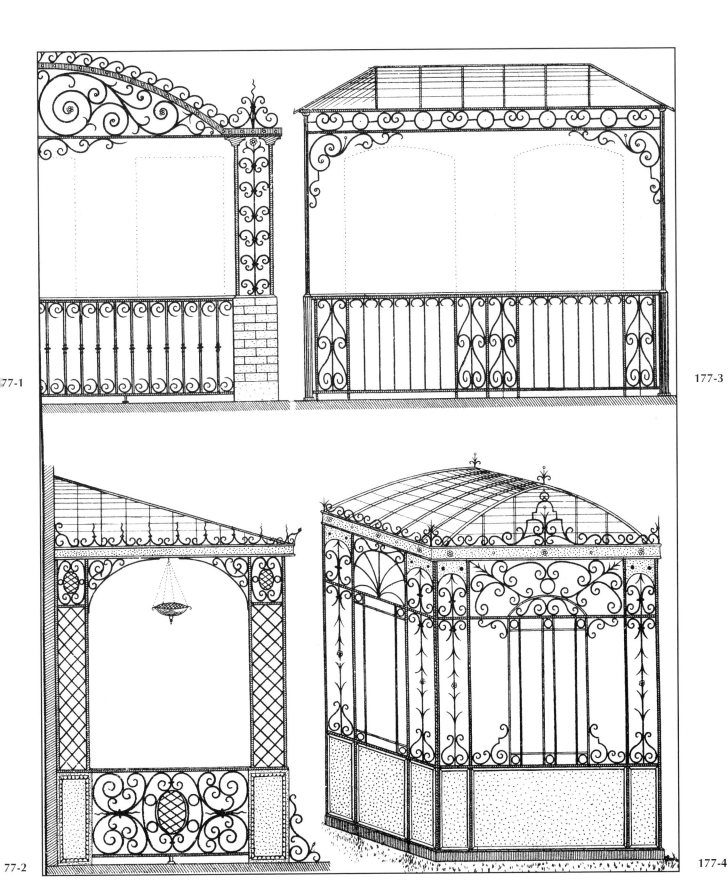

177-1

177-3

77-2

177-4

177

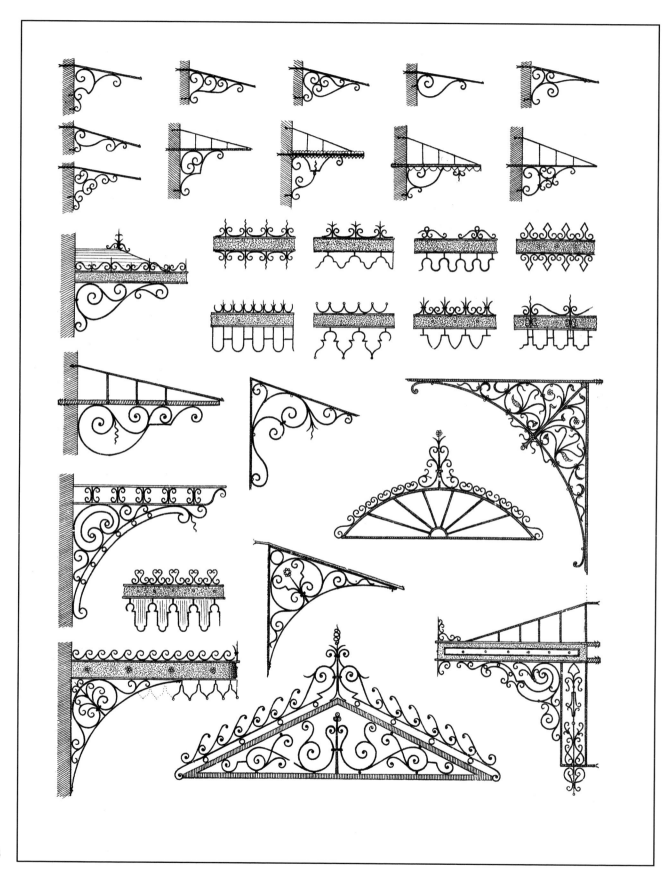

178: Canopies.
Marquises.
Vordächern.
Marquesinas.
Навесы.

H. Grave, *Travaux en fer forgé,* France, 1881.

179/181: Finials, France, 15th century.
Épis, France, XVᵉ siècle.
Epis, Frankreich, 15. Jh.
Remates, Francia, siglo XV.
Шпили, Франция, XV век.

E. Viollet-le-Duc, *Dictionnaire raisonné de l'architecture
française du XIᵉ au XVIᵉ siècle,* 1854–1868.

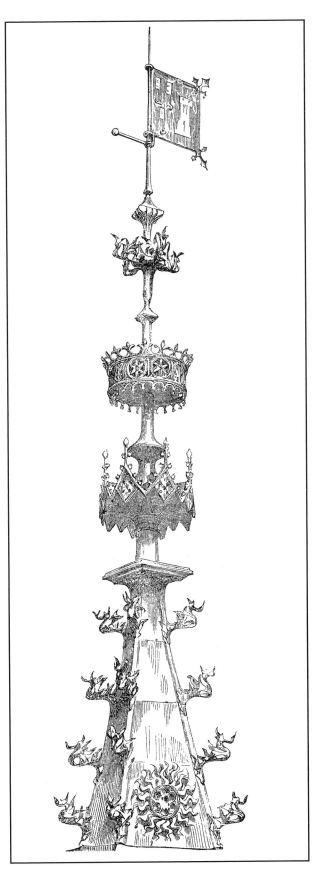

179

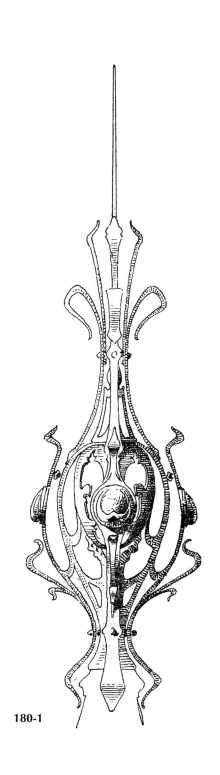

180-1

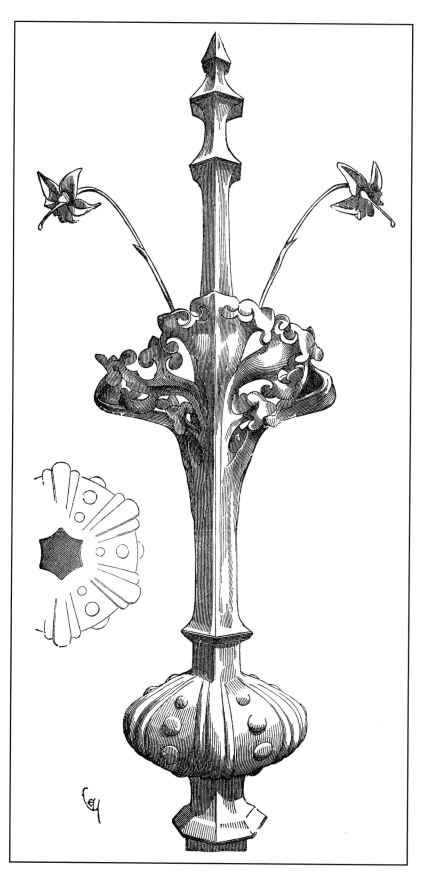

180-

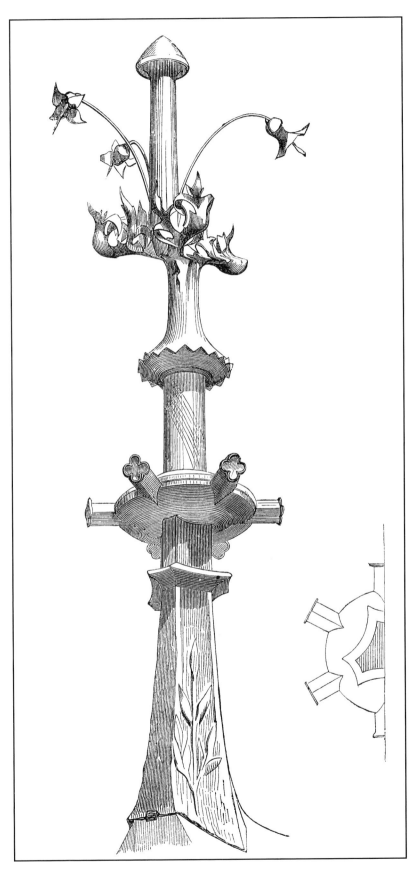

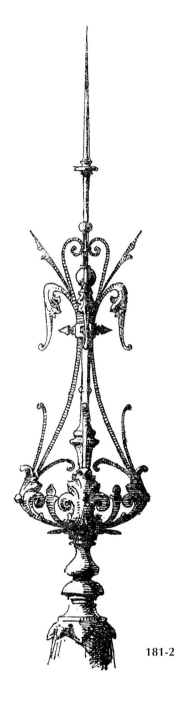

181-2

182: Finials, France,
19th century.
Épis, France, XIXᵉ siècle.
Epis, Frankreich, 19. Jh.
Remates, Francia,
siglo XIX.
Шпили, Франция,
XIX век.

Établissement
métallurgique A. Durenne.

183: Finials, France,
15th century.
Épis, France, XVᵉ siècle.
Epis, Frankreich, 15. Jh.
Remates, Francia, siglo XV.
Шпили, Франция,
XV век.

E. Viollet-le-Duc,
*Dictionnaire raisonné de
l'architecture française du XIᵉ
au XVIᵉ siècle.* 1854–1868.

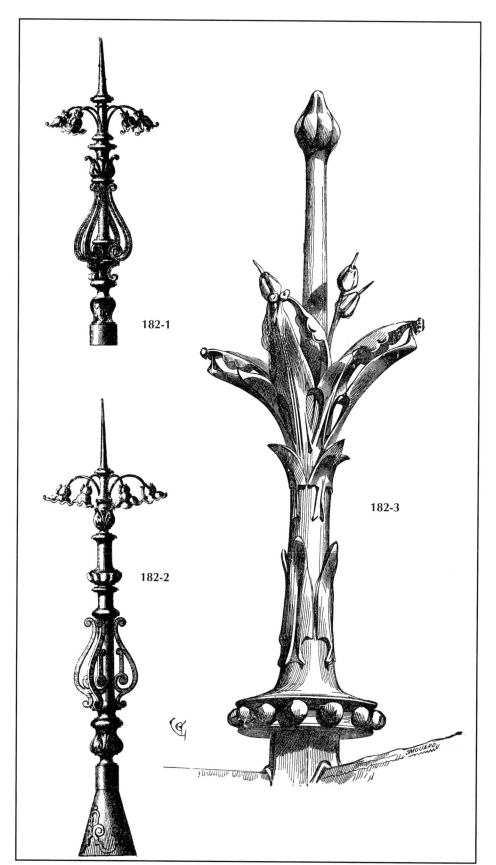

182-1

182-2

182-3

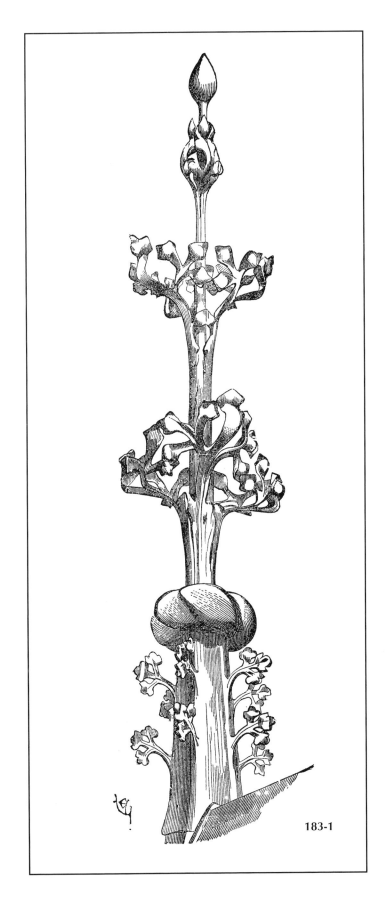

183-1

183-2

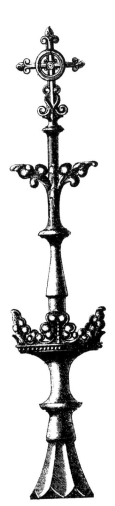

183-3

183

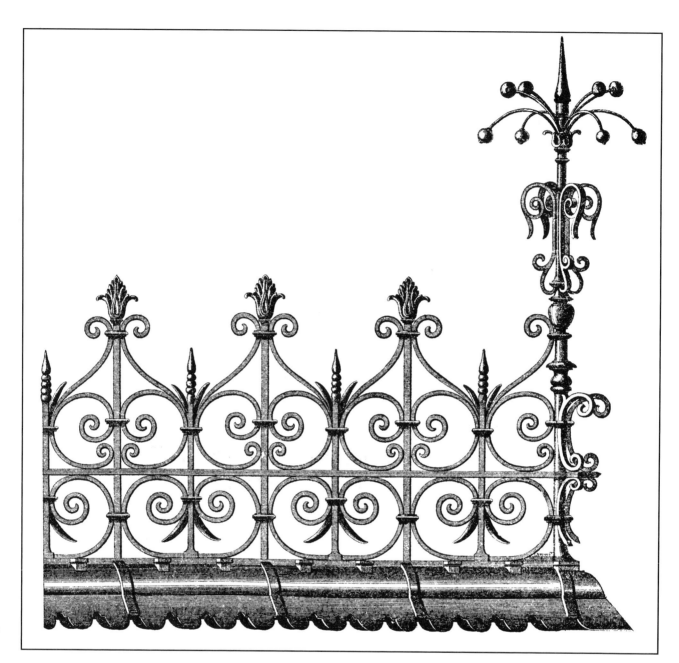

184

184/189: Copings.
Crêtes de faîtage.
Verfirstungsgipfel.
Cresterias de remates.
Коньки крыш.

E. Barberot, *Traité pratique de serrurerie*, Paris & Liège, 1925.

185

186-1

186-2

186-3

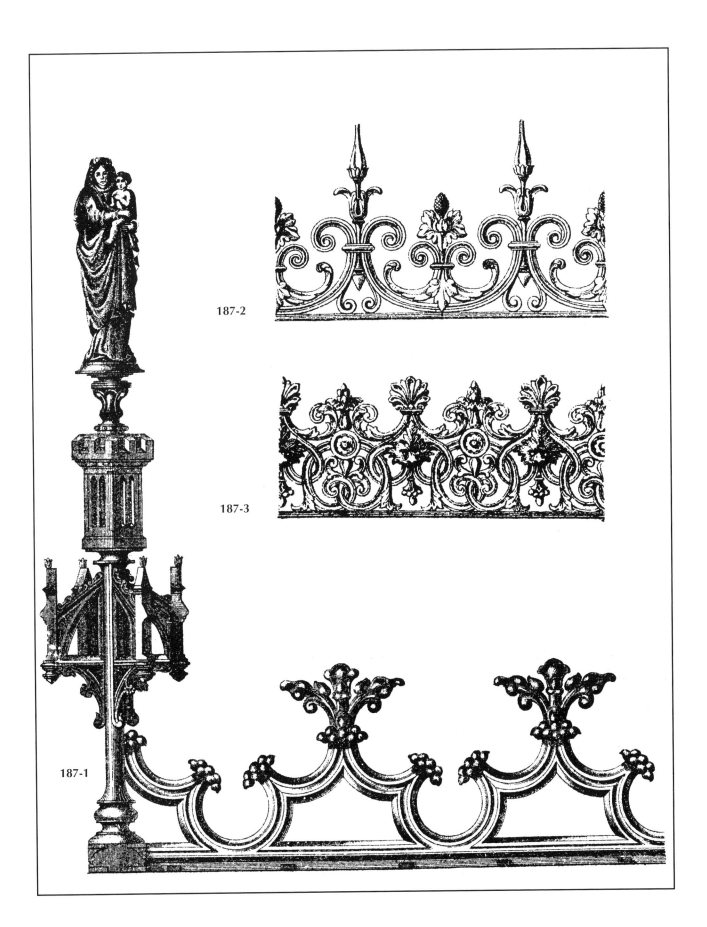

187-2

187-3

187-1

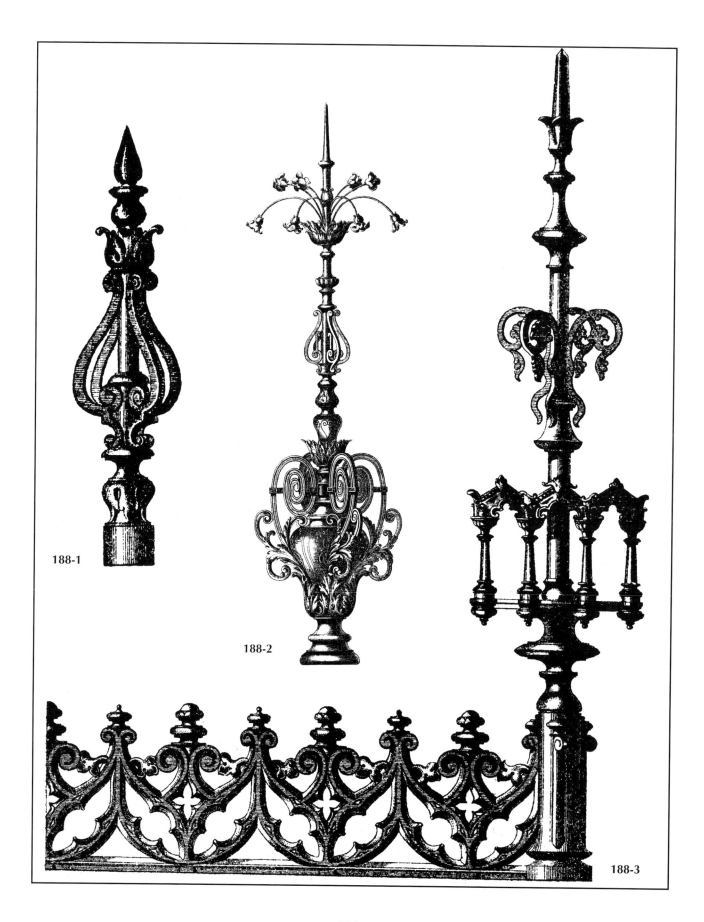

188-1

188-2

188-3

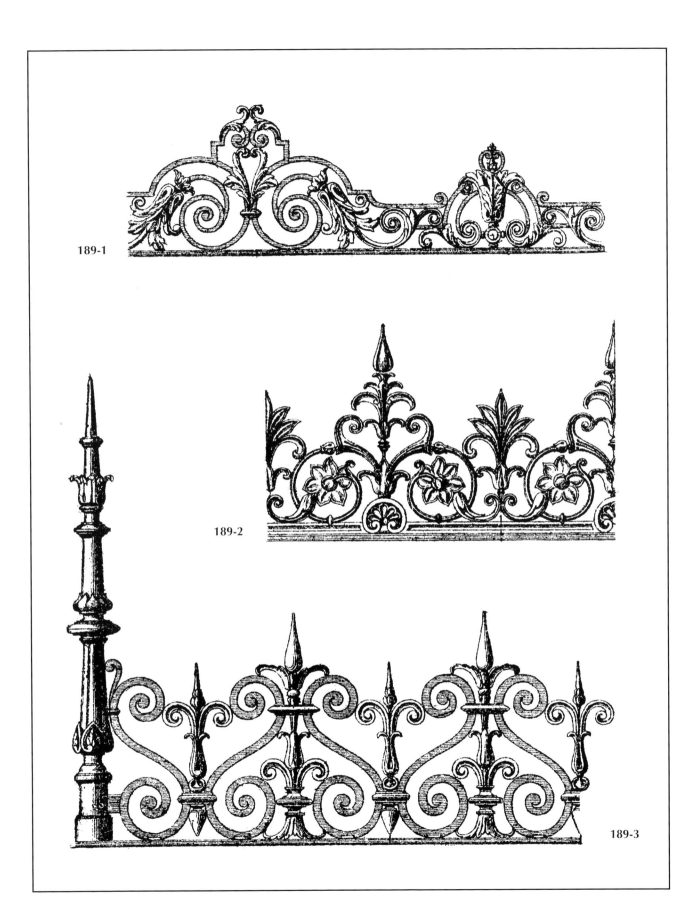

189-1

189-2

189-3

190: Coping, cresting, finial and belltower crosse, France, 19th century.
Crête, faîtière, épi et croix de clocher, France, XIXᵉ siècle.
Verfirstungsgipfel, Verzierung, Kreuz und Turmspitze, Frankreich, 19. Jh.
Remate, crestería, cobija y cruz de campanario, Francia, siglo XIX.
Шпиль, конек, черепица и крест на колокольне, Франция, XIX век.

Établissement Le Val d'Osne.

191: Kiosk. Kiosque. Pavillon. Kiosco. Беседка.

E. Barberot, *Traité pratique de serrurerie*, Paris & Liège, 1925.

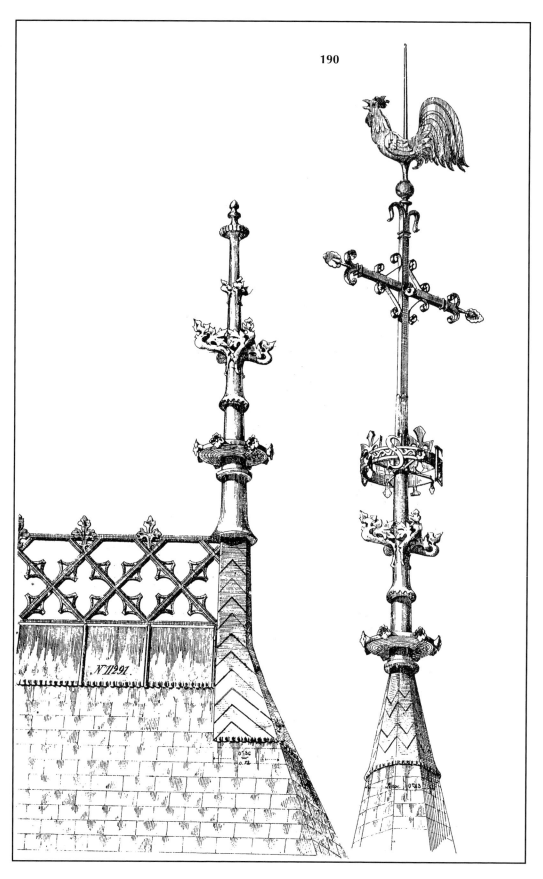

190

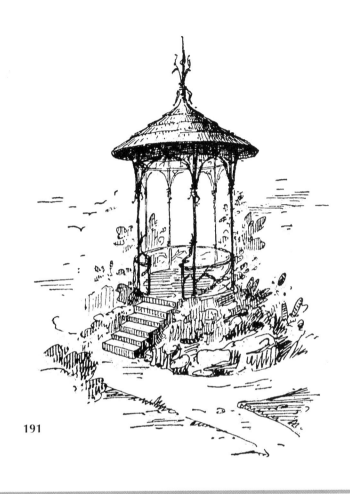

191

• Garden equipment • Éléments
de jardin • Gartenutensilien •
• Elementos de jardines •
• Садовые постройки •

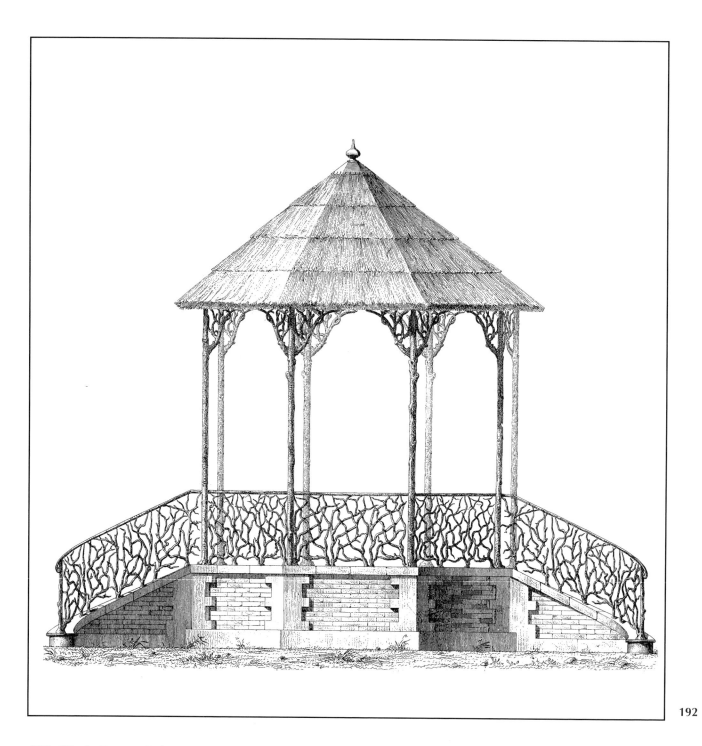

192: Kiosk, France, 19th century.
Kiosque, France, XIXᵉ siècle.
Pavillon, Frankreich, 19. Jh.
Kiosco, Francia, siglo XIX.
Беседка, Франция, XIX век.

Établissement Le Val d'Osne.

193 : Music Kiosks, France, 19th century.
Kiosques à musique, France, XIXᵉ siècle.
Musikpavillons, Frankreich, 19. Jh.
Kioscos, Francia, siglo XIX.
Музыкальный павильон, Франция, XIX век.

Établissement Carré.

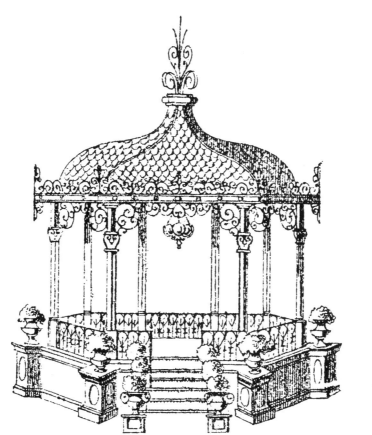

193-1

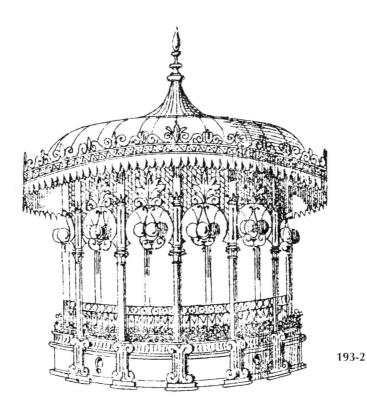

193-2

193

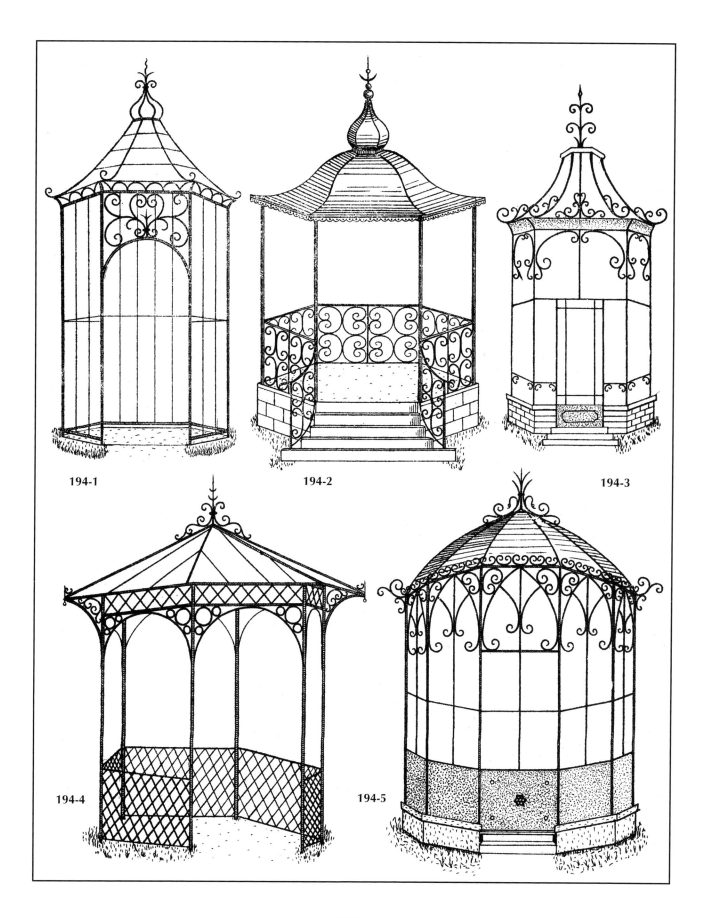

194-1

194-2

194-3

194-4

194-5

194

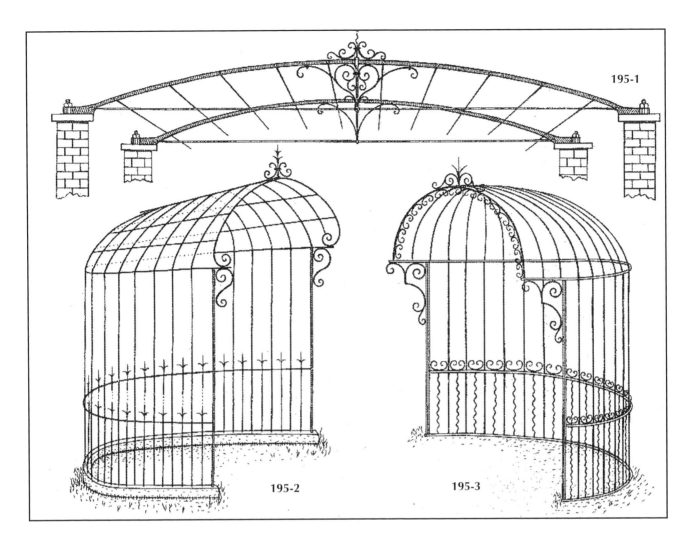

195-1

195-2

195-3

195: Bowers.
Tonnelles.
Gartenlaube.
Cenadores.
Своды беседок.

H. Grave, *Travaux en fer forgé,* France, 1881.

194: Kiosks and pavilions.
Kiosques et pavillons.
Pavillons.
Kioscos y pavillones.
Беседки и павильоны.

H. Grave, *Travaux en fer forgé,* France, 1881.

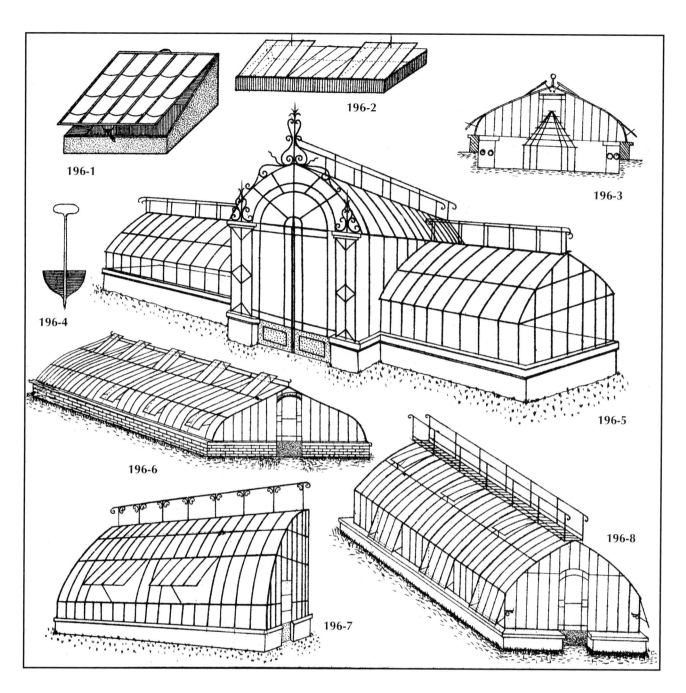

196: Greenhouses.
Serres.
Gewächshauser.
Invernaderos.
Парники.

H. Grave, *Travaux en fer forgé,* France, 1881.

197: Aviary.
Volière.
Vogelkäfig.
Pajarera.
Вольер.

E. Barberot, *Traité pratique de serrurerie*, Paris & Liège, 1925

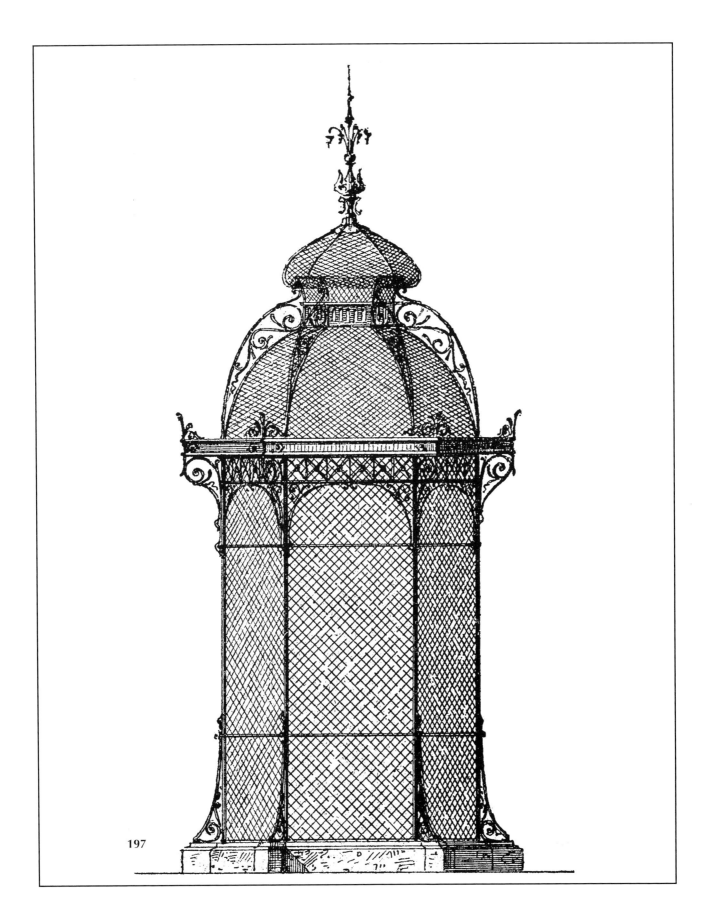

197

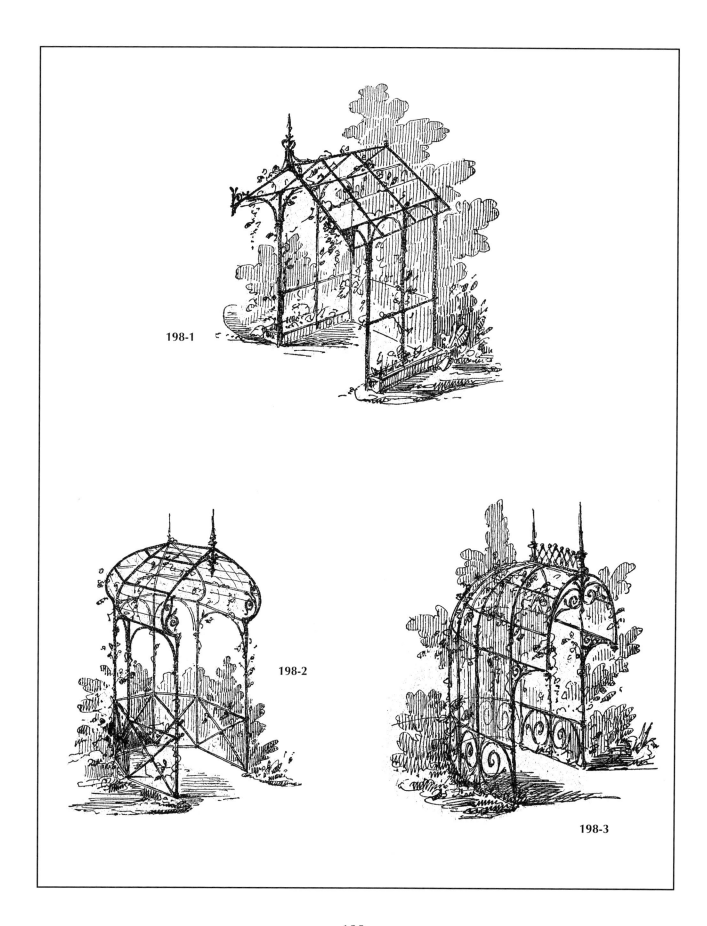

198-1

198-2

198-3

198: Bowers.
Tonnelles.
Gartenlaube.
Cenadores.
Своды беседок.

E. Barberot, *Traité pratique de serrurerie*,
Paris & Liège, 1925.

199: Aviary.
Volière.
Vogelkäfig.
Pajarera.
Вольер.

E. Barberot, *Traité pratique de serrurerie*,
Paris & Liège, 1925.

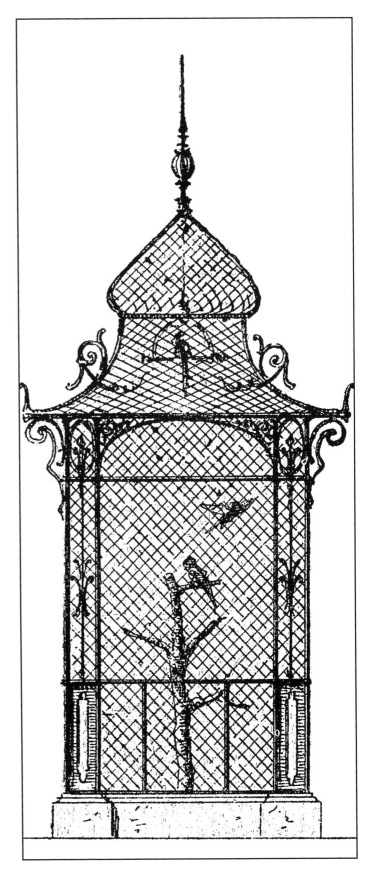

199

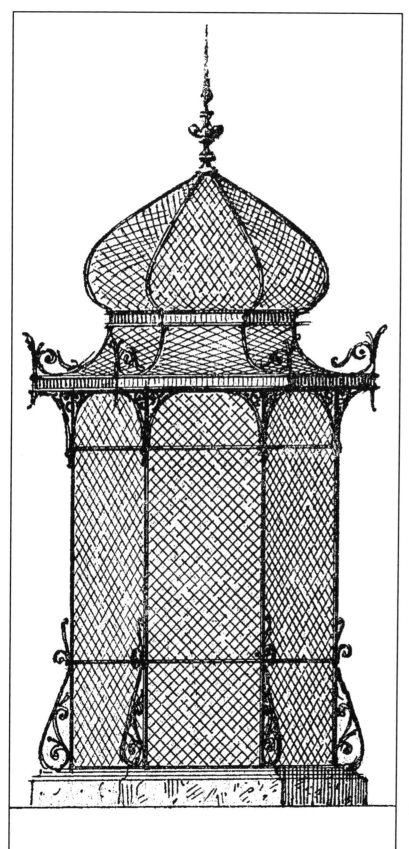

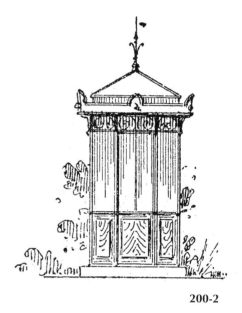

200-2

200/202:
Kiosks.
Kiosques.
Pavillons.
Kioscos.

E. Barberot, *Traité pratique de serrurerie*,
Paris & Liège, 1925.

200-1

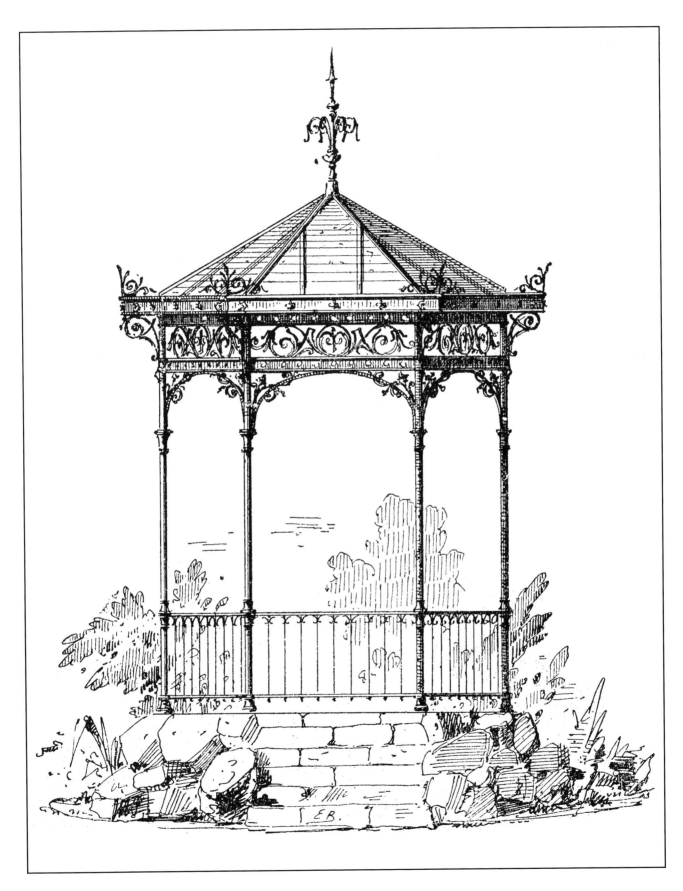

201

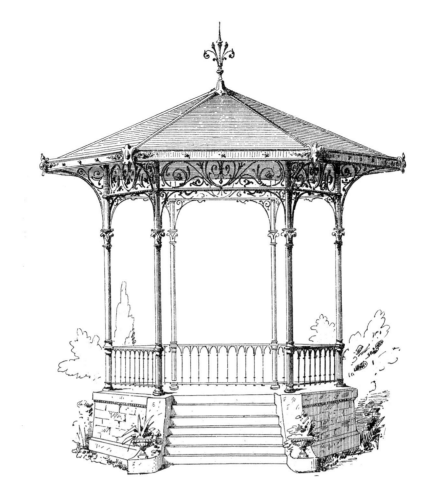

202-1

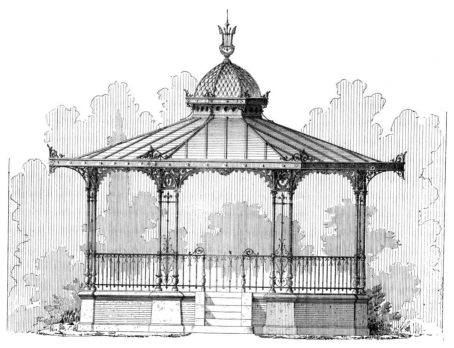

202-2

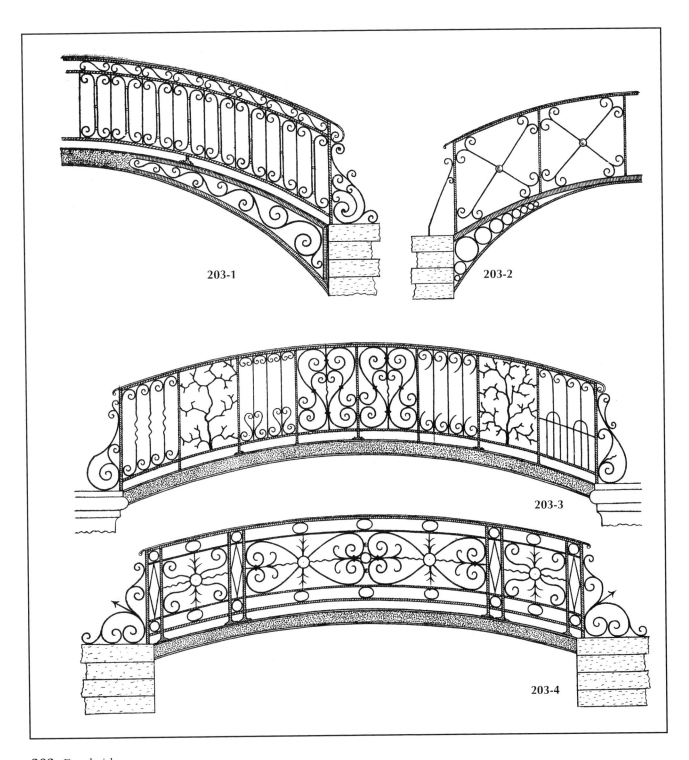

203-1

203-2

203-3

203-4

203: Footbridges.
Passerelles.
Passerelle.
Pasarelas.
Мостики.

H. Grave, *Travaux en fer forgé,* France, 1881.

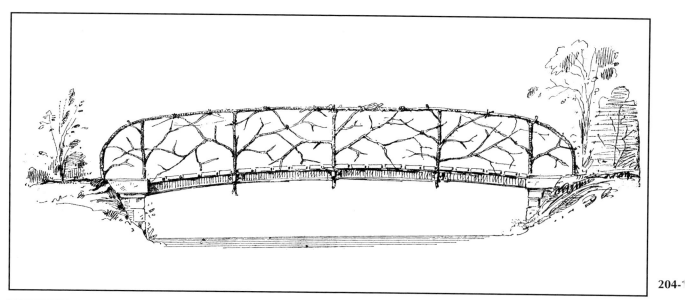

204-1

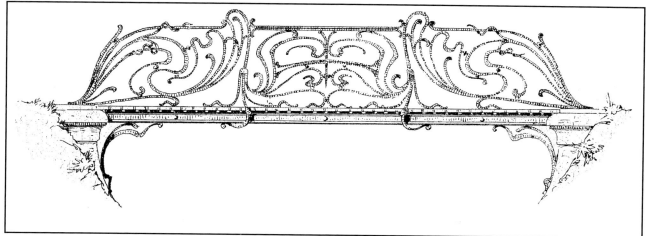

204-2

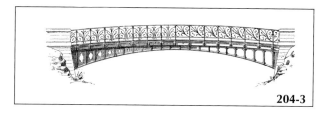

204-3

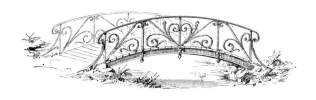

204-4

204: Footbridges.
Passerelles.
Passerelle.
Pasarelas.
Мостики.

E. Barberot, *Traité pratique de serrurerie*, Paris & Liège,
1925.

205/206: Garden benches, France,19th century.
Bancs de jardin, France, XIXᵉ siècle.
Gartenbänke, Frankreich, 19. Jh.
Bancos de jardines, Francia, siglo XIX.
Садовые скамейки, Франция, XIX век.

Établissement Le Val d'Osne.

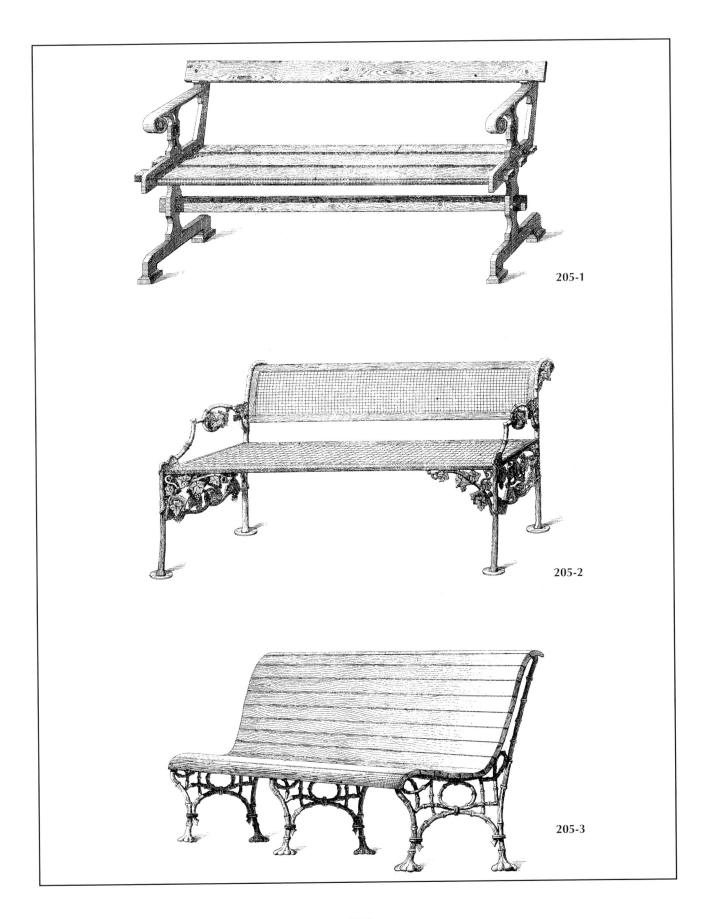

205-1

205-2

205-3

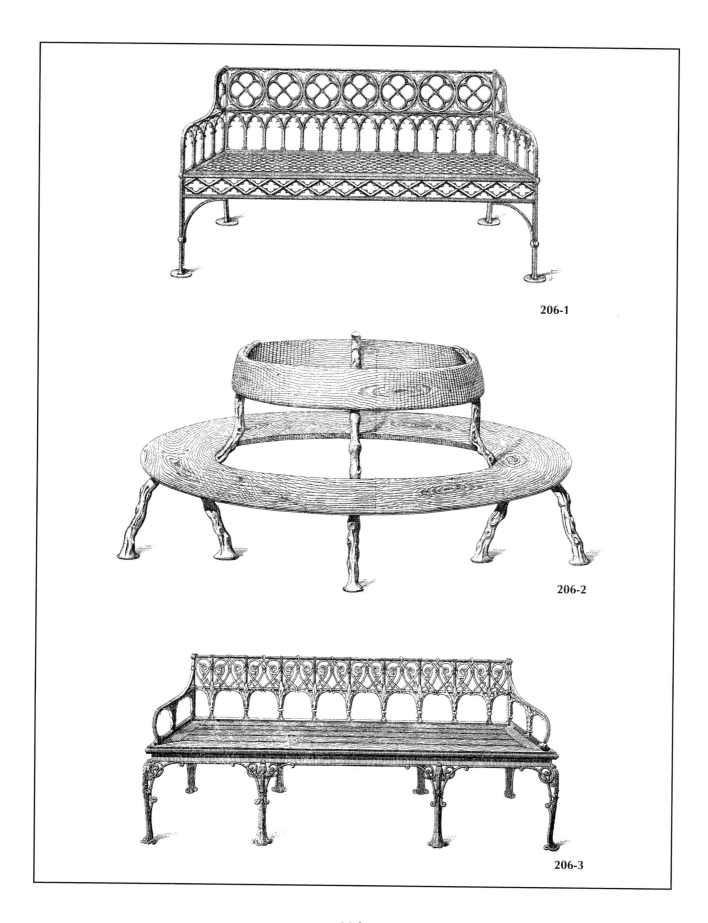

206-1

206-2

206-3

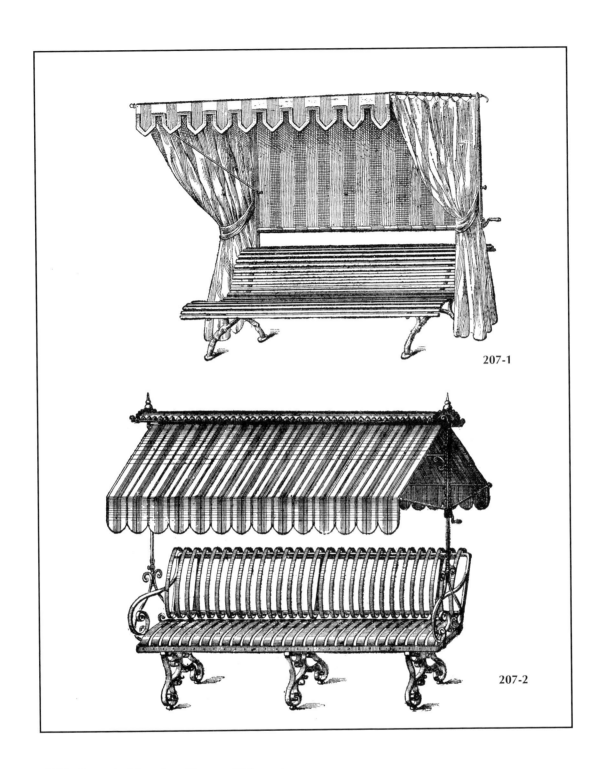

207-1

207-2

207: Canopied benches, France, 19th century.

Bancs-stores, France, XIXᵉ siècle.

Gartenbanküberdachungen, Frankreich, 19. Jh.

Bancos con toldos, Francia, siglo XIX.

Скамейки с тентом, Франция, XIX век.

Établissement Allez Frères.

208/210: Garden tools and equipment.
Équipements de jardins et outils horticoles.
Gartenausstattungen und Gartengeräte.
Equipos de jardines y herramientas hortícolas.
Садовый инвентарь.

H. Grave, *Travaux en fer forgé,* France, 1881.

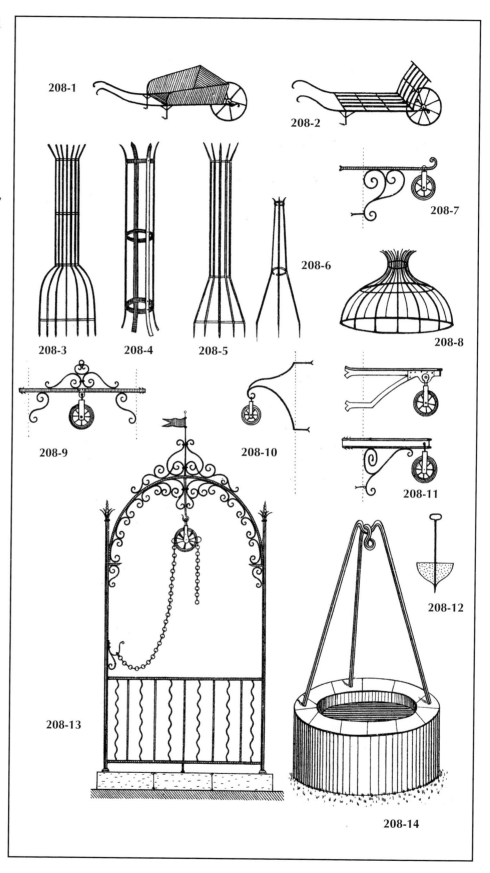

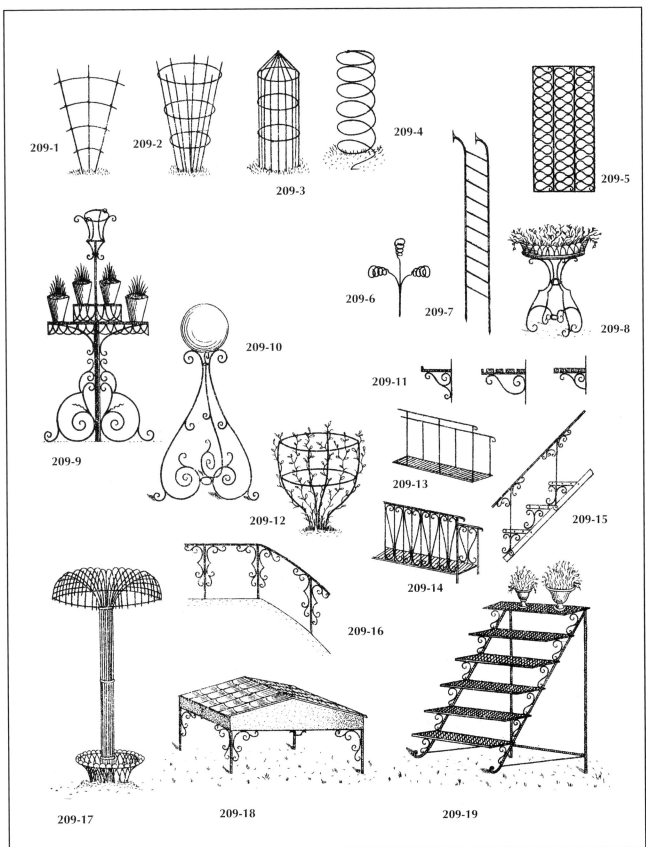

209-1

209-2

209-3

209-4

209-5

209-6

209-7

209-8

209-9

209-10

209-11

209-12

209-13

209-14

209-15

209-16

209-17

209-18

209-19

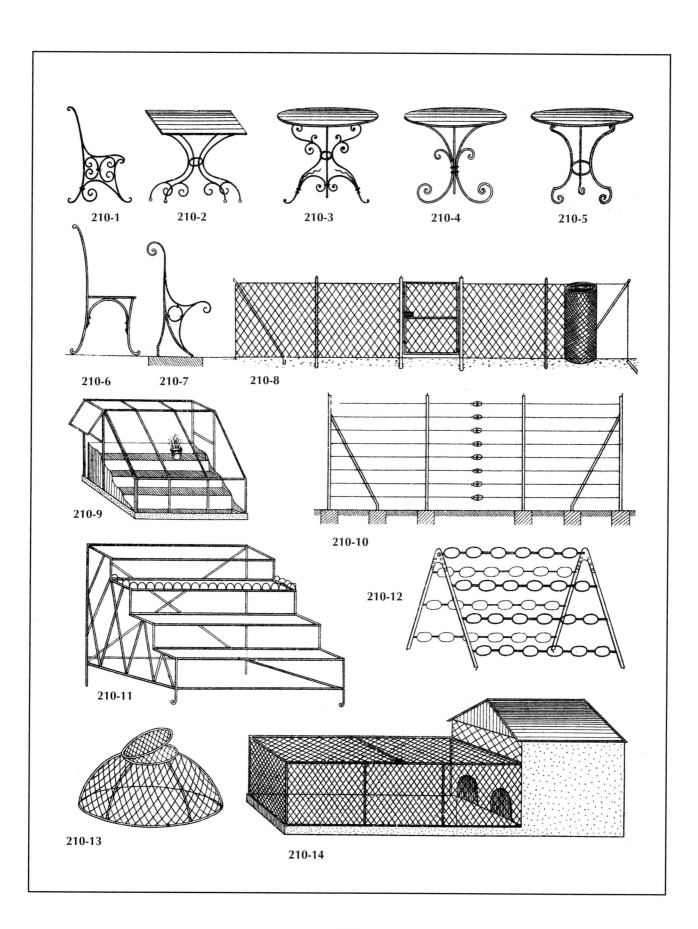

210-1

210-2

210-3

210-4

210-5

210-6

210-7

210-8

210-9

210-10

210-11

210-12

210-13

210-14

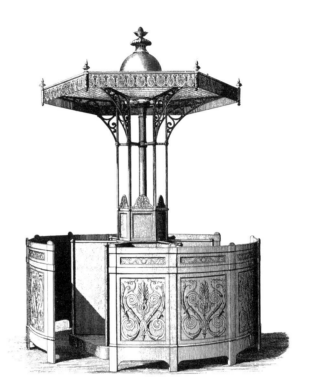

211

• Urban furniture • Mobilier urbain •
• Gegestände des öffentlichen Lebens •
• Mobiliario urbano •
• Садовый инвентарь •

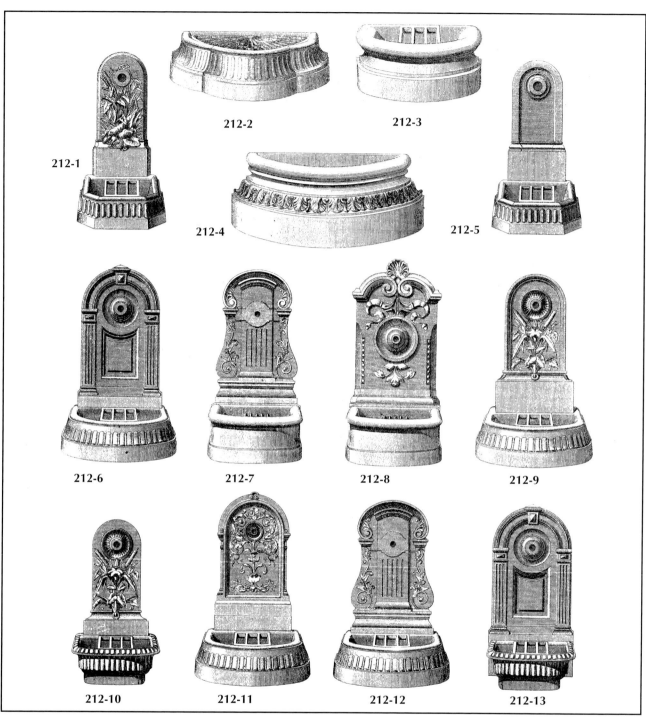

211: Circular urinal, France, 19th century.
Vespasienne circulaire, France, XIXe siècle.
Vespasienne in Kreisform, Frankreich, 19. Jh.
Urinario público circular, Francia, siglo XIX.
Круглый уличный писсуар, Франция, XIX век.

Établissement Le Val d'Osne.

212: Wall fountains and basins, France, 19th century.
Bassins et fontaines d'applique, France, XIXe siècle.
Bassins und Auffangbecken von Wasserquellanlagen,
Frankreich, 19. Jh.
Pilones y fuentes, Francia, siglo XIX.
Резервуары и фонтаны, Франция, XIX век.

Établissement Le Val d'Osne.

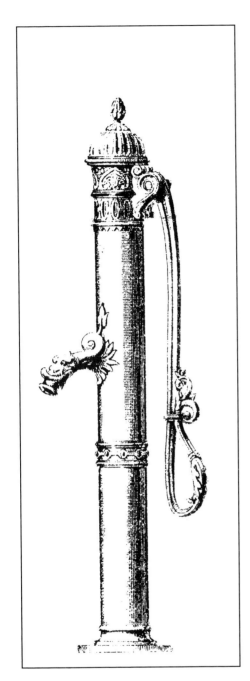

213-1

213 : Water pumps, France,
19th century.
Pompes à eau, France, XIXᵉ siècle.
Wasserpumpen, Frankreich, 19. Jh.
Bombas de agua, Francia, siglo XIX.
Водяной насос, Франция,
XIX век.

Établissement Le Val d'Osne.

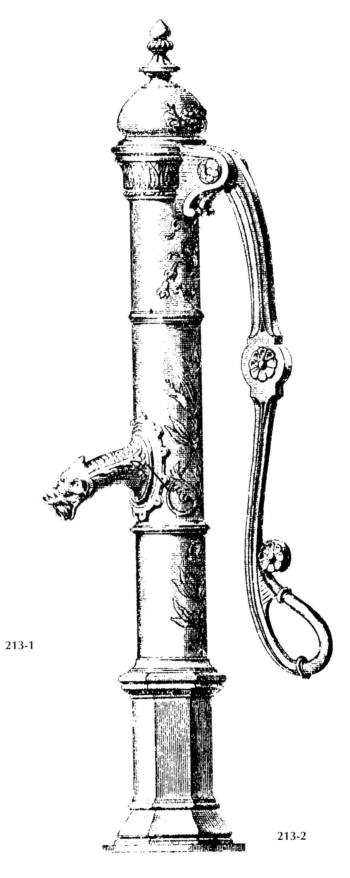

213-2

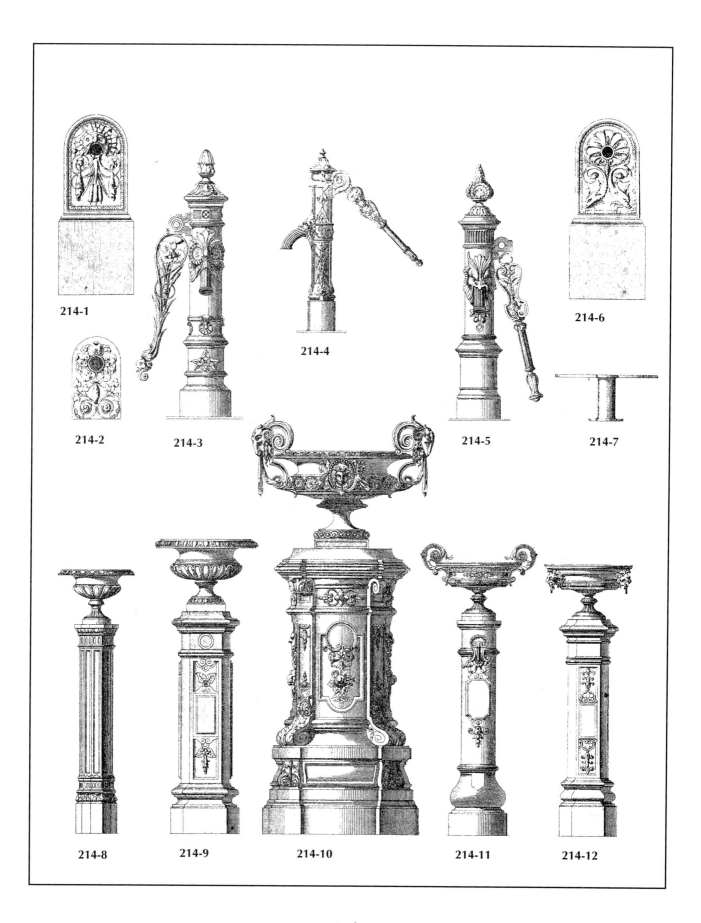

214-1

214-2

214-3

214-4

214-5

214-6

214-7

214-8

214-9

214-10

214-11

214-12

214: Pumps, fountains and columns, France, 19th century.

Pompes, fontaines et colonnes, France, XIXᵉ siècle.

Wasserpumpen, Standfontainen und Saülen, Frankreich, 19. Jh.

Bombas, fuentes y columnas, Francia, siglo XIX.

Насосы, фонтаны и колонны, Франция, XIX век.

Établissement métallurgique A. Durenne.

215/218: Street lamps.

Réverbères.

Stehlampen.

Farolas.

Уличные фонари.

I. and J. Taylor, *Ornamental Iron Work or Designs in the Present Taste*, London, *c.* 1795.

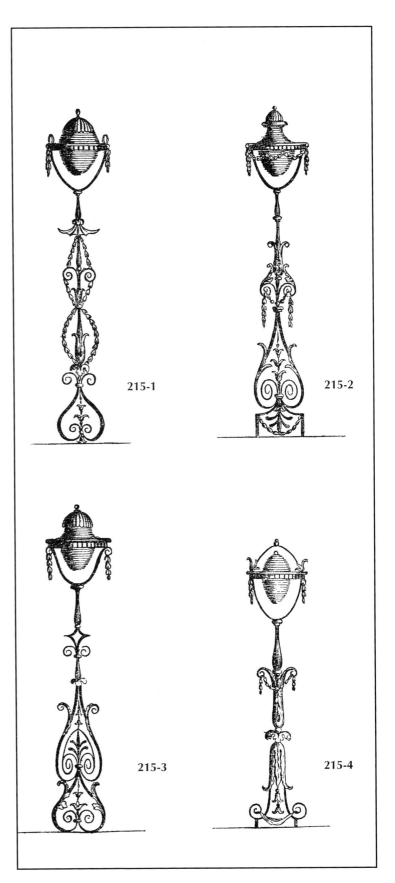

215-1

215-2

215-3

215-4

215

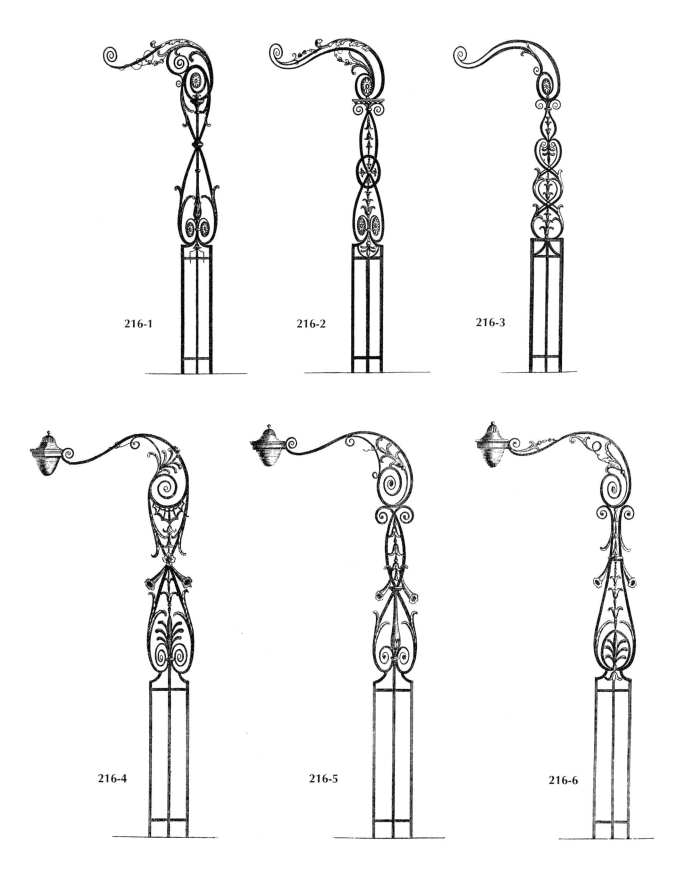

216-1

216-2

216-3

216-4

216-5

216-6

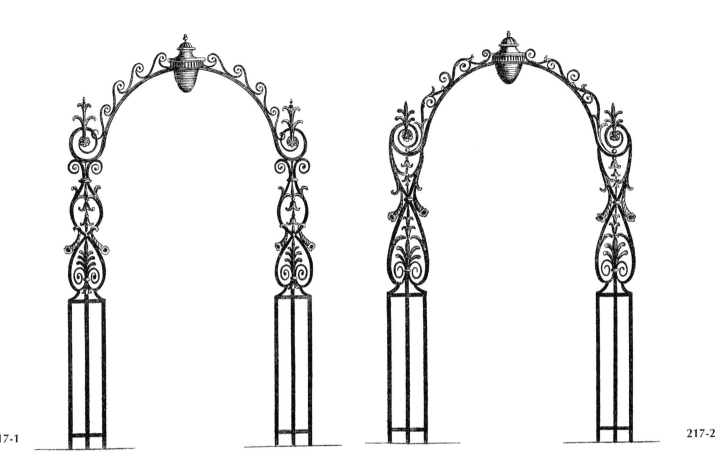

217-1

217-2

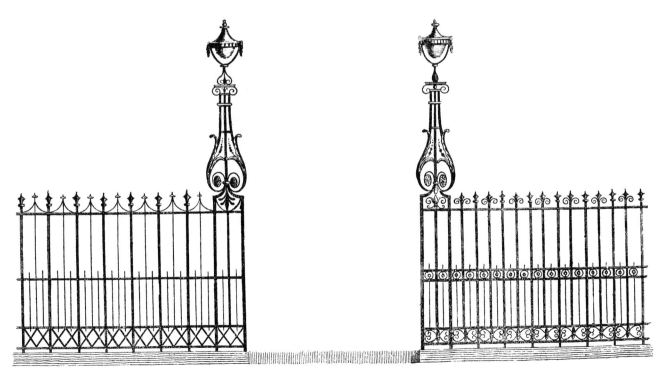

217-3

217

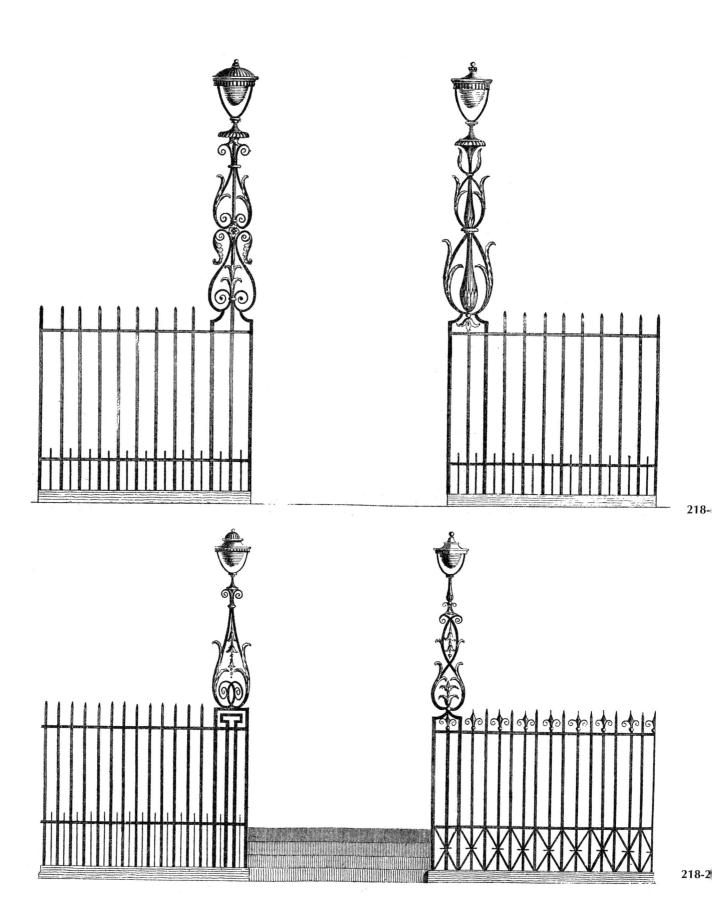

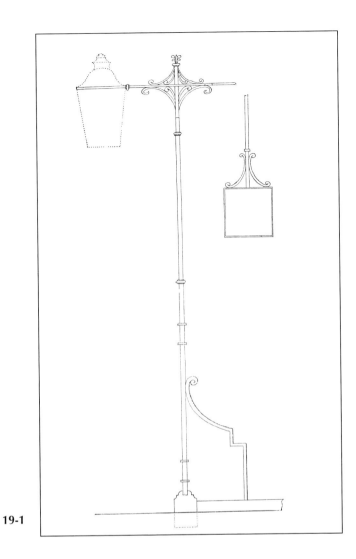

19-1

219: H. Holland. Streetlamps, England, *c.* 1800.
H. Holland. Réverbères, Angleterre, vers 1800.
H. Holland. Strassenlaternen, England, um 1800.
H. Holland. Farolas, Inglaterra, hacia 1800.
Х. Холланд. Уличные фонари, Англия,
ок. 1800.

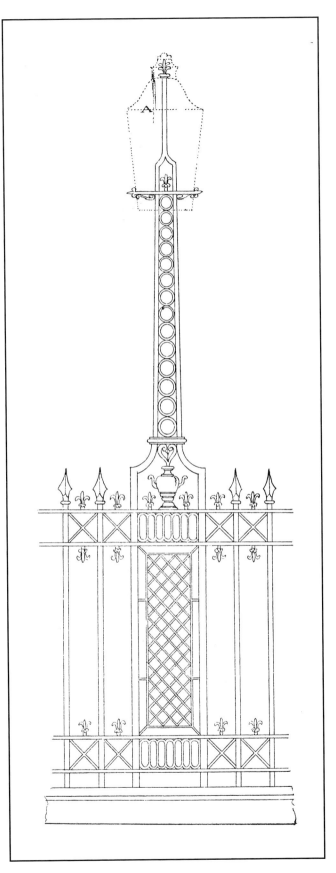

219-2

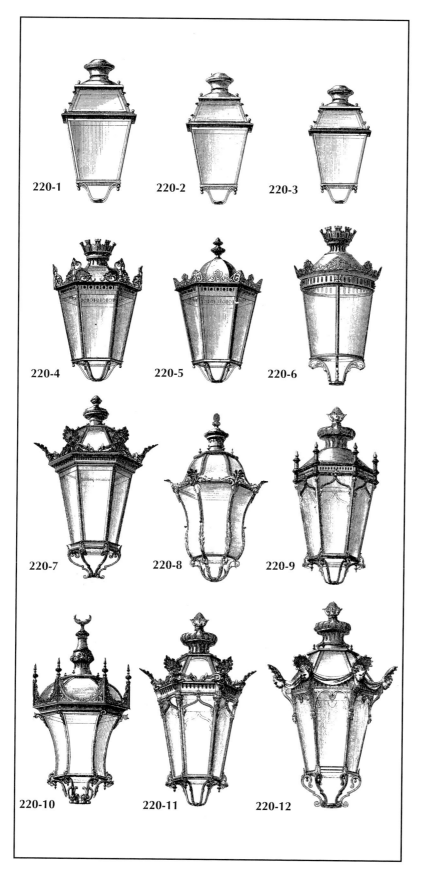

220: Lanterns, France, 19th century.
Lanternes, France, XIXe siècle.
Laternen, Frankreich, 19. Jh.
Linternas, Francia, siglo XIX.
Фонари, Франция, XIX век.

Établissement Le Val d'Osne.

221/224: Streetlamps, France,
19th century.
Réverbères, France, XIXe siècle.
Strassenlaternen, Frankreich, 19. Jh.
Farolas, Francia, siglo XIX.
Уличные фонари, Франция, XIX
век.

Établissement Le Val d'Osne.

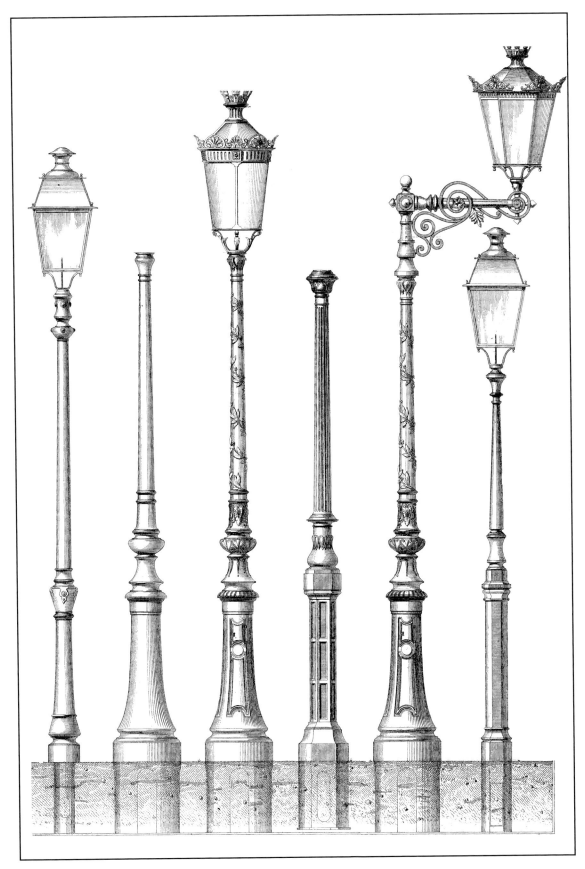

221

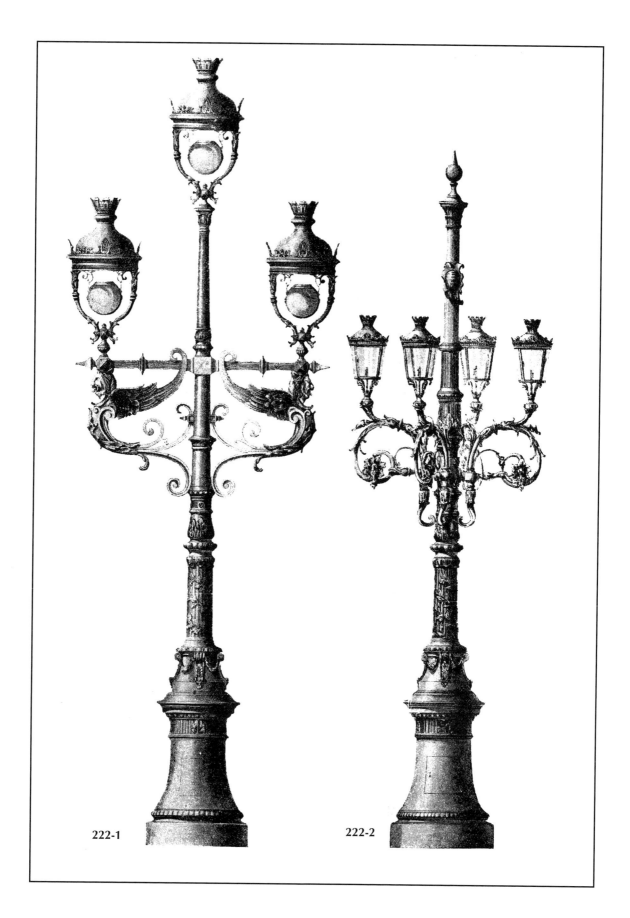

222-1   222-2

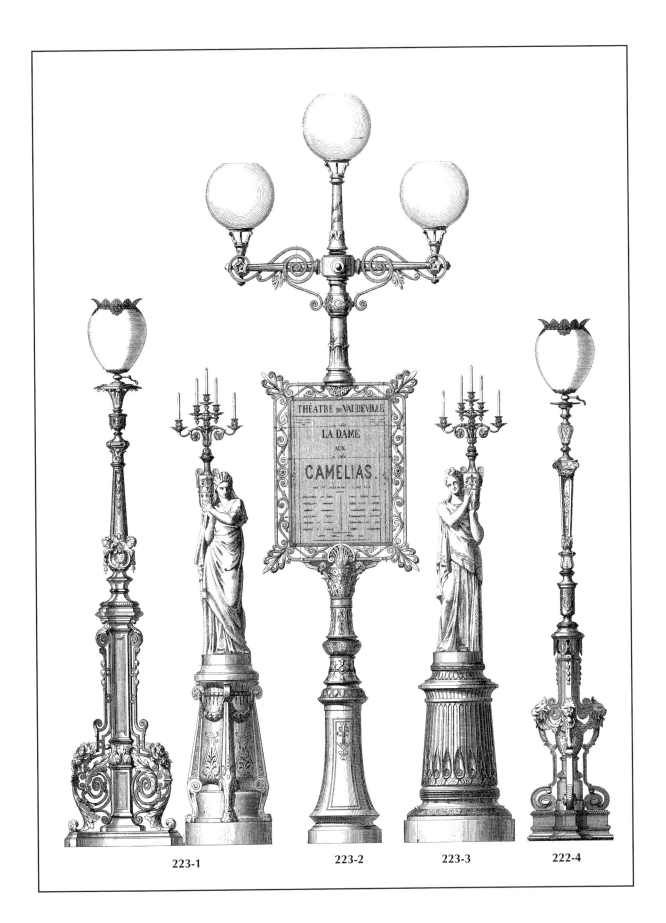

THÉATRE DU VAUDEVILLE

LA DAME
AUX
CAMELIAS.

223-1 223-2 223-3 222-4

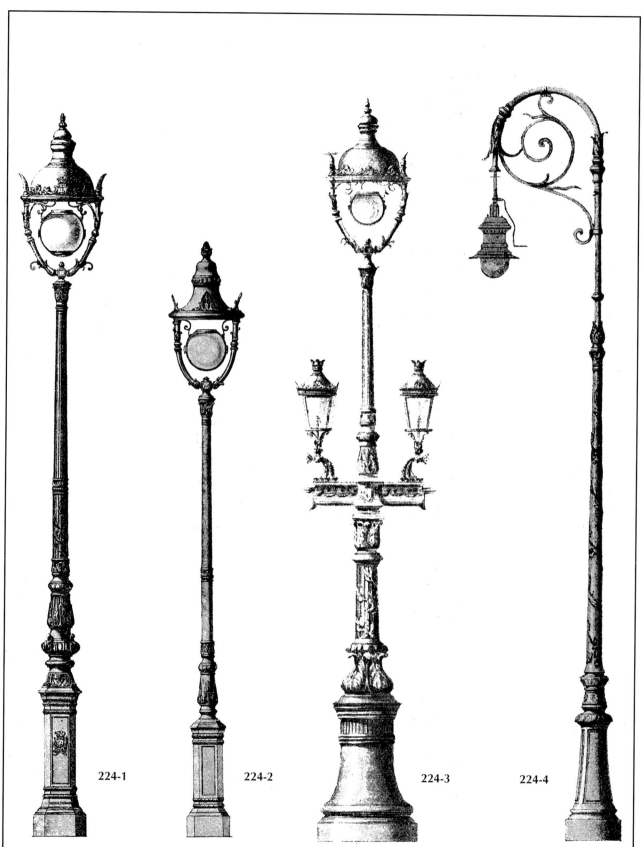

224-1   224-2   224-3   224-4

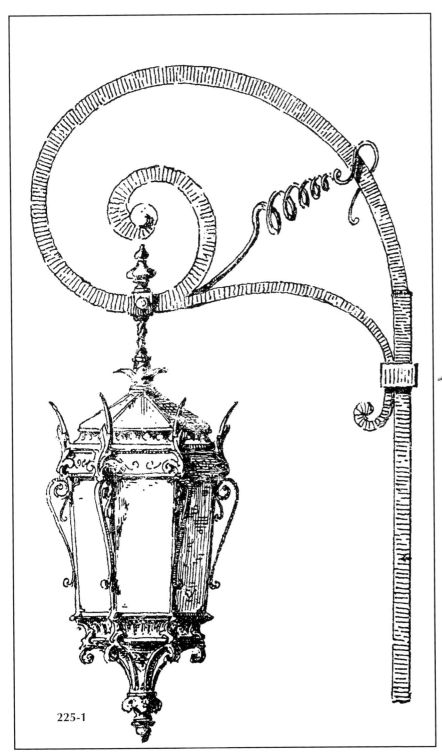

225-1

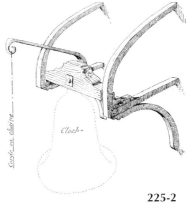

225-2

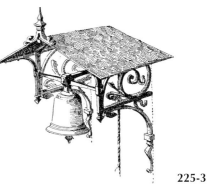

225-3

225-1: Lantern.
Lanterne.
Laterne.
Linterna.
Фонарь.

225-2: Bell stands.
Supports de cloche.
Aufhängungsmechanismen von
Glocken.
Soportes de campana.
Кронштейны для колокола.

E. Barberot, *Traité pratique de serrurerie*,
Paris & Liège, 1925.

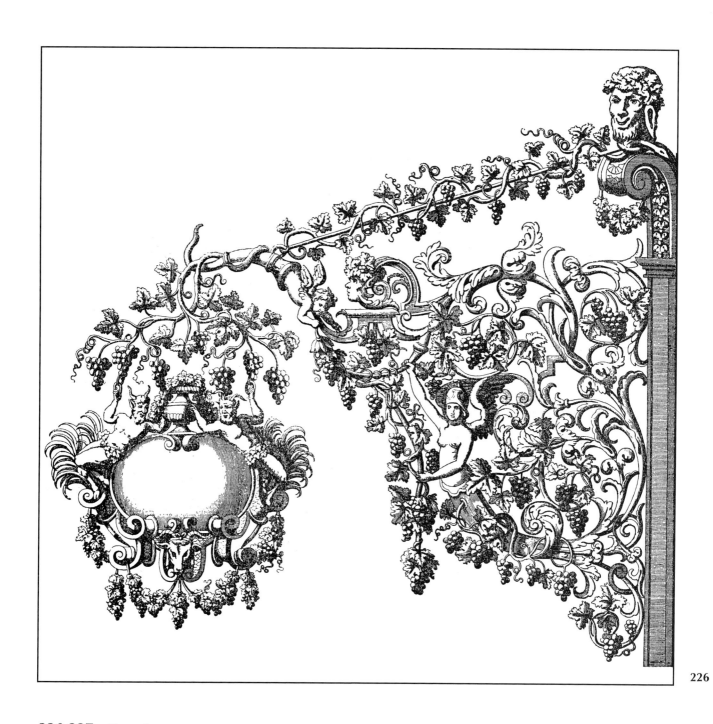

226

226.227 : Shop signs.
Enseignes de boutiques.
Türsschilder von Boutiquen.
Letreros de tiendas.
Вывески магазинов.

Jean Tijou, *A New Book of Drawings Invented and Designed by Jean Tijou*, London, 1690.

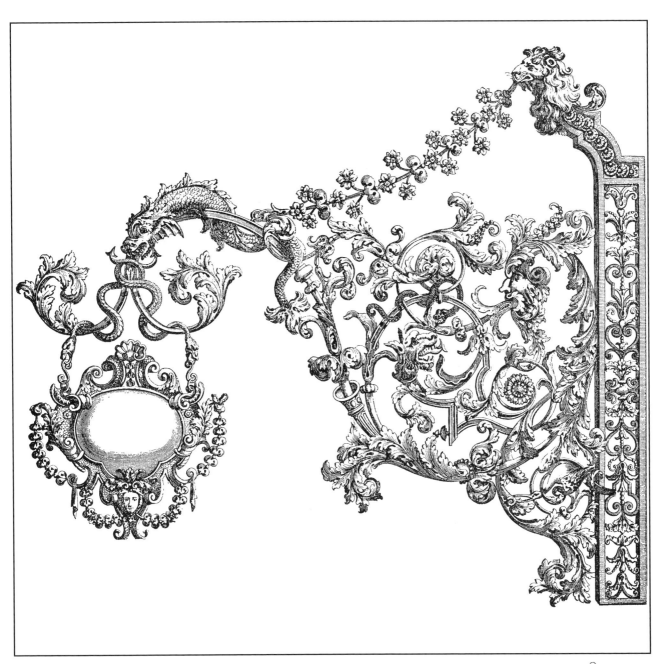

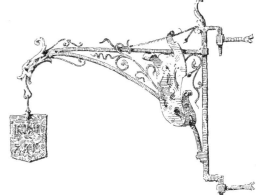

227-2

228-1, 228-2: Lantern brackets.
Porte-lanterne.
Laternenständer.
Portafarol.
Кронштейн для фонаря.

W. Ince and J. Mayhew, *Universal System of Household Furniture*, London, 1762.

228-3, 228-4, 228-5, 228-6, 228-7:
Sign brackets.
Porte-enseignes.
Ladenschild.
Gancho de letrero.
Крюки для вывески.

W. and J. Welldon, *The Smith's Right Hand,* London, 1765.

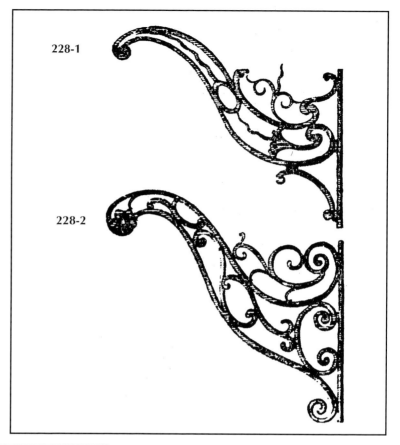

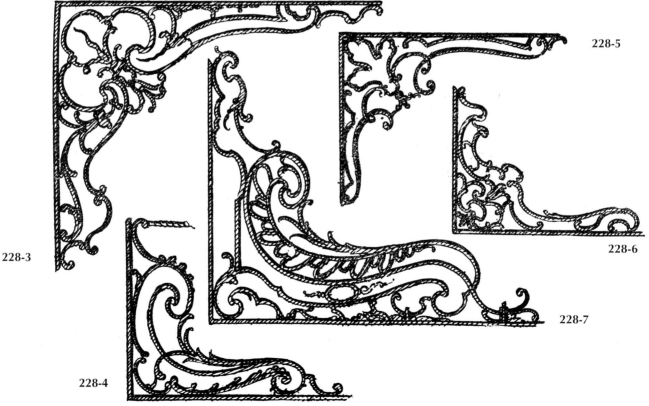

229-1: Lamp posts.
Réverbères.
Stehlampen.
Farolas.
Фонари.

J. Carter, *The Builder's Magazine,* London, 1779.

229-2: Sign brackets.
Porte-enseignes.
Aufhängungsmechanismen.
Gancho de letrero.
Крюки для вывески.

W. and J. Welldon, *The Smith's Right Hand,*
London, 1765.

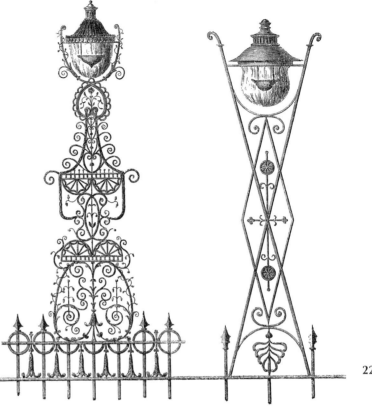

229-1

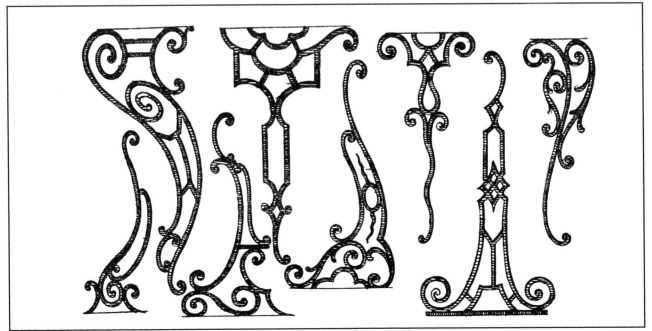

229-2

229

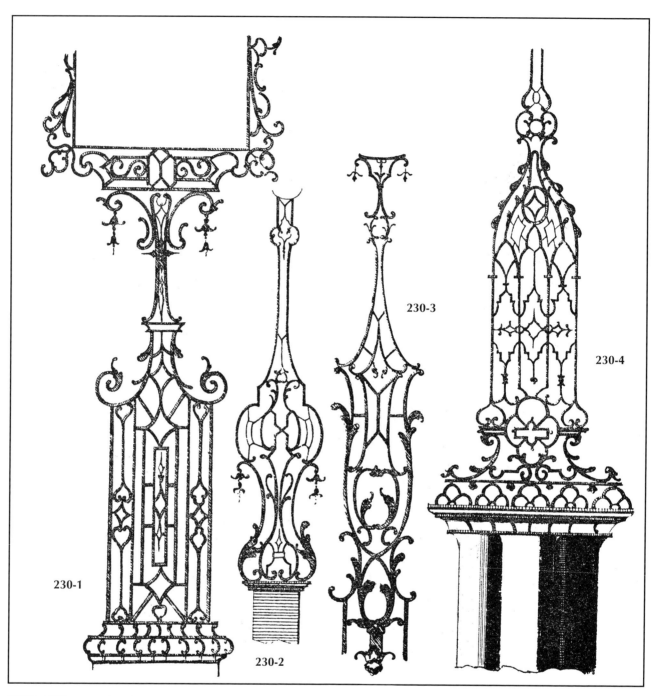

230, 231: Sign brackets.
Porte-enseignes.
Schilderbefestigungen.
Ganchos de letrero.
Крюки для вывески.

J. Jores, *A New Book of Iron Work containing a great variety of Designs*, London, 1759.

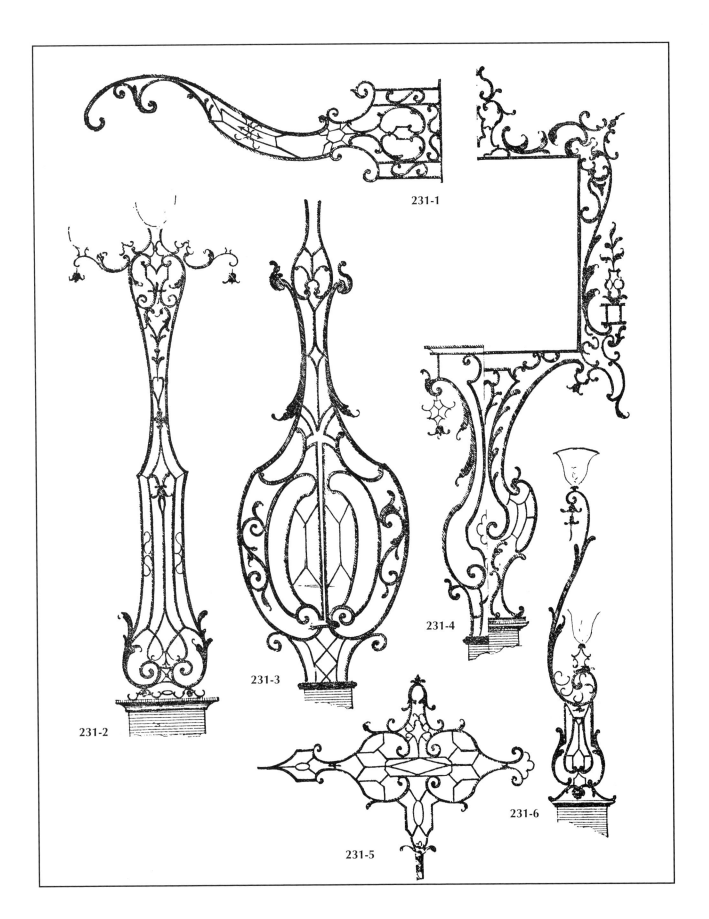

231-1

231-2

231-3

231-4

231-5

231-6

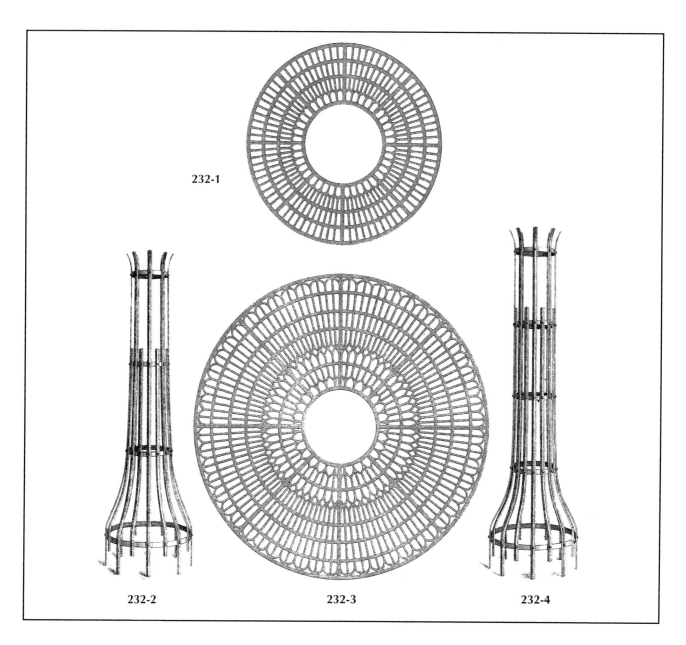

232-1

232-2   **232-3**   **232-4**

232: Tree grille and corset, France, 19th century.
Grilles et corsets d'arbres, France, XIXe siècle.
Gitter und andere Baumstützen, Frankreich, 19. Jh.
Rejas para los árboles,Francia, siglo XIX.
Решетки для деревьев, Франция, XIX век.

Établissement Le Val d'Osne.

233: Signposts, France, 19th century.
Poteaux indicateurs, France, XIXe siècle.
Strassenschilder, Frankreich, 19. Jh.
Postes indicadores, Francia, siglo XIX.
Столбы с указателями, Франция, XIX век.

Établissement Le Val d'Osne.

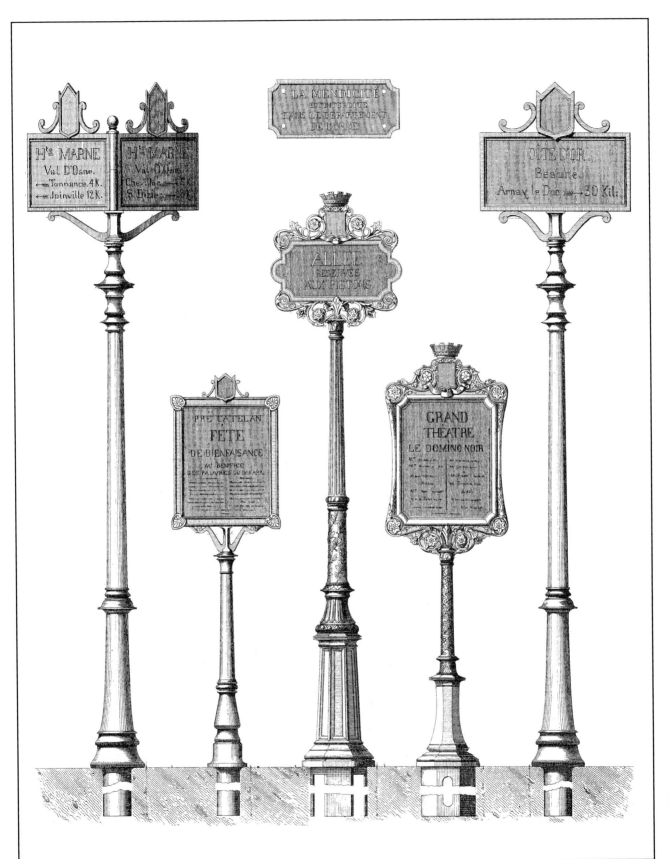

233

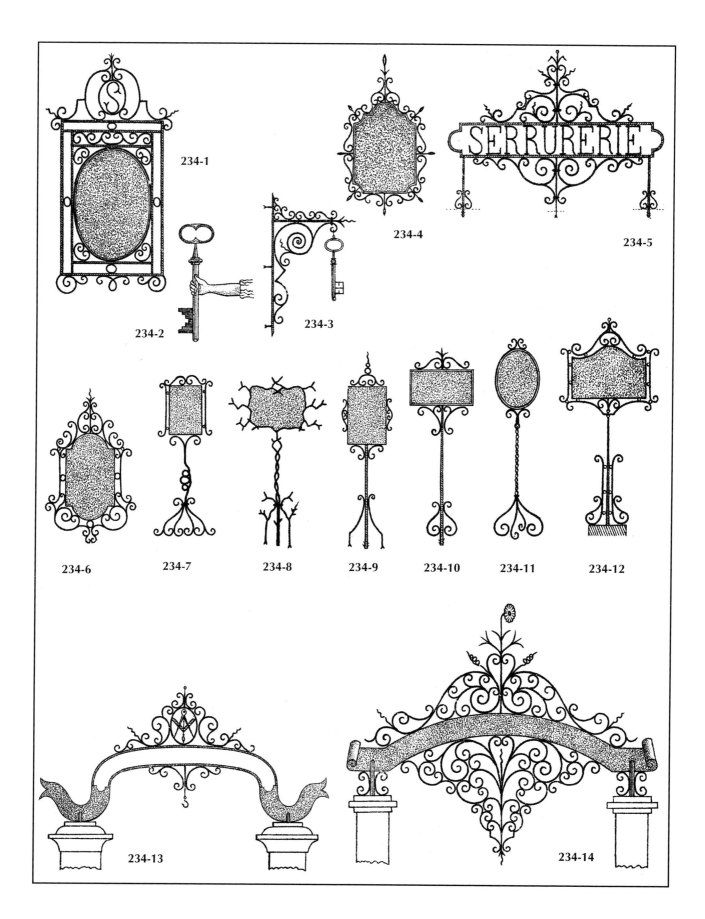

234-1

234-2

234-3

234-4

SERRURERIE

234-5

234-6

234-7

234-8

234-9

234-10

234-11

234-12

234-13

234-14

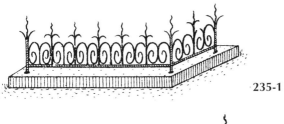

235-1

235-2

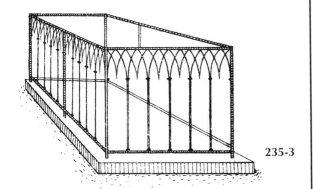

235-3

234: Signs.
Enseignes.
Schilder.
Letreros.
Указатели.

H.Grave, *Travaux en fer forgé,* France, 1881.

235/236: Grave fences.
Entourages de tombe.
Grabumrandungen.
Rejas de sepulcros.
Кладбищенские ограды.

H. Grave, *Travaux en fer forgé,* France, 1881.

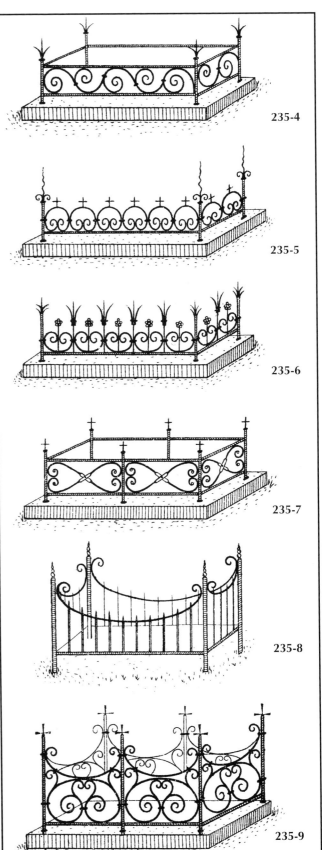

235-4

235-5

235-6

235-7

235-8

235-9

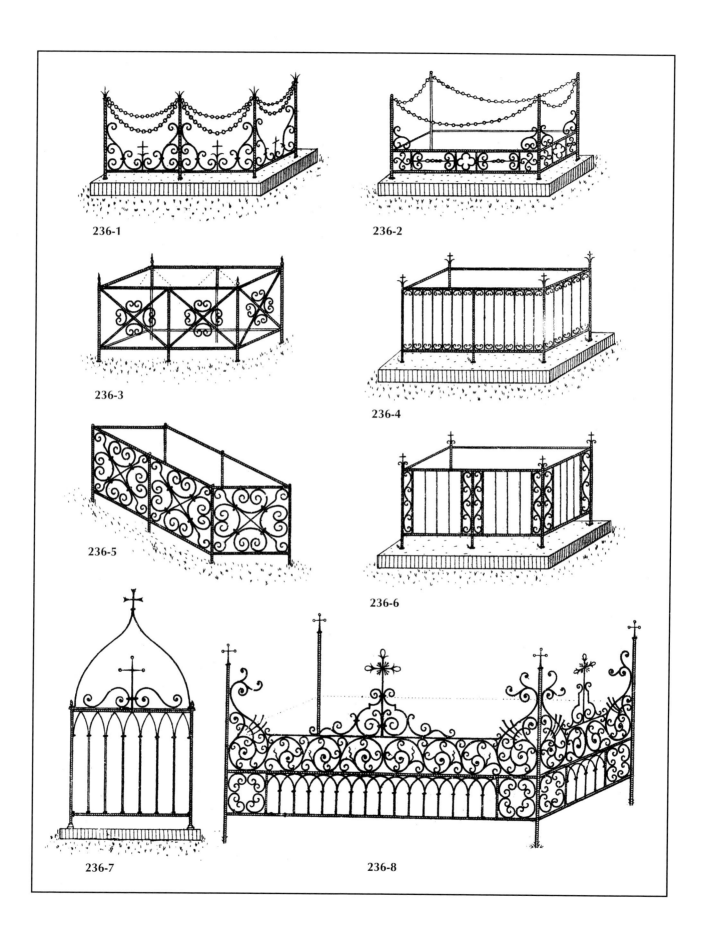

236-1

236-2

236-3

236-4

236-5

236-6

236-7

236-8

236

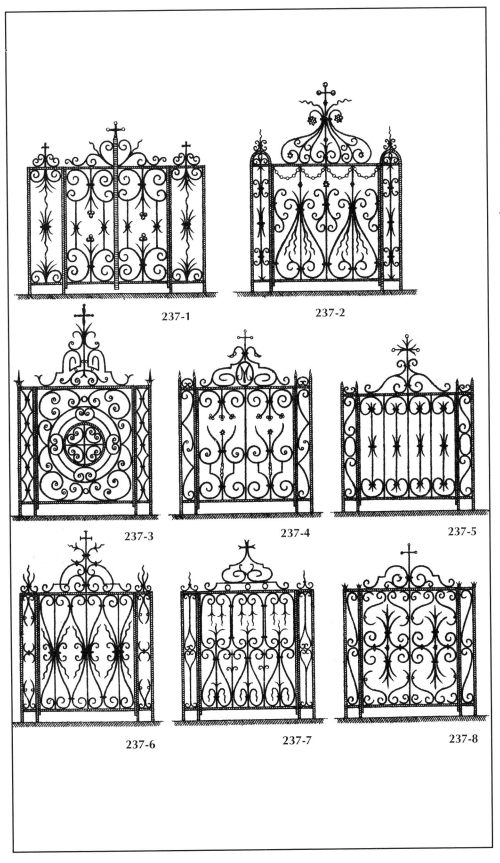

237: Tomb doors.
Portes de tombe.
Eingangstüren zu
Grabmahlanlagen.
Puertas de sepulcros.
Двери кладбищенских
оград.

H. Grave, *Travaux en fer forgé,* France, 1881.

237-1

237-2

237-3

237-4

237-5

237-6

237-7

237-8

238: Burial vault doors,
France, 19th century
Portes de caveau, France,
XIXe siècle.
Türen zu Grabmahlanlagen,
Frankreich, 19. Jh.
Puertas de sepulcros,
Francia, siglo XIX.
Двери склепов,
Франция, XIX век.

Établissement Le Val
d'Osne.

239: Burial vault doors.
Portes de caveau.
Türen zu Grabmahlanlagen.
Puertas de sepulcros.
Двери склепов.

H. Grave, *Travaux en fer
forgé,* France, 1881.

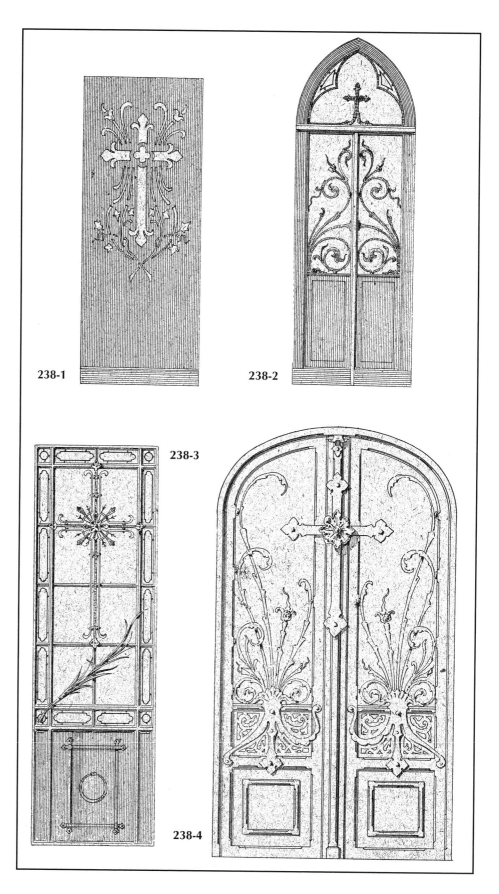

238-1

238-2

238-3

238-4

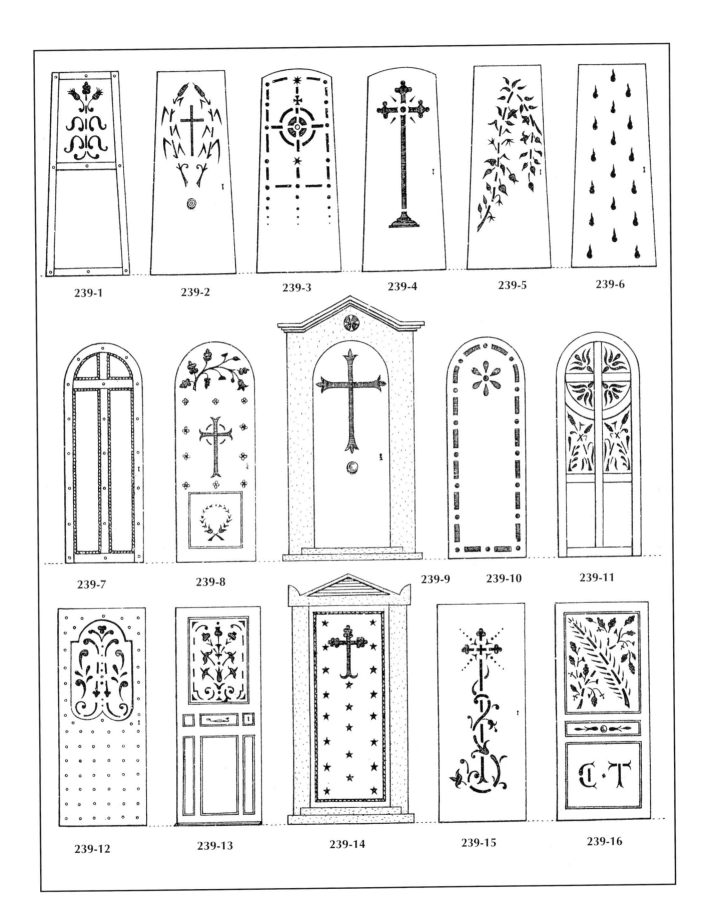

239-1 239-2 239-3 239-4 239-5 239-6

239-7 239-8 239-9 239-10 239-11

239-12 239-13 239-14 239-15 239-16

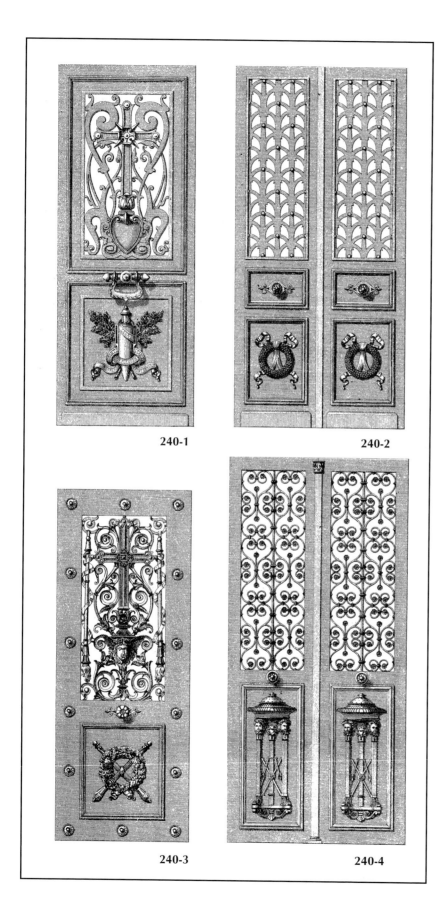

240-1

240-2

240-3

240-4

240: Burial vault doors, France, 19th century.
Portes de caveau, France, XIXe siècle.
Türen zu Grabmahlanlagen, Frankreich, 19. Jh.
Puertas de sepulcros, Francia, siglo XIX.
Франция, XIX век.

Établissement Le Val d'Osne.

241: Funeral crosses, France, 19th century.
Croix funéraires, france, XIXe siècle. Grabkreuze, Frankreich, 19. Jh.
Cruces funerarias, Francia, siglo XIX.
Погребальные кресты, Франция, XIX век.

Établissement Le Val d'Osne.

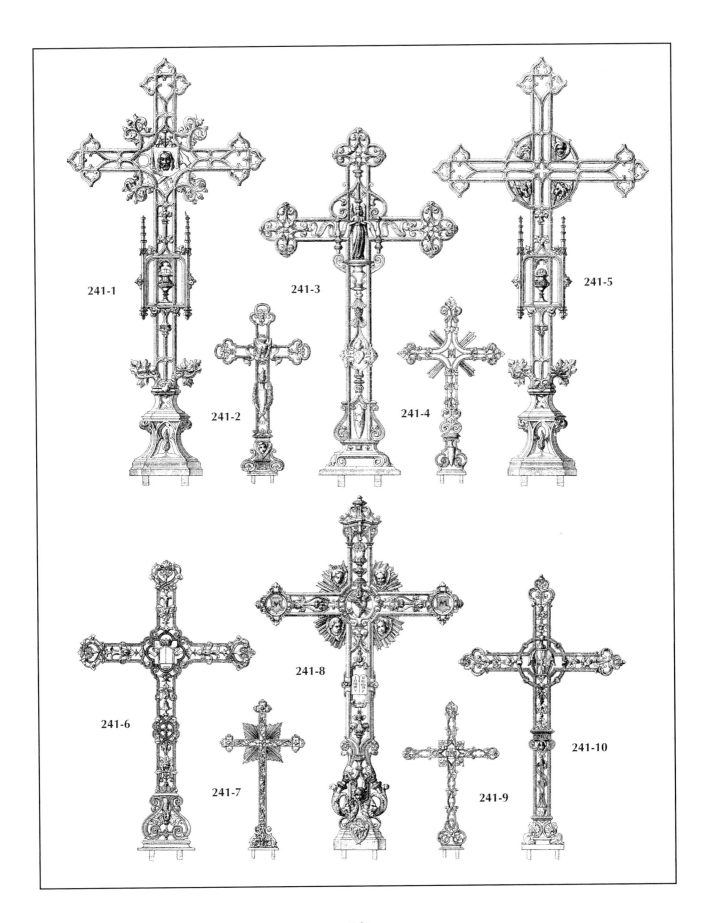

241-1

241-2

241-3

241-4

241-5

241-6

241-7

241-8

241-9

241-10

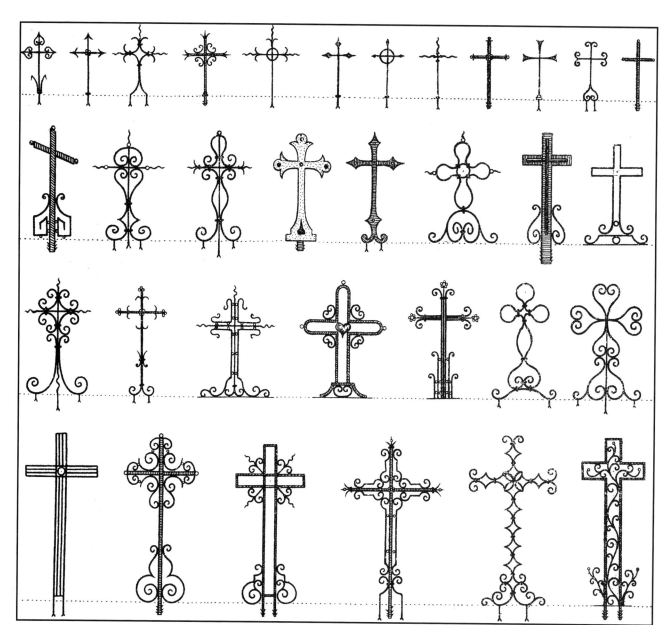

242

242: Grave crosses.
Croix de tombes.
Grabkreuze.
Cruces de sepulcros.
Могильные кресты.

H. Grave, *Travaux en fer forgé,* France, 1881.

243: Funeral ornaments, France, 19th century.
Ornements funéraires, France, XIXe siècle.
Grabornamente, Frankreich, 19. Jh.
Ornamentos funerarios, Francia, siglo XIX.
Погребальные орнаменты, Франция, XIX век.

Établissement Le Val d'Osne.

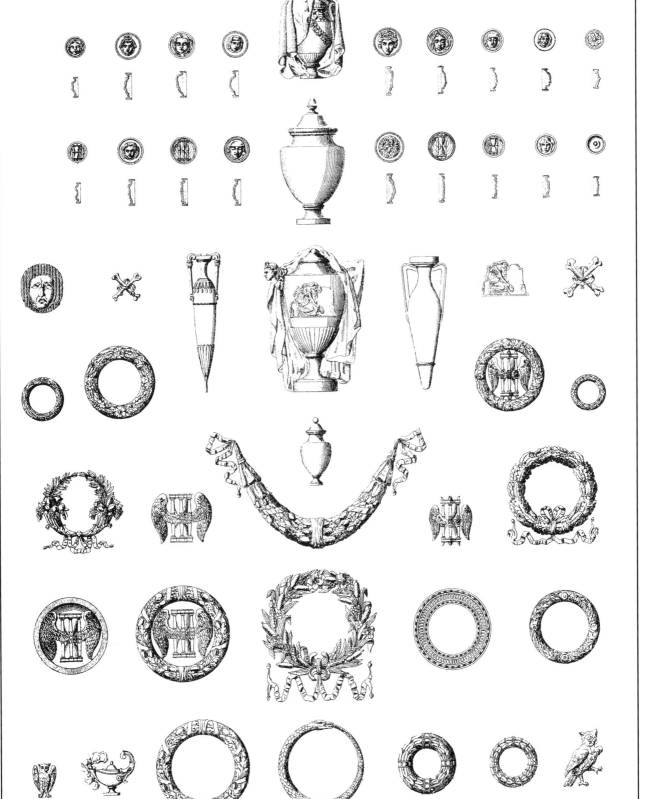

243

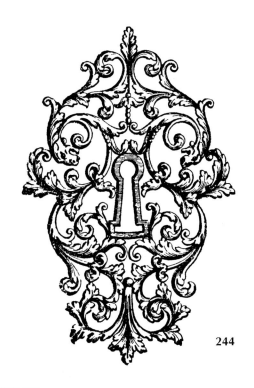

244

• Locksmithing • Serrurerie •
• Kunstschlosserei • Cerrajería •
• Замки •

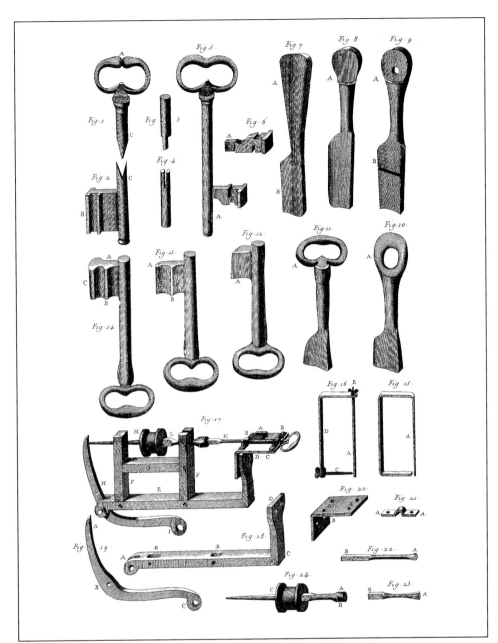

244: Lock.
Serrure.
Beschlag eines Schlosses.
Cerradura.
Замок.

Jean Tijou, *A New Book of Drawings Invented and Designed by Jean Tijou*, London, 1690.

245/249: Locksmithing components.
Éléments de serrurerie.
Schlossteile.
Elementos de cerrajería.
Скобяные изделия и слесарные инструменты.

Diderot & D'Alembert,
L'Encyclopédie, Paris, 1751–1772.

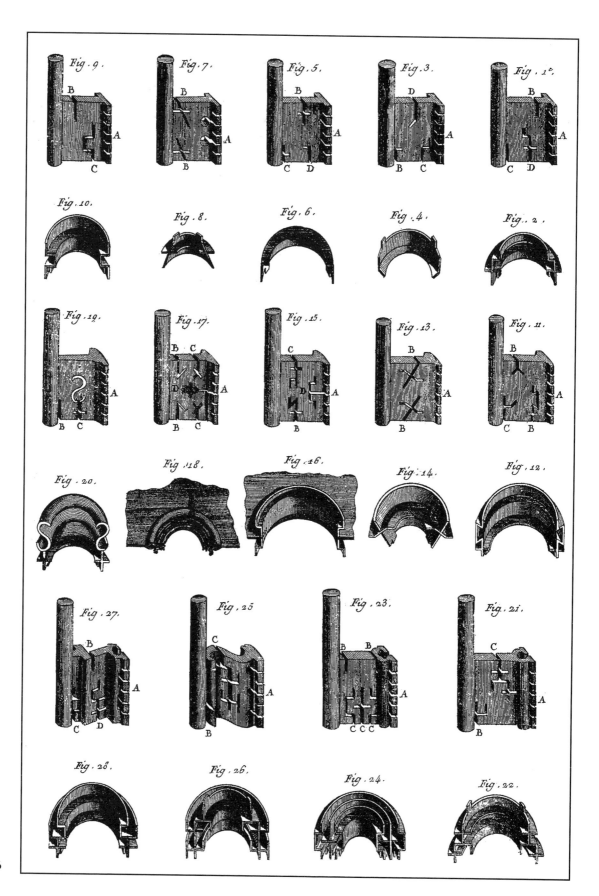

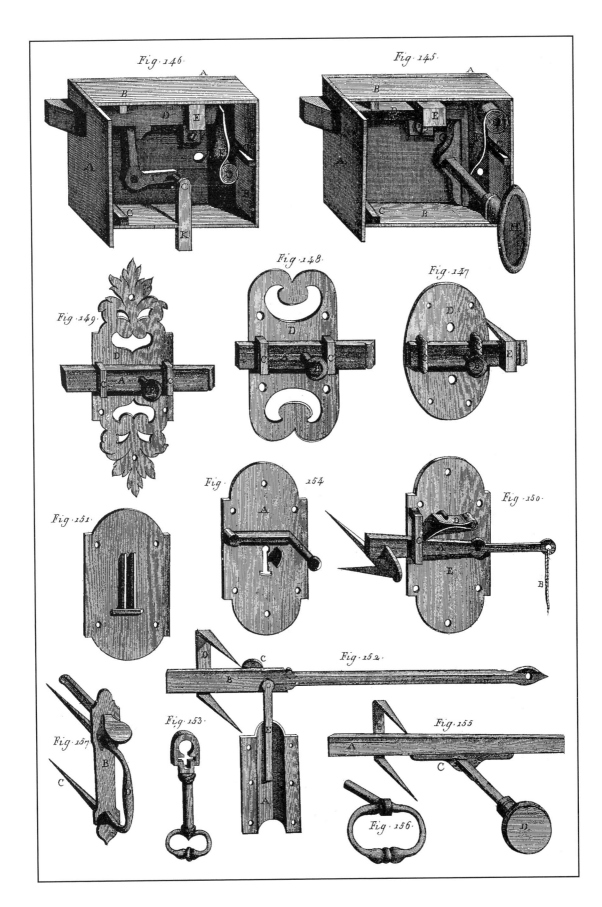

247

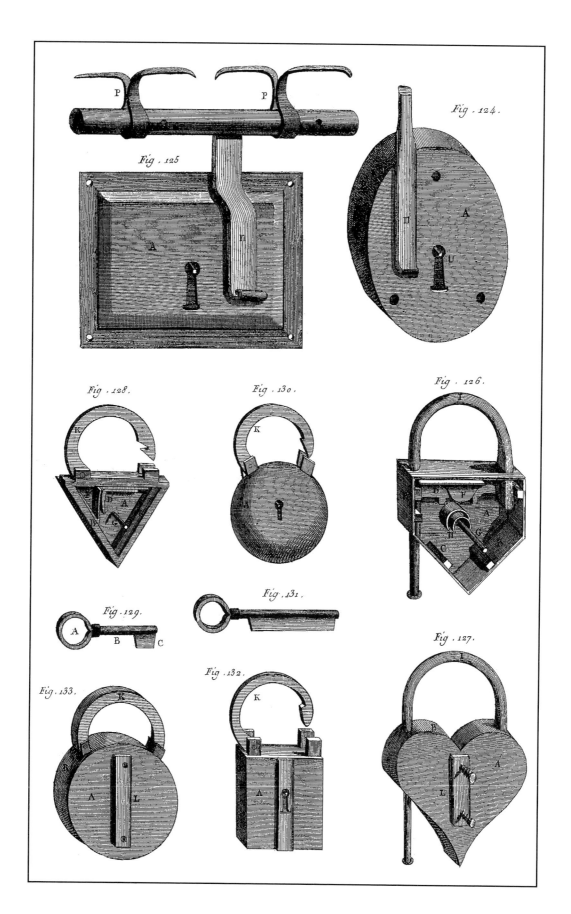

Fig. 124.

Fig. 125

Fig. 128.

Fig. 130.

Fig. 126.

Fig. 129.

Fig. 131.

Fig. 127.

Fig. 133.

Fig. 132.

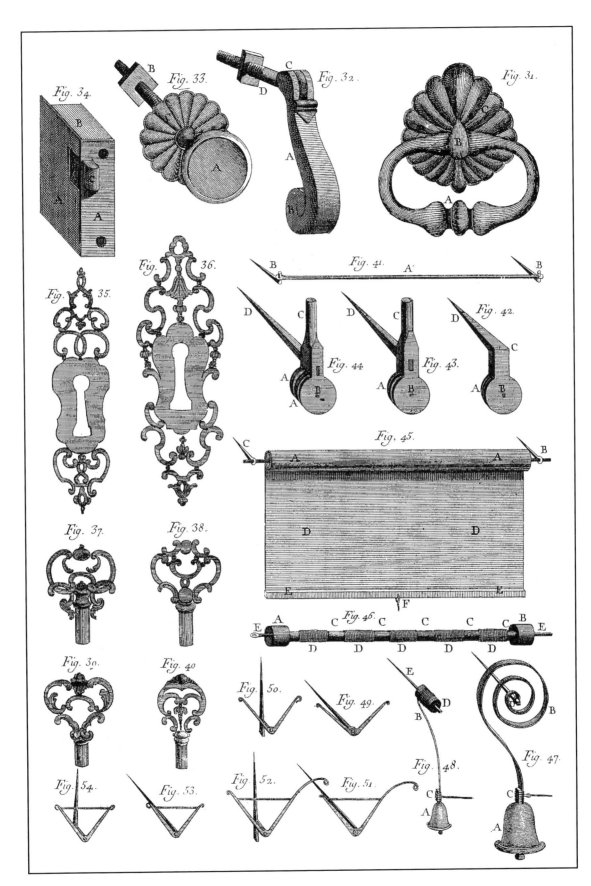

Fig. 34.
Fig. 33.
Fig. 32.
Fig. 31.
Fig. 36.
Fig. 35.
Fig. 41.
Fig. 42.
Fig. 44.
Fig. 43.
Fig. 45.
Fig. 37.
Fig. 38.
Fig. 46.
Fig. 39.
Fig. 40.
Fig. 50.
Fig. 49.
Fig. 48.
Fig. 47.
Fig. 54.
Fig. 53.
Fig. 52.
Fig. 51.

249

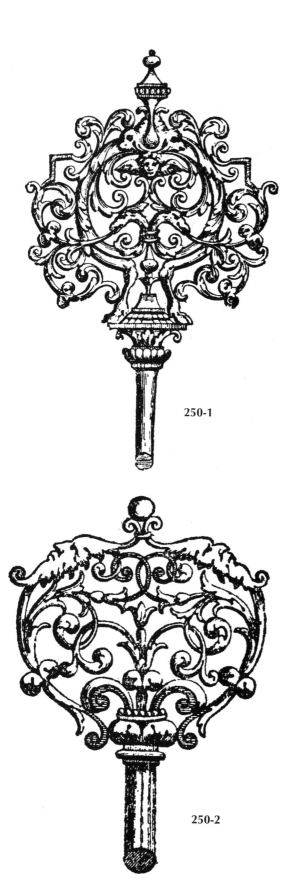

250-1

250-2

250/251: Keys.
Clefs.
Schlüssel.
Llaves.
Ключи.

Jean Tijou, *A New Book of Drawings Invented and Designed by Jean Tijou*, London, 1690.

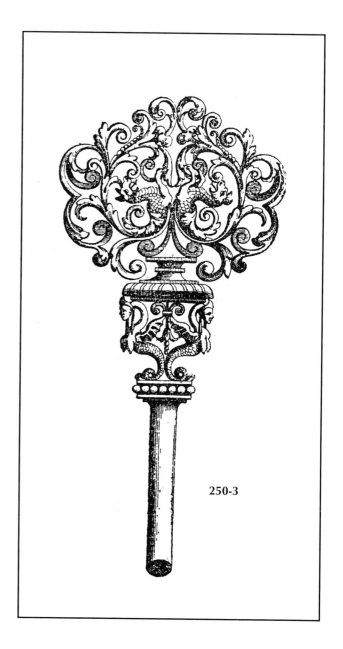

250-3

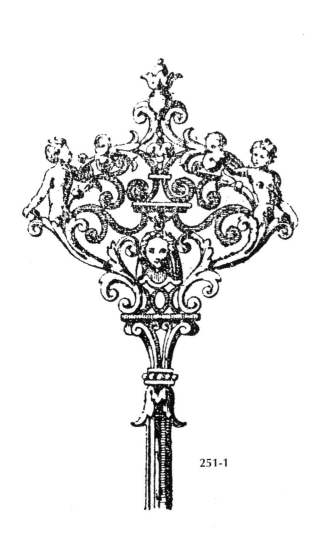

251-1

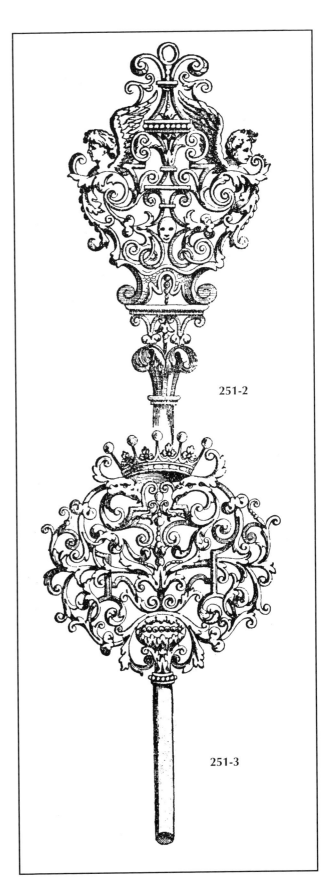

251-2

251-3

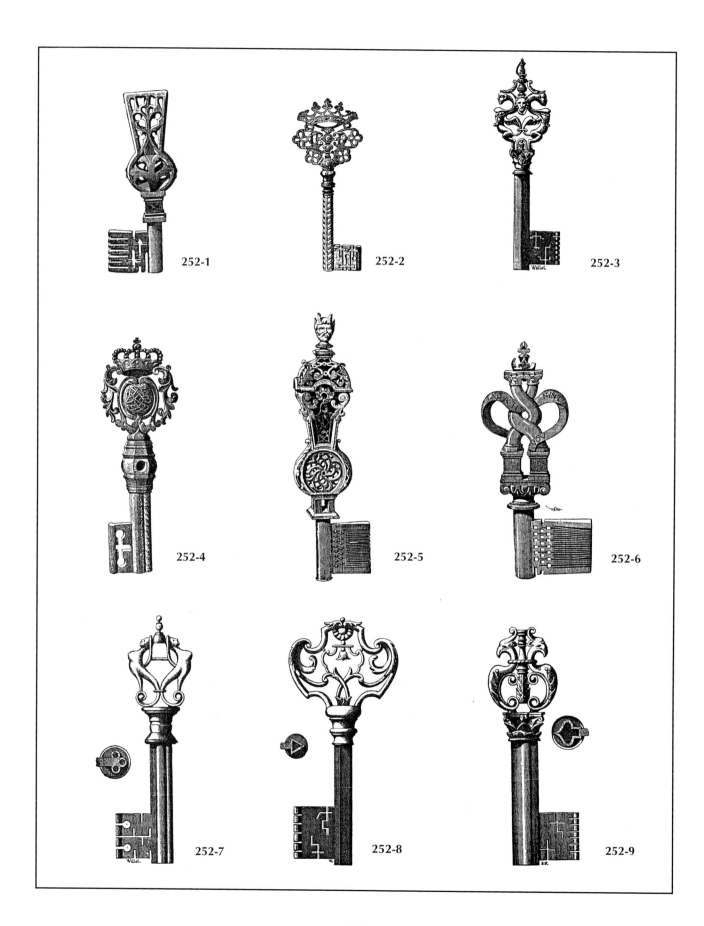

252-1

252-2

252-3

252-4

252-5

252-6

252-7

252-8

252-9

252: Keys, France, 16th and 17th centuries.
Clefs, France, XVIᵉ et XVIIᵉ siècles.
Schlüssel, Frankreich, 16. und 17. Jh.
Llaves, Francia, siglos XVI y XVII.
Ключи, Франция, XVI-XVII века.

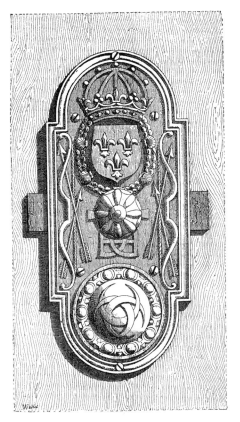

253-1

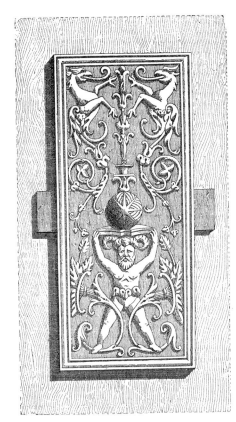

253-2

253-3

253-4

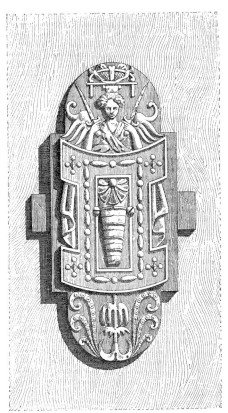

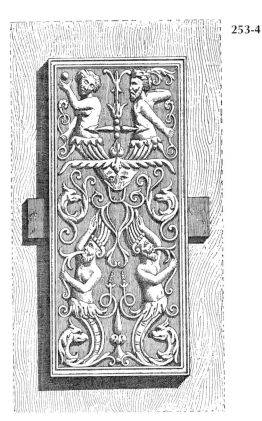

253: Bolts, France, 16th century.
Verrous, France, XVIᵉ siècle.
Riegel, Frankreich, 16. Jh.
Cerrojos, Francia, siglo XVI.
Засов, Франция, XVI век.

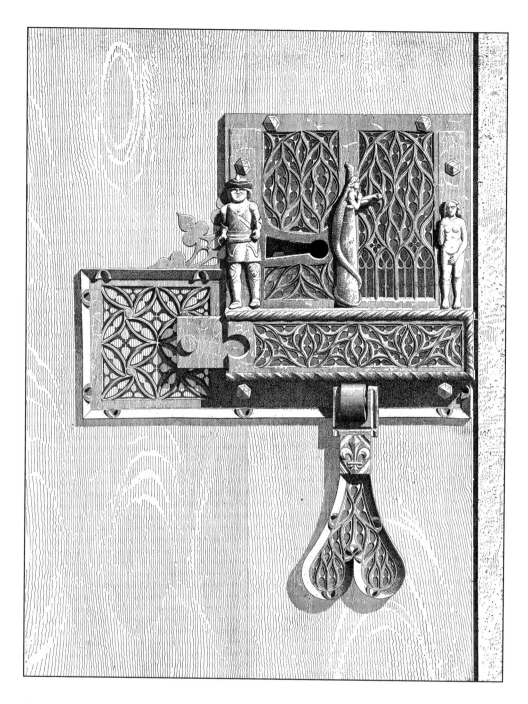

254: Bolt and escutcheon, France, 15th century.
Verrou et entrée de serrure, France, XVe siècle.
Riegel und Schlossbeschlag, Frankreich, 15. Jh.
Cerrojo y cerradura, Francia, siglo XV.
Засов и замочная скважина, Франция, XV век.

254

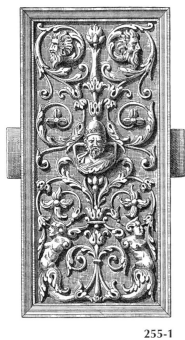

255-1

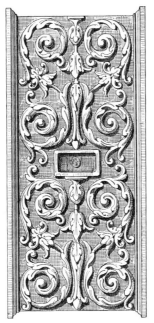

255-2

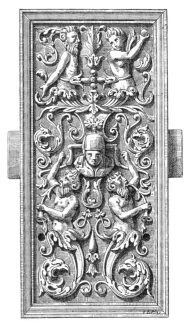

255-3

255-1: Bolts, France, 16th century.
Verrous, France, XVIe siècle.
Riegel, Frankreich, 16. Jh.
Cerrojos, Francia, siglo XVI.
Засов, Франция, XVI век.

255-2: Locks, France, 16th century.
Serrures, France, XVIe siècle.
Schlösserbeschlag, Frankreich, 16. Jh.
Cerraduras, Francia, siglo XVI.
Замки, Франция, XVI век.

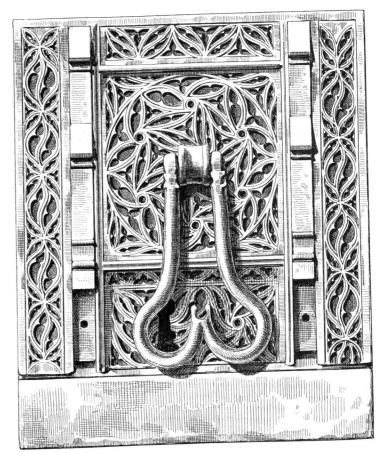

255-4

256-1: Locks, France, 15th century.
Serrures, France, XVᵉ siècle.
Schlösser, Frankreich, 15. Jh.
Cerraduras, Francia, siglo XV.
Замки, Франция, XVI век.

256-2: Bolt, France, 15th century.
Verrou, France, XVᵉ siècle.
Riegel, Frankreich, 15. Jh.
Cerrojo, Francia, siglo XV.
Засов, Франция, XV век.

E. Viollet-le-Duc, *Dictionnaire raisonné de l'architecture française du XIᵉ au XVIᵉ siècle.*
1854–1868.

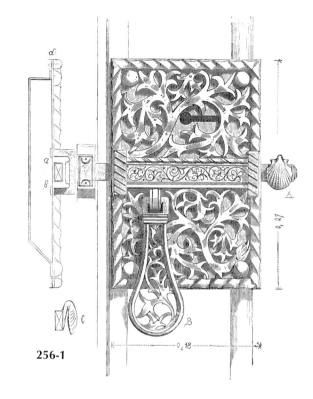

256-1

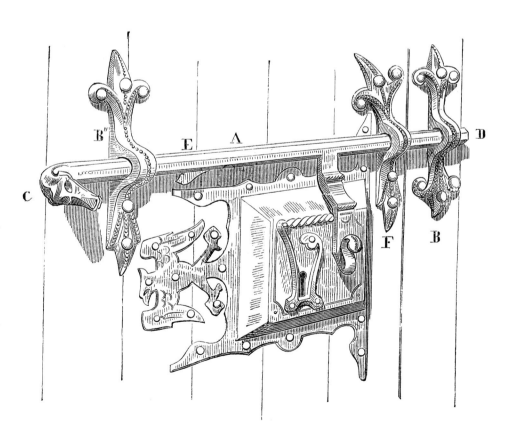

256-2

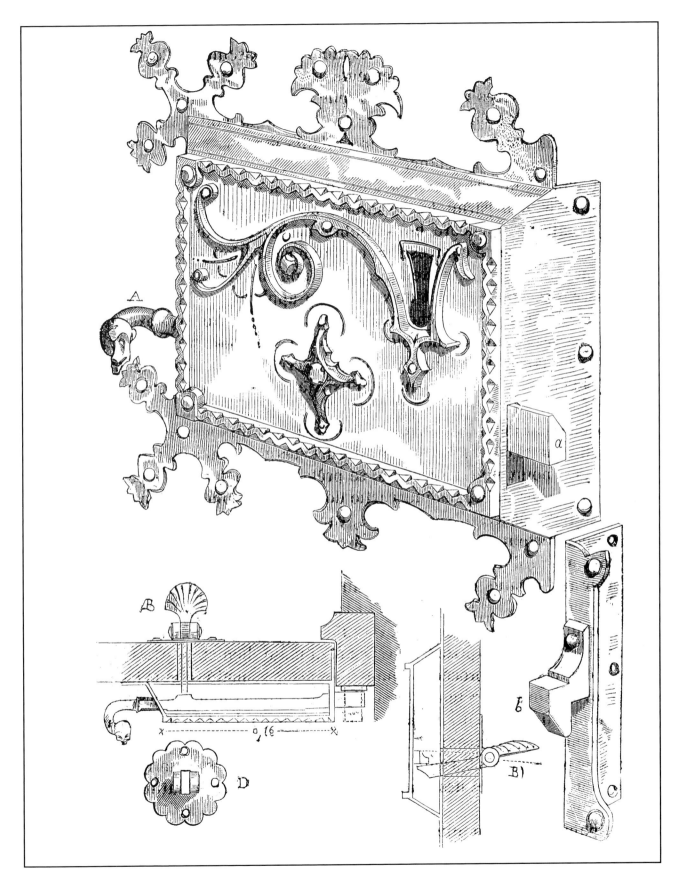

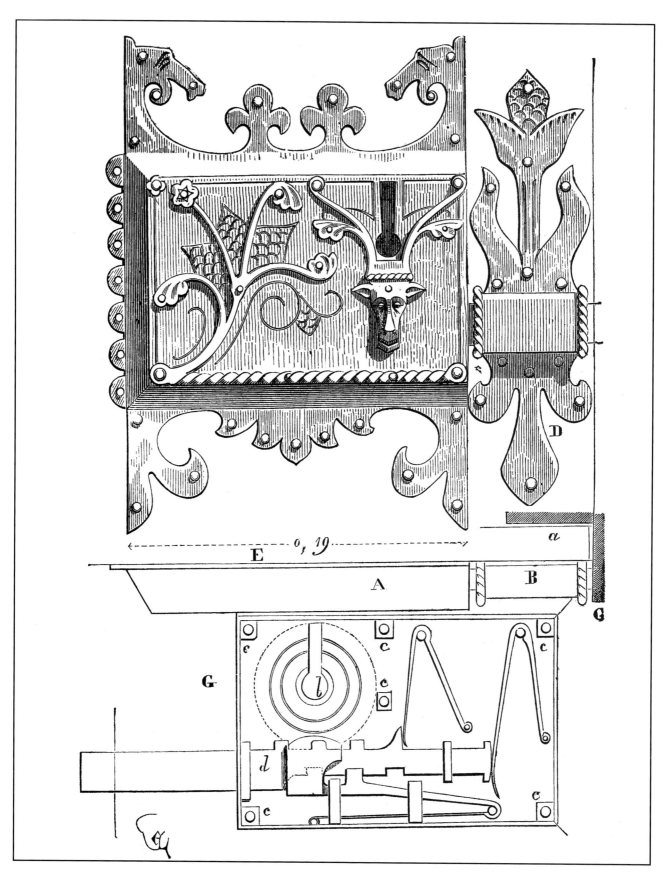

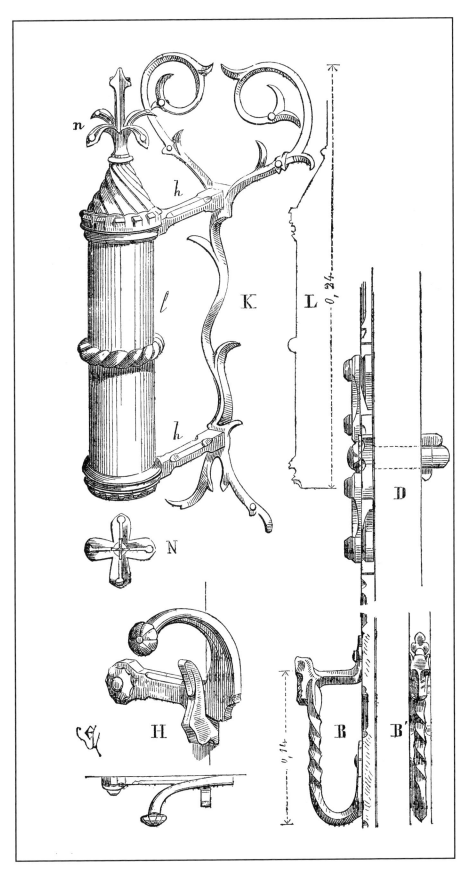

257/258: Locks, France, 14th and 15th centuries.
Serrures, France, XIVᵉ et XVᵉ siècles.
Schlösser, Frankreich, 14. und 15. Jh.
Cerraduras, Francia, siglos XIV y XV.
Замки, Франция, XVI век.

E. Viollet-le-Duc, *Dictionnaire raisonné de l'architecture française du XIᵉ au XVIᵉ siècle.* 1854–1868.

259: Locksmithing components, France, mid–15th century.
Éléments de serrurerie, France, milieu du XVᵉ siècle.
Schlossteile, Frankreich, Mitte, 15. Jh.
Elementos de cerrajería, Francia, medio del siglo XV.
Скобяные изделия, Франция, середина XV века.

E. Viollet-le-Duc, *Dictionnaire raisonné de l'architecture française du XIᵉ au XVIᵉ siècle.* 1854–1868.

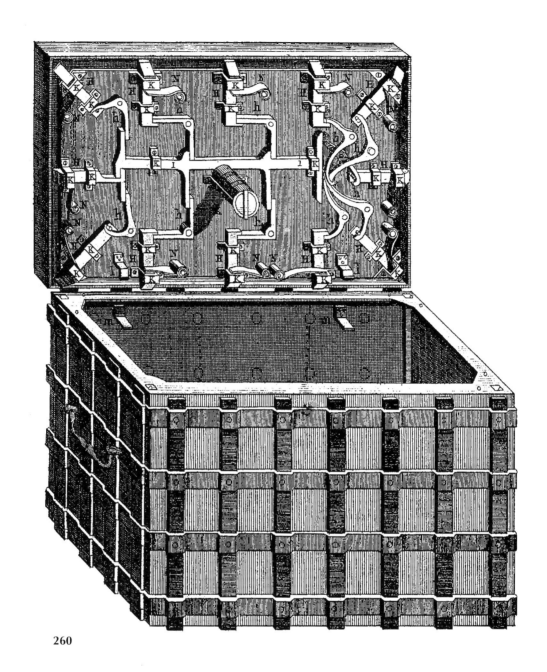

260

260: Casket lock with twelve strong points.
Serrure de coffre à douze fermetures.
Schloss eines Koffers mit zwölf Schlössern.
Soldadura de cofre con doce cierres.
Сундук с двенадцатью запорами.

Diderot & D'Alembert, *L'Encyclopédie*, Paris, 1751–1772.

261 : Locksmithing components.
Éléments de serrurerie.
Schlossteile.
Elementos de cerrajería.
Скобяные изделия.

Diderot & D'Alembert, *L'Encyclopédie*, Paris, 1751–1772.

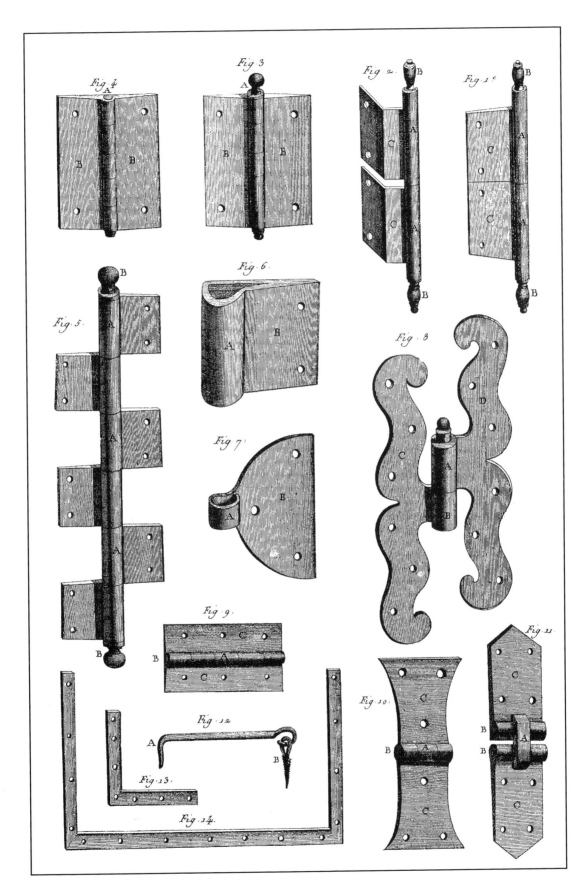

261

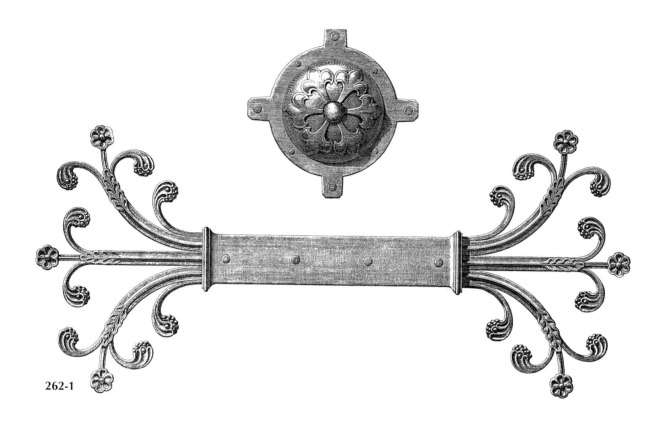

262-1

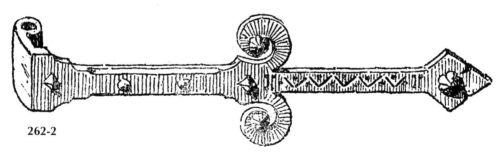

262-2

262-1: Stud and strap hinge of the cathedral of Rouen, France, 13th century.
Clou et penture de la cathédrale de Rouen, France, XIIIᵉ siècle.
Nagel und Türbeschlag der Kathedrale von Rouen. Frankreich, 13. Jh.
Clavo y pernio de la catedral de Rouen, Francia, siglo XIII.
Гвоздь и петля собора в Руане, Франция, XIII век.

262-2: Strap hinges, France, 13th century.
Pentures, France, XIIIᵉ siècle.
Türbeschläge, Frankreich, 13. Jh.
Pernios, Francia, siglo XIII.
Петли, Франция, XIII век.

E. Viollet-le-Duc, *Dictionnaire raisonné de l'architecture française du XIᵉ au XVIᵉ siècle.* 1854–1868.

263/269: Strap hinges, France, 12th and 13th centuries.
Pentures, France, XIIᵉ et XIIᵉ siècles.
Türbeschläge, Frankreich, 12. und 13. Jh.
Pernios, Francia, siglo XII y XIII.
Петли, Франция, XII-XIII века.

E. Viollet-le-Duc, *Dictionnaire raisonné de l'architecture française du XIᵉ au XVIᵉ siècle.* 1854–1868.

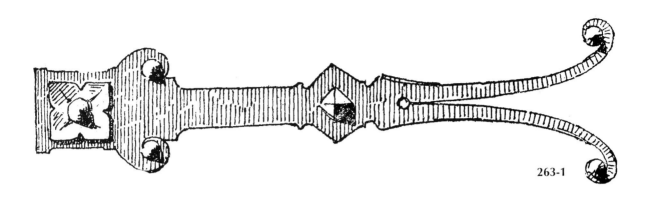

263-1

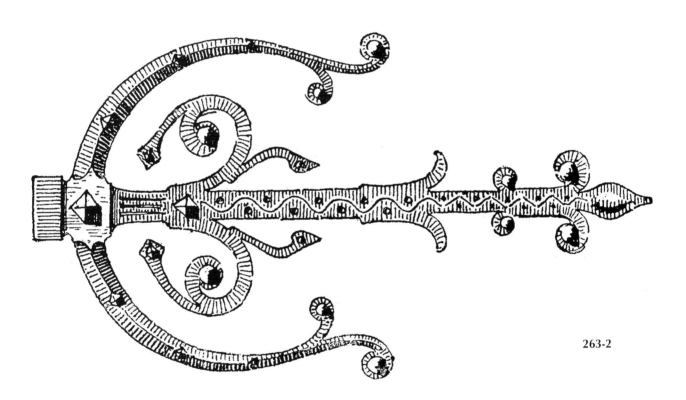

263-2

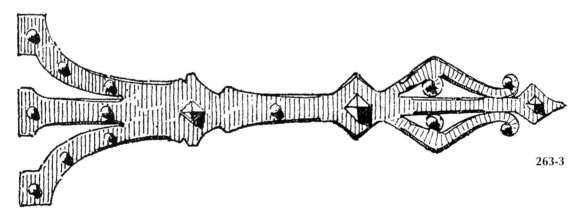

263-3

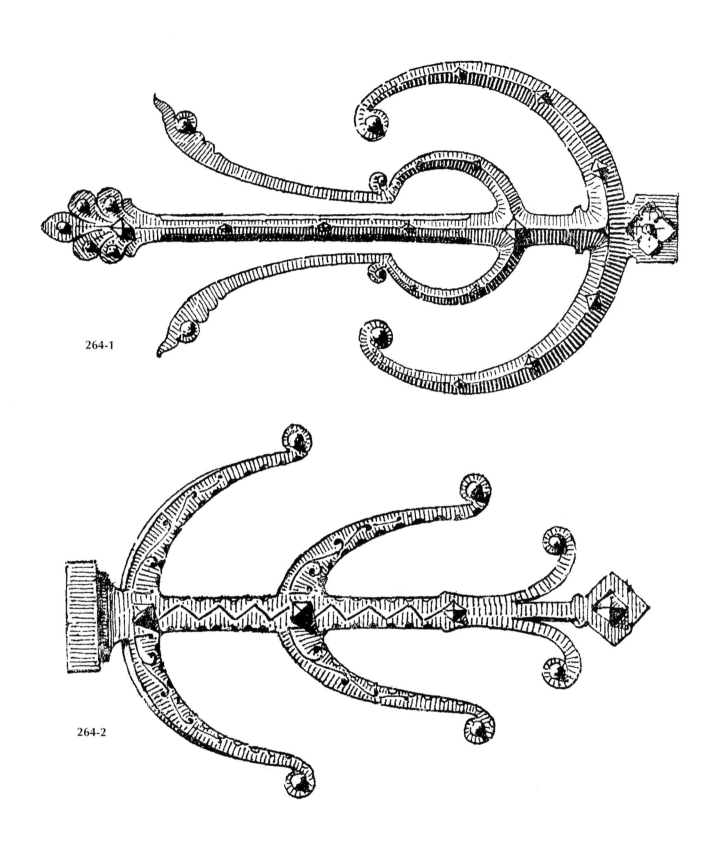

264-1

264-2

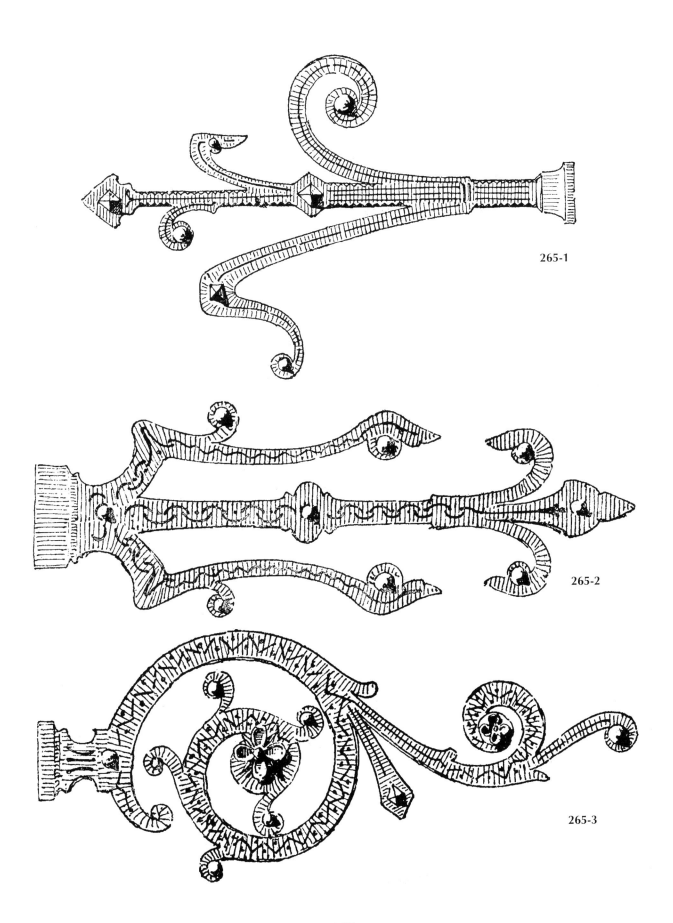

265-1

265-2

265-3

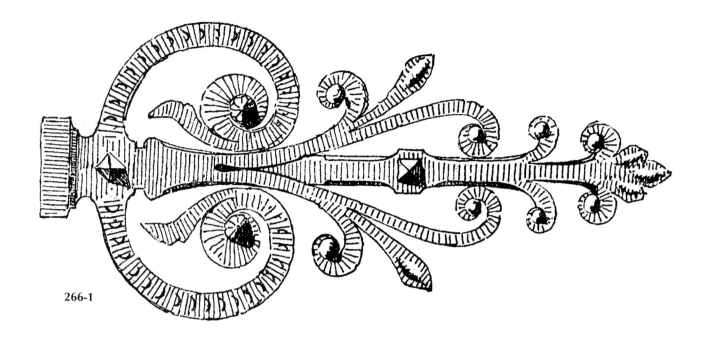

266-1

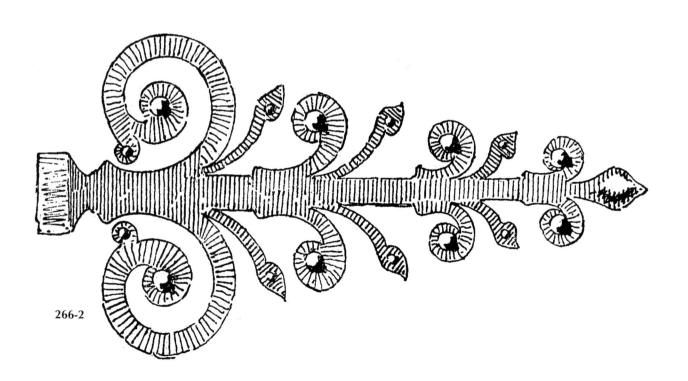

266-2

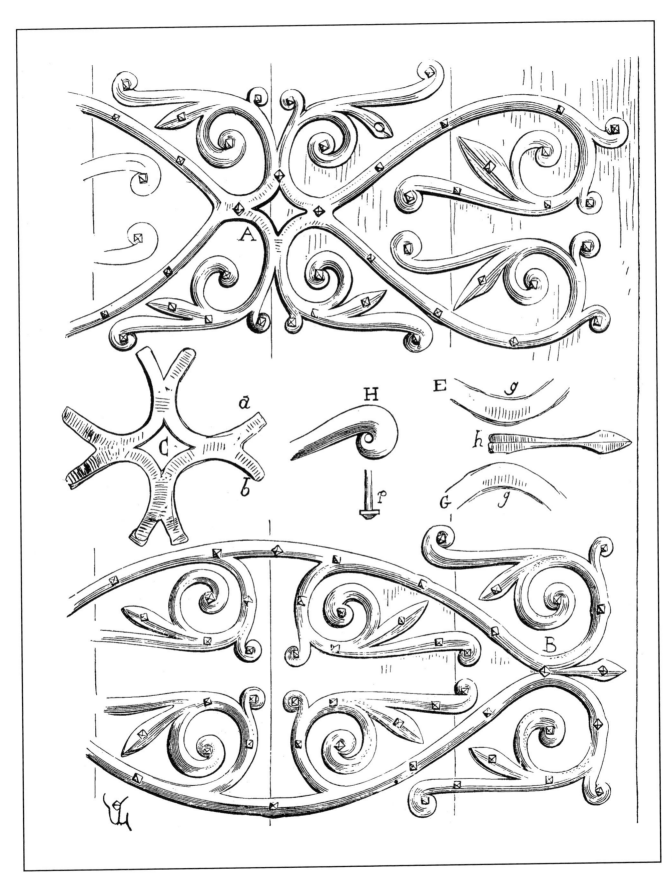

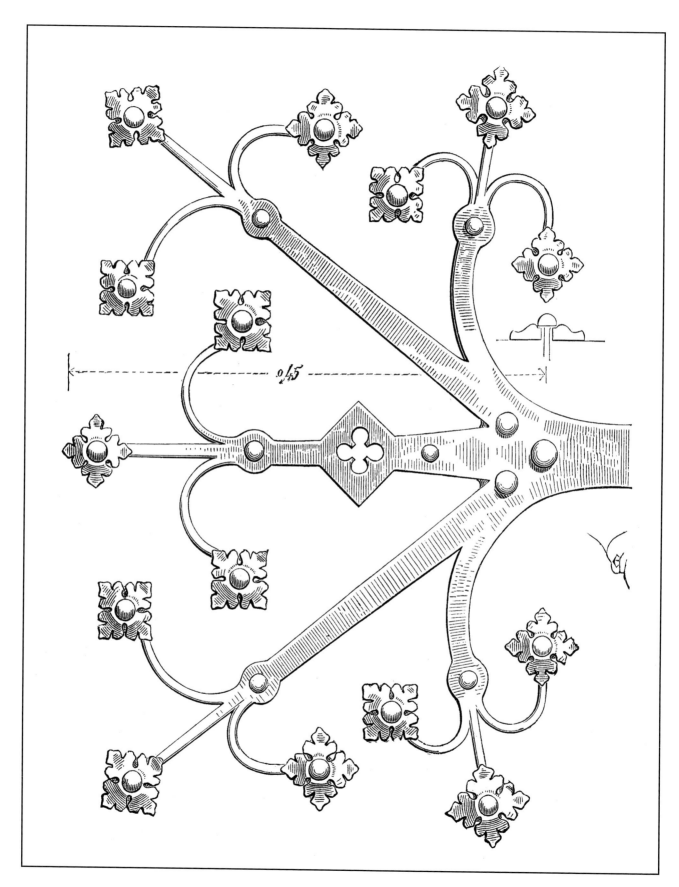

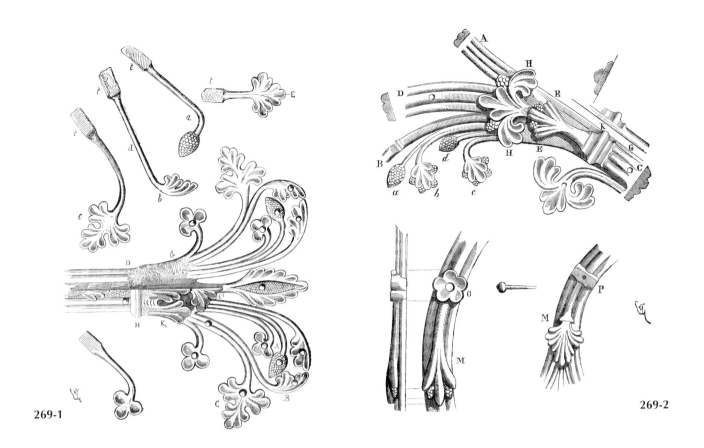

269-1

269-2

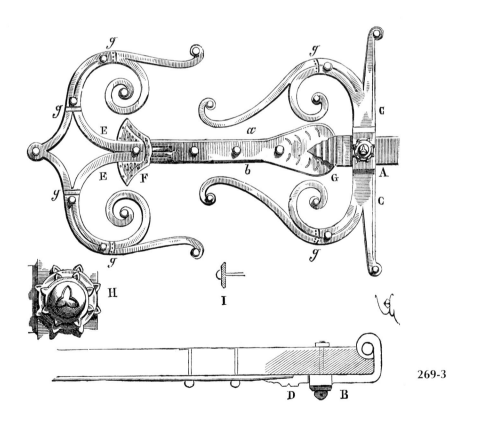

269-3

269

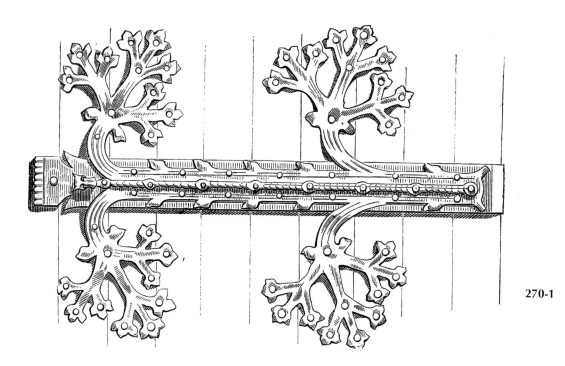

270-1

270-1: Strap hinge, France, 13th century.
Penture, France, XIIIe siècle.
Türbeschlag, Frankreich, 13. Jh.
Pernio, Francia, siglo XIII.
Петли, Франция, XIII век.

270-2: Hinges, France, 15th century.
Charnières, France, XVe siècle.
Scharniere, Frankreich, 15. Jh.
Charnelas, Francia, siglo XV.
Шарнирные петли, Франция, XV век.

E. Viollet-le-Duc, *Dictionnaire raisonné de l'architecture française du XIe au XVIe siècle*. 1854–1868.

271: Candlestick, France, late 11th century.
Chandelier, France, fin du XIe siècle.
Leuchter, Frankreich, ende 11. Jh.
Candelero, Francia, fin del siglo XI.
Подсвечник, Франция, конец XI века.

E. Viollet-le-Duc, *Dictionnaire raisonné du mobilier français de l'époque carolingienne à la Renaissance,* 1858–1875.

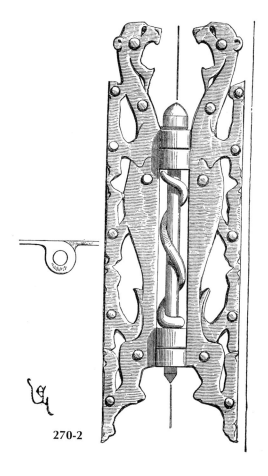

270-2

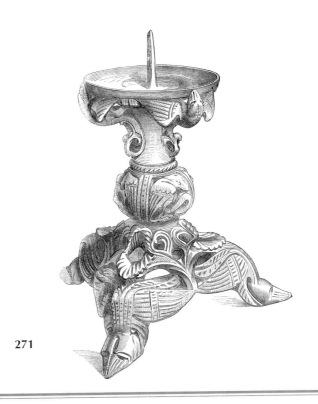

271

• Household and religious objects •
• Objets domestiques et religieux •
• Haushalts und
Religionsgegenstände •
• Objetos domésticos y religiosos •
• Домашняя и церковная утварь •

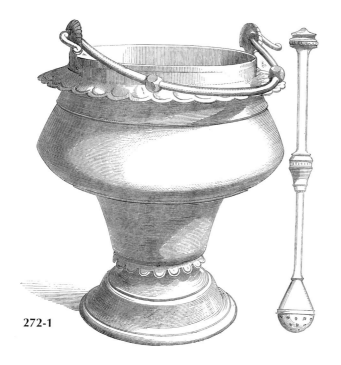

272-1

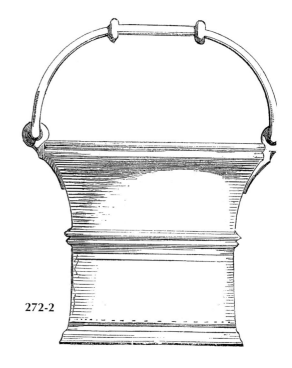

272-2

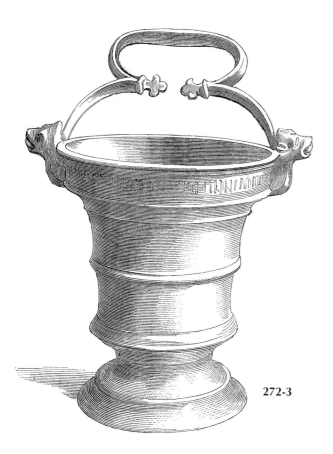

272-3

272: Holy water basins, France, 15th century.
Bénitiers portatifs, France, xvᵉ siècle.
Weihwasserbecken, Frankreich, 15. Jh.
Acetres, Francia, siglo XV.
Кропильница, Франция, XV век.

E. Viollet-le-Duc, *Dictionnaire raisonné du mobilier français de l'époque carolingienne à la Renaissance*, 1858-1875.

273: Candlesticks, France, 12th to 14th centuries.
Chandeliers, France, XIIᵉ au XIVᵉ siècles.
Leuchter, Frankreich, 12. bis 14. Jh.
Candelos, Francia, siglo XII hasta XIV.
Подсвечники, Франция, XII-XIV века.

E. Viollet-le-Duc, *Dictionnaire raisonné du mobilier français de l'époque carolingienne à la Renaissance,* 1858–1875.

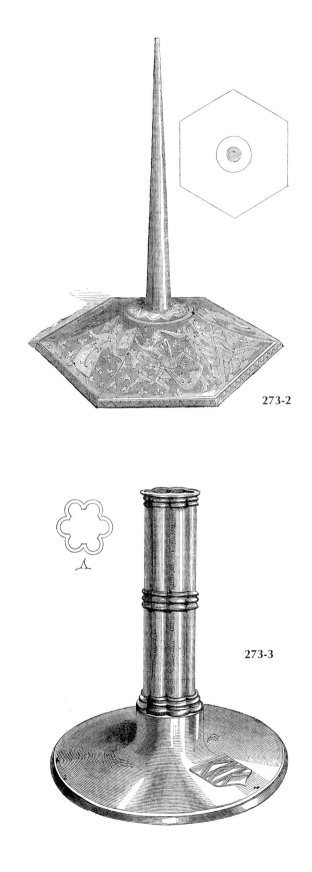

273-2

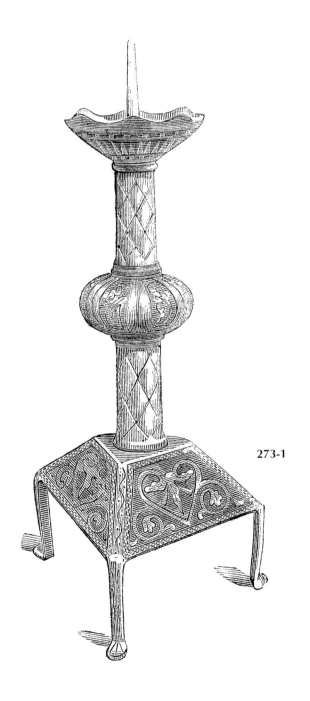

273-1

273-3

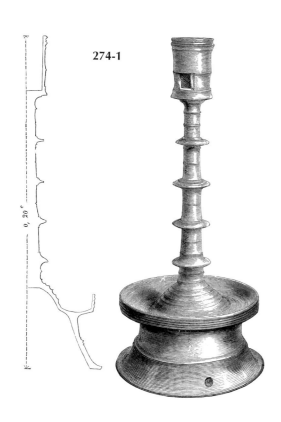

274-1: Candlestick, France, reign of Charles VII.
Chandelier, France, époque Charles VII.
Leuchter, Frankreich, Epoche Charles VII.
Candelo, Francia, época Carlos VII.
Подсвечник, Франция, время правления
Карла VII.

274-2: Candelabra, France, 14th century.
Candélabre, France, XIV siècle.
Kerzenständer, Frankreich, 14. Jh.
Candelabro, Francia, siglo XIV.
Канделябр, Франция, XIV век.

E. Viollet-le-Duc, *Dictionnaire raisonné du mobilier
français de l'époque carolingienne à la Renaissance.* 1858–
1875.

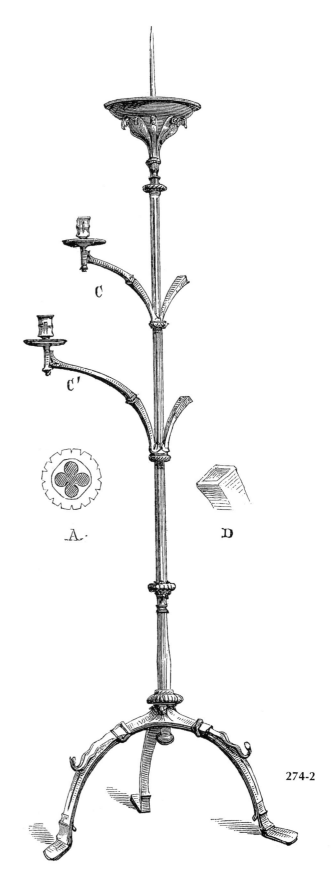

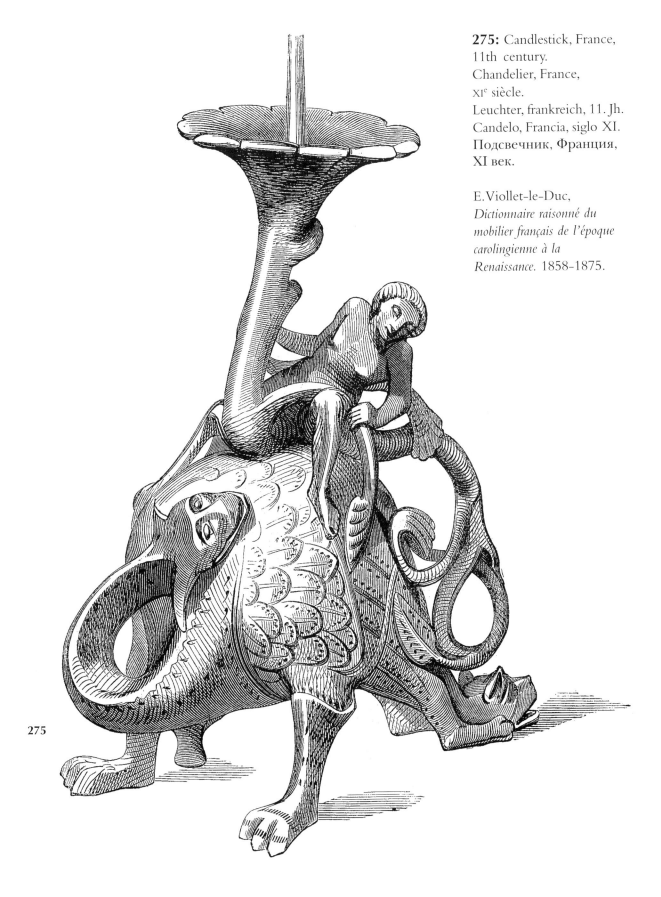

275: Candlestick, France,
11th century.
Chandelier, France,
XIᵉ siècle.
Leuchter, frankreich, 11. Jh.
Candelo, Francia, siglo XI.
Подсвечник, Франция,
XI век.

E. Viollet-le-Duc,
*Dictionnaire raisonné du
mobilier français de l'époque
carolingienne à la
Renaissance.* 1858–1875.

275

276-1: Hand warmer, France, 16th century.
Chaufferette à mains, France, XVIᵉ siècle.
Handwärmer, Frankreich, 16. Jh.
Calientapiés, Francia, siglo XVI.
Грелка для рук, Франция, XVI век.

276-2: Candle snuffers, France,
16th century.
Mouchettes, France, XVIᵉ siècle.
Kerzenlöscher, Frankreich, 16. Jh.
Despabiladeras, Francia, siglo XVI.
Щипцы для снятия нагара, Франция,
XVI век.

E. Viollet-le-Duc, *Dictionnaire raisonné du
mobilier français de l'époque carolingienne à la
Renaissance.* 1858-1875.

277-1: Bowls, France, 14th century.
Écuelles, France, XIVᵉ siècle.
Napfen, Frankreich, 14. Jh.
Escudillas, Francia, siglo XIV.
Миски, Франция, XIV век.

277-2: Cast iron mortars, France,
15th century.
Mortiers en fonte, France, XVᵉ siècle.
Mörtel aus Gusseisen, Frankreich, 15. Jh.
Morteros de hierro, Francia, siglo XV.
Железные ступки, Франция, XV век.

E. Viollet-le-Duc, *Dictionnaire raisonné du
mobilier français de l'époque carolingienne à la
Renaissance.* 1858-1875.

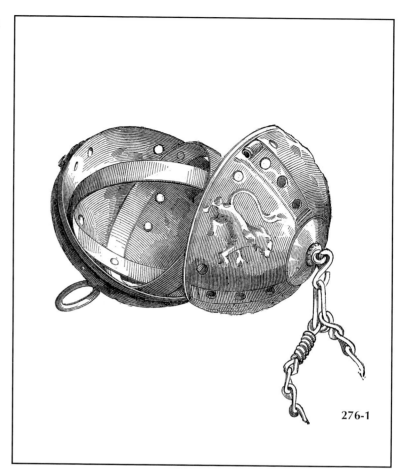

276-1

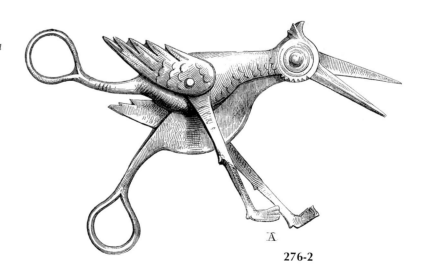

276-2

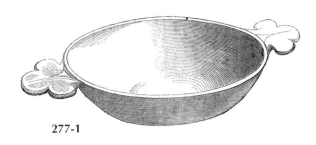

277-1

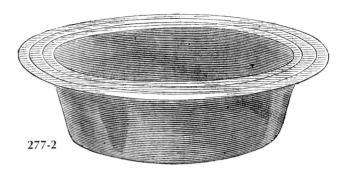

277-2

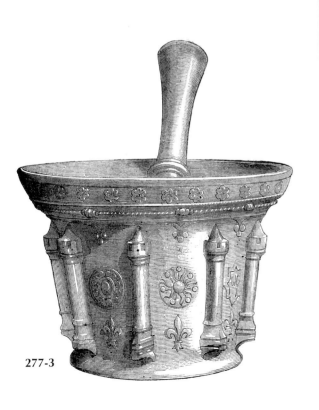

277-3

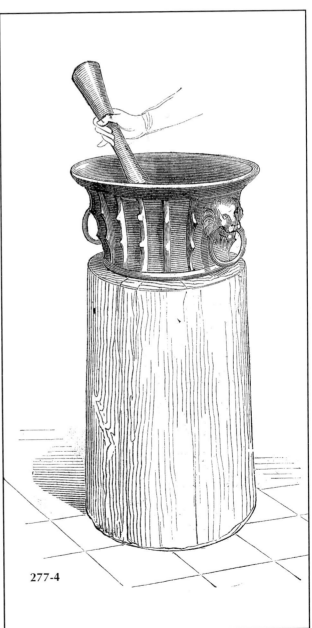

277-4

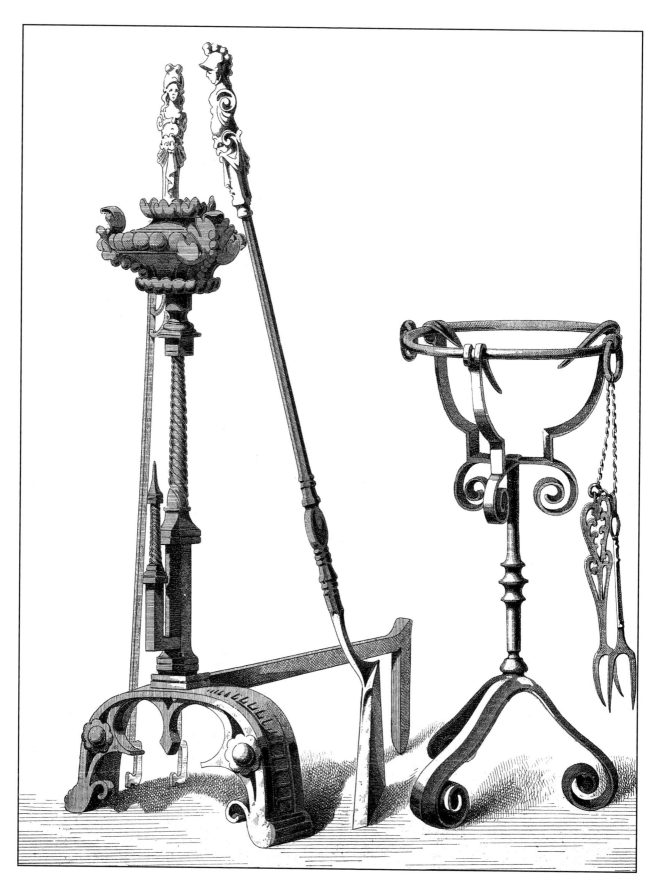

278/279: Andirons, France, 15th century. Chenets, France, XVᵉ siècle. Feuerböcke, Frankreich, 15. Jh. Morillos, Francia, siglo XV. Подставки для дров, Франция, XV век.

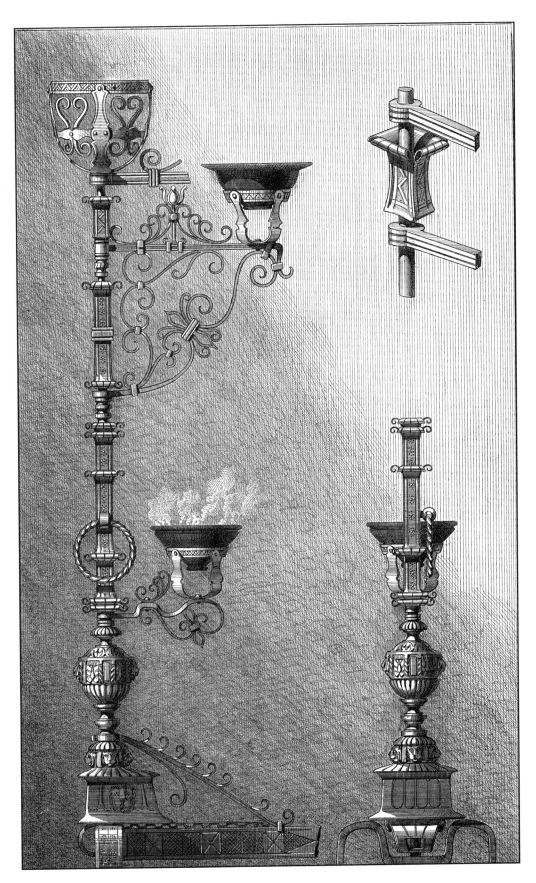

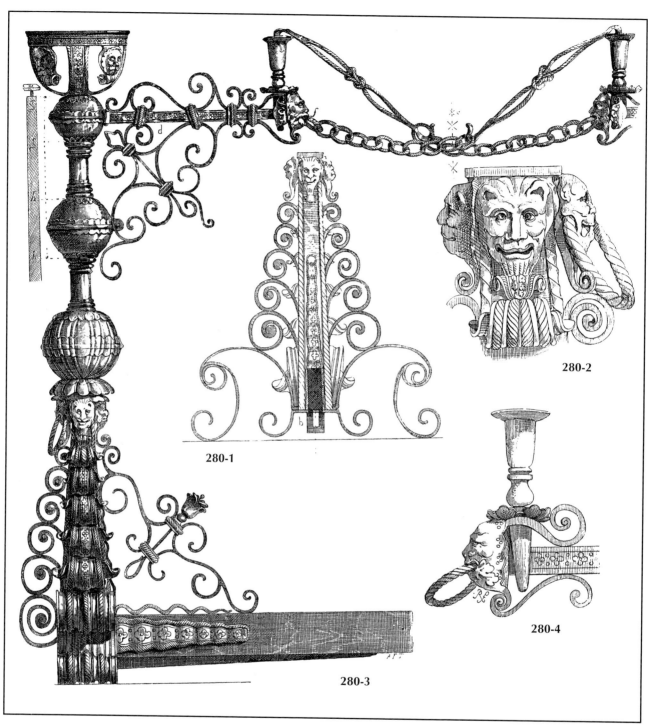

280: Andirons, Italy, 16th century.
Chenets, Italie, XVIᵉ siècle.
Feuerböcke, Italien, 16. Jh.
Morillos, Italia, siglo XVI.
Подставки для дров, Италия, XVI.

281: Candelabra, Spain, 14th century.
Candélabres, Espagne, XIVᵉ siècle.
Kandelaber, Spanien, 14. Jh.
Candelabros, España, siglo XIV.
Канделябры, Испания, XIV век.

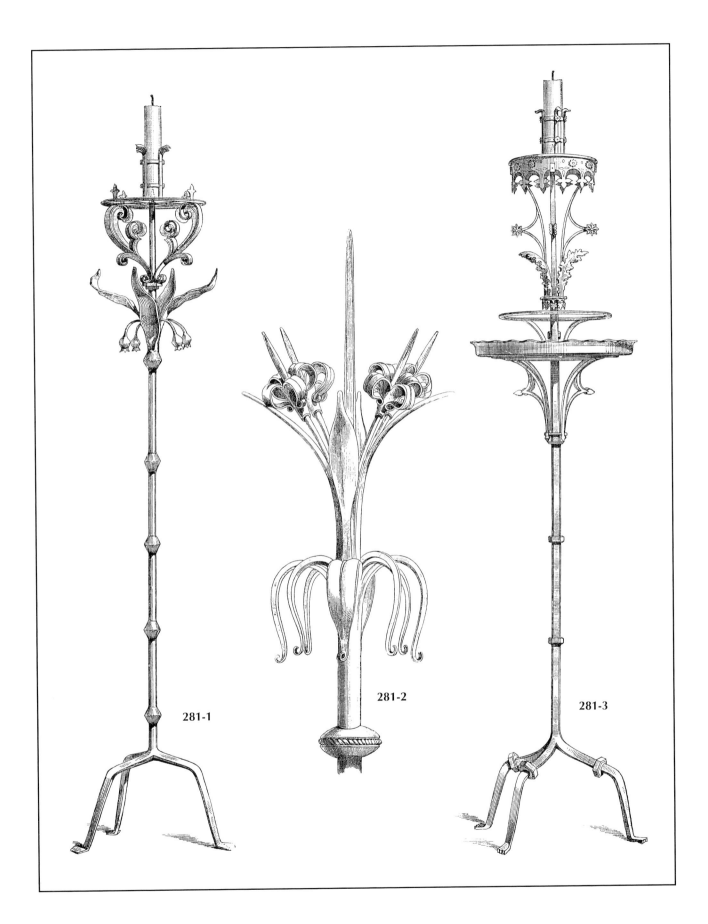

281-1

281-2

281-3

282: Candelabra, Belgium,
17th century
Candélabre, Belgique,
XVIIe siècle.
Kandelaber, Belgien, 17. Jh.
Candelabro, Bélgica,
siglo XVII.
Канделябр, Бельгия,
XVII век.

283/284: Vases, France, 19th
century.
Vases, France, XIXe siècle.
Vasen, Frankreich, 19. Jh.
Vasos, Francia siglo XIX.
Вазы, Франция, XIX век.

Établissement Le Val d'Osne.

285: Cast-iron beds, France,
19th century.
Lits en fonte, France, XIXe
siècle.
Betten aus Gusseisen,
Frankreich, 19. Jh.
Camas de hierro, Francia,
siglo XIX.
Железные кровати,
Франция, XIX век.

Établissement Le Val d'Osne.

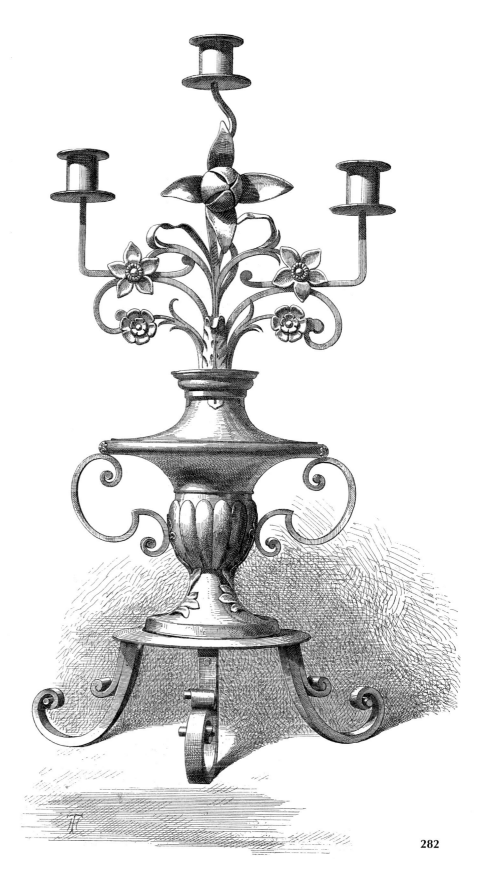

282

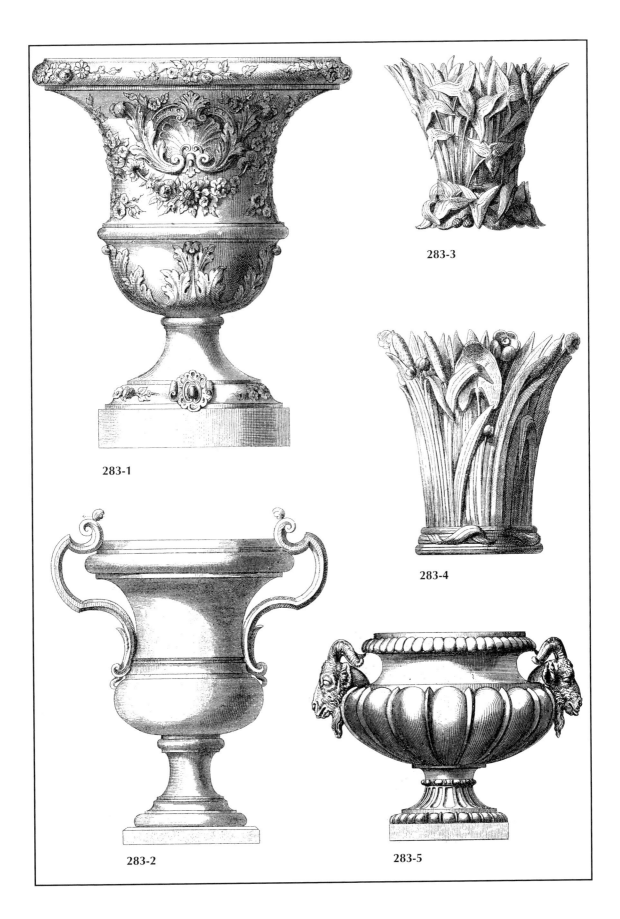

283-1

283-3

283-4

283-2

283-5

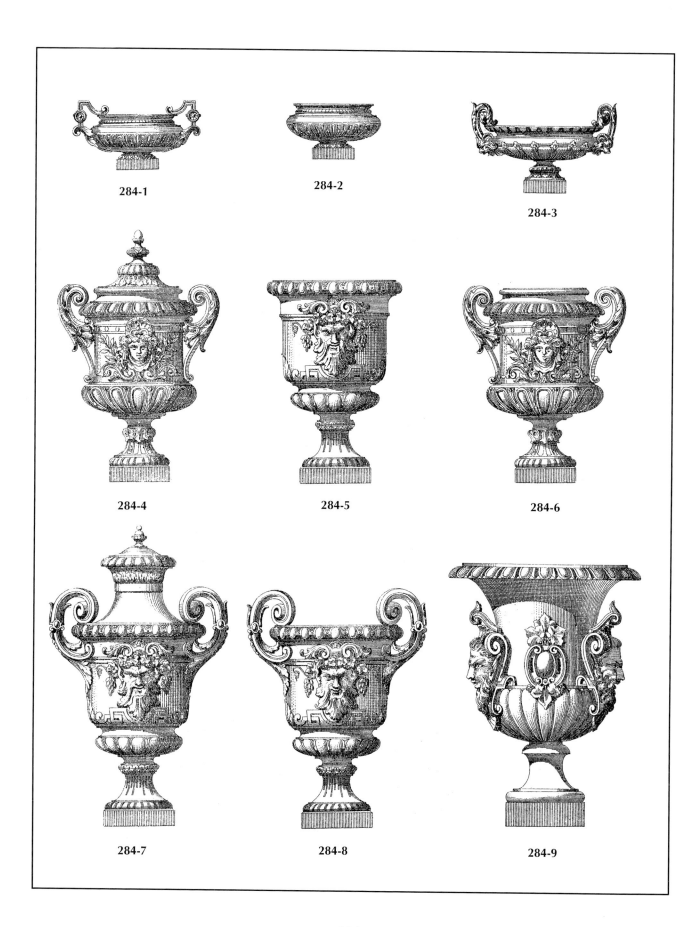

284-1

284-2

284-3

284-4

284-5

284-6

284-7

284-8

284-9

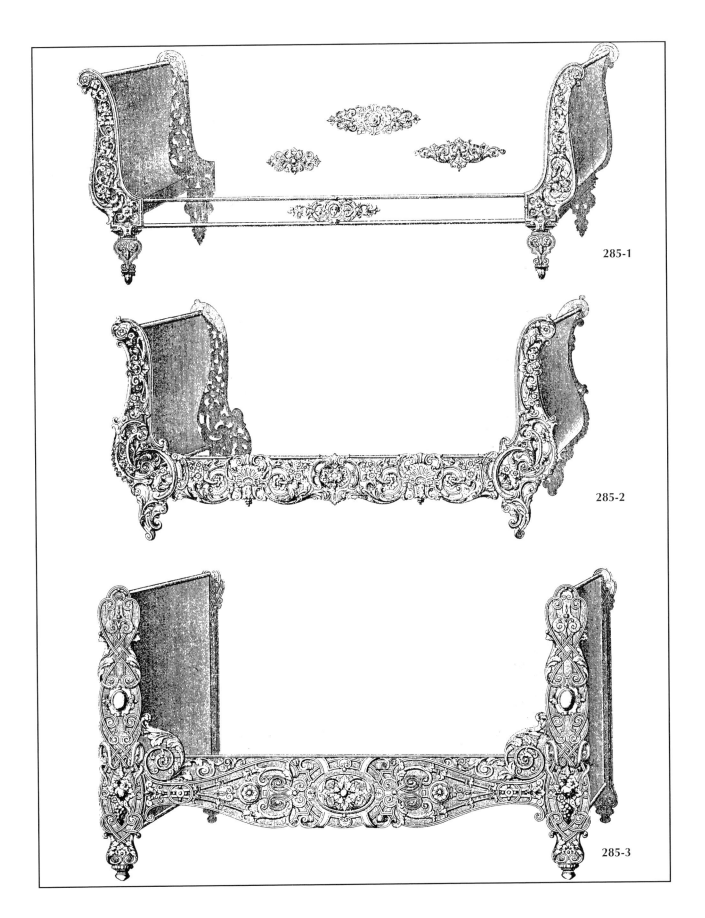

285-1

285-2

285-3

Achevé d'imprimer
en mai 2004
en Slovaquie (CEE)
Dépôt légal 2e trimestre 2004